Extending Dynamics 365 Customer Engagement Apps with Low Code

Create tailor-made Dynamics 365 CE apps using the powerful low-code capabilities of Power Platform

Nicolás Andrés Fernández

BIRMINGHAM—MUMBAI

Extending Dynamics 365 Customer Engagement Apps with Low Code

Group Product Manager: Alok Dhuri
Publishing Product Manager: Harshal Gundetty
Senior Editor: Nisha Cleetus
Technical Editor: Pradeep Sahu
Copy Editor: Safis Editing
Project Coordinator: Manisha Singh
Proofreader: Safis Editing
Indexer: Rekha Nair
Production Designer: Prashant Ghare
Business Development Executive: Uzma Sheerin
Marketing Coordinators: Deepak Kumar and Rayyan Khan

Production reference: 1161222

Published by Packt Publishing Ltd.

Livery Place
35 Livery Street
Birmingham
B3 2PB, UK.

ISBN 978-1-80323-231-7

www.packt.com

This book marks a great professional milestone for me, but it has been made possible only thanks to the example of hard work that Susana, my mother, has given me since I was a child, the accompaniment and support that Noelia, my wife, gives me daily, and the motivation that Guadalupe, my daughter, inspires in me to be the role model that she needs me to be.

– Nicolás Andrés Fernández

Contributors

About the author

Nicolás Andrés Fernández started his career in the Dynamics 365 CE and Power Platform industry in 2014. In 2018, he started to actively participate in the Dynamics 365 and Power Platform technical community, something he continues to do to date. In 2020, he was awarded the title of Most Valuable Professional by Microsoft for the first time. Nicolás is currently a solutions director at HCLTech, in charge of the Dynamics 365 CE and Power Platform pre-sales team in the EMEA and APAC regions.

Nicolás also leads a number of community initiatives within Power 365 Initiatives.

I would especially like to thank my wife Noelia and my daughter Guadalupe, for their unconditional support and encouragement throughout every professional adventure I have taken.

About the reviewers

Wilmer Alcivar is originally from Ecuador and got started in the CRM world in 2012. On-Premise Dynamics CRM 2011 was the first version he got his hands on – what a great version! He is a big Juventus fan and likes to spend time with his girlfriend, trying all kinds of beers, playing video games, and trying his best to keep up with the new features of Power Platform. He moved to Uruguay in 2015 to expand his technical knowledge, but Wilmer moved to Amsterdam earlier this year for new professional challenges. He loves the vibe of the city and the kind people.

Mario Trueba Cantero began his programming career at the age of 8 when he realized that it was easier to code in C++ than study to become a doctor. In 2011, he moved to the UK and was introduced to the MS Dynamics CRM, and the rest is history. Mario brings over a decade of Dynamics 365 and Power Platform experience, having worked with several high-profile customers across a myriad of industries. For the last 14 years, he has been working exclusively with Microsoft technologies. His ability to understand and articulate the value of Microsoft technologies, and in particular, Dynamics and Power Platform, to customers is second to none. Currently, Mario is working as the global lead for low-code and ESG at KPMG and living in Spain with his family.

Table of Contents

Part 2: Extending Dynamics 365 Customer Engagement Applications

3

Extending Dynamics 365 Customer Engagement Native Applications 31

4

Building Applications with Dynamics 365 Customer Engagement 63

Part 3: Building Custom Processes for Dynamics 365 Customer Engagement Applications

7

Automations in Dynamics 365 Customer Engagement Apps   145

8

Working with Data   175

9

Integrating Artificial Intelligence into Processes   205

Part 4: No-Code/Low-Code Bots for Dynamics 365 Customer Engagement

10

Customer-Facing Bots   241

11

Enabling Bots to Users   263

Part 5: Working with Advanced Dashboards and Reports with Dynamics 365 Customer Engagement

12

Reporting Dashboards with Dynamics 365 Customer Engagement Data   279

13

Embedded Dashboards and Reports in Dynamics 365 Customer Engagement   295

Index   311

Other Books You May Enjoy   320

Preface

Hey, you! If you're here, it's because Dynamics 365 Customer Engagement is part of your day-to-day life, either because you work on projects as an implementer (as an architect or consultant), or perhaps as an administrator or citizen developer of an organization that has Dynamics 365 Customer Engagement implemented.

Dynamics 365 Customer Engagement enables organizations to control each point of contact that the customer has with it, from the Sales, Service (both Customer and Field Service), and Marketing standpoints, creating a unique and personalized customer experience. Dynamics 365 Customer Engagement, formerly known as CRM, has evolved a lot during the past several years. Projects have changed from being mostly custom developed to almost no development required. A key challenge is not knowing the possibilities and limitations of the no-code/low-code approach with Dynamics 365 Customer Engagement, leveraging Power Platform. Because of this, solution designs often include duplications of native functionality or unnecessarily complex development.

This does not mean that Dynamics 365 Customer Engagement projects no longer require custom developments. Rather, the evolution of Power Platform enables us to think of new solutions that were not available before.

Power Platform allows us to extend native Dynamics 365 Customer Engagement applications in terms of UX, data processing, integrations, and automations, among others.

Understanding how the no-code/low-code project approach works in Dynamics 365 Customer Engagement, including what is possible with each of the Power Platform solutions, will help you to provide more value with your projects, increase productivity, and ensure a more scalable and maintainable solution.

Having no-code, low-code, and pro-code options presents us with three key challenges:

- The first is to understand what we mean by no-code/low-code.

- Next is understanding the possibilities of extending Dynamics 365 Customer Engagement with a no-code/low-code approach.

- And finally, to correctly triage different solution approaches in order to correctly identify when we can provide a solution with a native capability, when we should extend the project with a no-code/low-code approach, and when the best option for a solution is custom development.

Who this book is for

Understanding how and why to extend Dynamics 365 Customer Engagement applications with a no-code/low-code approach is critical for solution architects responsible for implementation. However, this is something every consultant and developer should learn.

There are two main enterprise areas for which this topic is relevant:

- **Presales**: Both presales architects and presales consultants are the first technical people a customer will talk to and discuss the solution with. Understanding what is possible with no-code/low-code when extending Dynamics 365 Customer Engagement, along with the limitations, is very important to set expectations and create the right solution from the beginning of an engagement.

- **Delivery**: Architects and consultants involved in the delivery of a project are responsible for the design and technical decisions for the solution. Understanding how and why to extend Dynamics 365 Customer Engagement applications with Power Platform is a key responsibility to ensure the success and scalability of an implementation.

What this book covers

Chapter 1, Dynamics 365 Customer Engagement and No-Code/Low-Code, provides an understanding of the no-code/low-code concept for extending Dynamics 365 Customer Engagement applications with Power Platform.

Chapter 2, Extending Dynamics 365 Customer Engagement with a No-Code/Low-Code Approach, we will explore the most common use cases in which Dynamics 365 Customer Engagements applications are extended. It also includes key concepts on extensibility capabilities that will be expanded upon in the following chapters.

Chapter 3, Extending Dynamics 365 Customer Engagement Native Applications, provides a basic understanding of Dataverse and the key concepts of the Dynamics 365 Customer Engagement data model. It also provides an introduction to the most relevant aspects that need to be considered when you extend a native application.

Chapter 4, Building Applications with Dynamics 365 Customer Engagement, we will learn the different types of applications you can build on top of Dynamics 365 Customer Engagement, including model-driven apps, canvas apps, and portals.

Chapter 5, Dynamics 365 Customer Engagement with Custom Embedded Applications, discusses the different ways we can embed a canvas app in a Dynamics 365 Customer Engagement application. It includes details on how to embed a canvas app and how to build a custom page.

Chapter 6, Extending Your Apps with AI and Mixed Reality, provides an introduction to AI Builder models and how to start working with your own custom models.

Chapter 7, Automations in Dynamics 365 Customer Engagement Apps, we will explore how to empower users by creating automations such as cloud flows. It also includes an analysis of the most common scenarios in the context of Dynamics 365 Customer Engagement applications, with examples so you can start creating your own automations.

Chapter 8, Working with Data, we will discover the real scenarios of Dynamics 365 Customer Engagement implementations where it was required to work with data. It also includes an analysis of the possible solutions to these scenarios using Power Platform.

Chapter 9, Integrating Artificial Intelligence into Processes, we will explore how we can make use of the models that AI Builder offers us in our business processes for text processing scenarios, forms processing, and predictive models.

Chapter 10, Customer-Facing Bots, provides an introduction to Power Virtual Agents and how we can deploy bots in customer-facing scenarios.

Chapter 11, Enabling Bots for Users, we will understand how to leverage Power Virtual Agents for our end users.

Chapter 12, Reporting Dashboards with Dynamics 365 Customer Engagement Data, provides an introduction to connecting Dynamics 365 Customer Engagement with Power BI. It also includes the initial steps for creating reports and dashboards.

Chapter 13, Embedded Dashboards and Reports in Dynamics 365 Customer Engagement, provides an understanding of how we can embed dashboards and reports in Dynamics 365 Customer Engagement applications without the need for code or development.

To get the most out of this book

You'll need to have an understanding of the basics of Dynamics 365 Customer Engagement applications and Dataverse.

Software covered in the book	Licenses required
Dynamics 365 Sales	Dynamics 365 Sales Enterprise or Premium
Dynamics 365 Customer Service	Dynamics 365 Customer Service Enterprise
Dynamics 365 Field Service	Dynamics 365 Field Service
Dynamics 365 Marketing	Dynamics 365 Marketing
Power Apps	Not required as the Dynamics 365 Enterprise license includes permissions for Power Apps
Power Automate	Not required as the Dynamics 365 Enterprise license includes permissions for Power Automate
Power Virtual Agents	Power Virtual Agents
Power BI	Power BI Pro
AI Builder	AI Builder credits

Download the color images

We also provide a PDF file that has color images of the screenshots and diagrams used in this book. You can download it here: `https://packt.link/Fikc4`.

> **Tips or important notes**
> Appear like this.

Get in touch

Feedback from our readers is always welcome.

General feedback: If you have questions about any aspect of this book, email us at `customercare@packtpub.com` and mention the book title in the subject of your message.

Errata: Although we have taken every care to ensure the accuracy of our content, mistakes do happen. If you have found a mistake in this book, we would be grateful if you would report this to us. Please visit `www.packtpub.com/support/errata` and fill in the form.

Any errata related to this book can be found at `https://github.comPacktPublishing/Extending-Dynamics-365-Customer-Engagement-Apps-with-Low-Code`.

Piracy: If you come across any illegal copies of our works in any form on the internet, we would be grateful if you would provide us with the location address or website name. Please contact us at `copyright@packt.com` with a link to the material.

If you are interested in becoming an author: If there is a topic that you have expertise in and you are interested in either writing or contributing to a book, please visit `authors.packtpub.com`.

Share Your Thoughts

Once you've read *Extending Dynamics 365 Customer Engagement Apps with Low Code*, we'd love to hear your thoughts! Scan the QR code below to go straight to the Amazon review page for this book and share your feedback.

https://packt.link/r/1803232315

Your review is important to us and the tech community and will help us make sure we're delivering excellent quality content.

Download a free PDF copy of this book

Thanks for purchasing this book!

Do you like to read on the go but are unable to carry your print books everywhere? Is your eBook purchase not compatible with the device of your choice?

Don't worry, now with every Packt book you get a DRM-free PDF version of that book at no cost.

Read anywhere, any place, on any device. Search, copy, and paste code from your favorite technical books directly into your application.

The perks don't stop there, you can get exclusive access to discounts, newsletters, and great free content in your inbox daily

Follow these simple steps to get the benefits:

1.   Scan the QR code or visit the link below

https://packt.link/free-ebook/9781803232317

2.   Submit your proof of purchase
3.   That's it! We'll send your free PDF and other benefits to your email directly

Part 1: Introduction of No-Code/ Low-Code for Dynamics 365 Customer Engagement

Beyond an obvious understanding that "no-code/low-code" implies no complex developments, there are still several implications for a project and a solution that features this approach. In this part, we will cover the different aspects to consider when we talk about no-code or low-code technology with Dynamics 365 Customer Engagement. In this part, you will get an overview of what no-code or low-code means in the context of Dynamics 365 Customer Engagement applications.

This part has the following chapters:

- *Chapter 1, Dynamics 365 Customer Engagement and No-Code/Low-Code*
- *Chapter 2, Extending Dynamics 365 Customer Engagement with a No-Code/Low-Code Approach*

1

Dynamics 365 Customer Engagement and No-Code/Low-Code

Over the last few years, we have heard and read many times about *no-code/low-code* technologies, but what does it really mean when we talk about a platform such as Dynamics 365 Customer Engagement?

As most of us already know, Dynamics 365 Customer Engagement, also known as Dynamics CRM, offers a series of applications with out-of-the-box functionality to solve specific use cases for sales, customer service, field service, marketing, and project operations scenarios. However, far from being a canned product that we have to take and accept as it comes, the Power Platform allows us to adapt out-of-the-box Dynamics 365 Customer Engagement applications and create new applications that can integrate with each other, without the need for any development.

In this first chapter, we will learn why and since when we can consider Dynamics 365 Customer Engagement related to a no-code/low-code development platform, and the constraints that it can present when we face a project.

By the end of the chapter, you will have learned how to position the Power Platform no-code/low-code platform surrounding Dynamics 365 Customer Engagement projects, and what some of the most important challenges are that this new no-code/low-code paradigm introduces, as well as new opportunities.

In this chapter, we will cover the following topics:

- Understanding Dynamics 365 Customer Engagement DNA
- Low-code is not necessarily low cost
- Exploring new opportunities and challenges

Technical requirements

To work with Dynamics 365 Customer Engagement, it is necessary to have an environment with one of the supported licenses. However, the topics covered in this chapter do not require any Dynamics 365 applications.

The following is required for this chapter:

- Any Dynamics 365 Customer Engagement License (any of the available ones) with administrator permissions in the environment
- A supported browser

Understanding Dynamics 365 Customer Engagement DNA

To understand why Dynamics 365 Customer Engagement is closely linked with the no-code / low-code concept, first, we must look at the platform's key components to see what it is and what it is built on.

We know that, technically, Dynamics 365 Customer Engagement applications (Sales, Marketing, Customer Service, Field Service, and Project Operations) are model-driven apps built by Microsoft, so they are known as first-party applications. And so, as in all model-driven apps, the core component of the applications is **Dataverse**.

To quote the official definition from Microsoft, Dataverse is a *Powerful data service and app platform to quickly build enterprise-grade apps with automated business processes.*

Without going into too much detail about Dataverse, it is important to highlight the aspects that make it up:

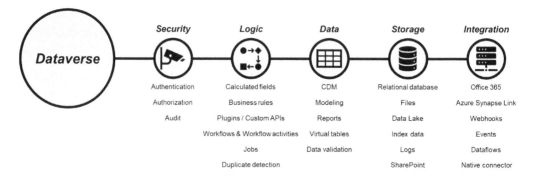

Figure 1.1 – A high-level Dataverse description

As we can see in the preceding diagram, Dataverse offers different capabilities for the design and modeling of applications, including aspects of great importance such as security or business logic, with capabilities ranging from no-code to pro-code.

Now, considering Dataverse is a relatively new concept, let's review the origin of this product to understand how closely it relates to Dynamics 365 Customer Engagement.

The XRM concept was used since the first versions of Dynamics CRM to describe the platform's ability to model and bring to life applications that respond to different business needs in an agile, integrated, secure, and easy-to-maintain way. The definition coined by Microsoft in 2015 was *XRM is a business applications framework designed to accelerate the development of line-of-business (LOB) applications through reusable applications services that can be adapted and extended to create many unique applications.*

With the launch of Power Apps, Microsoft understood that it had to formalize this concept under a specific product, so Common Data Service was born. After a first attempt to build this framework from scratch, in the Common Data Service 2.0 version, Microsoft took as a base what Dynamics CRM had been having for years as the core of its applications. Finally, and after some stumbling around for a name change, Common Data Service was renamed Dataverse.

For this reason, what we know today as Dataverse is a core part of that XRM framework for building applications with a no-code/low-code approach that we have known since the first versions of Dynamics CRM. Therefore, Dynamics 365 Customer Engagement has all the conditions and capabilities to be extended, without code, by using Power Platform.

To find out what Dynamics 365 Customer Engagement looks like inside, and how we can extend it without code, we simply have to access the maker portal (`https://make.powerapps.com`) and select the **Solutions** section:

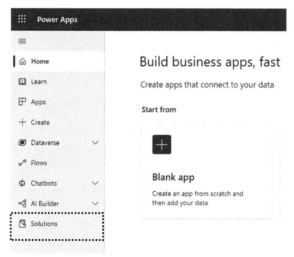

Figure 1.2 – The Solutions area in the makers portal

Here, we can see the different native Dynamics 365 Customer Engagement solutions and even create one from scratch. Once created, we can add the Dynamics 365 Customer Engagement components we need.

Now, you understand what the core component of Dynamics 365 Customer Engagement Apps is and how Dataverse makes it a no-code/low-code platform.

Low-code is not necessarily low cost

It is very common to assume that a low-code platform implies a low-cost project, when in fact, there is no direct relationship between the two. Sometimes, this becomes more difficult to explain when we are working with Dynamics 365 Customer Engagement as a base solution, which already brings a native data model, a series of business processes, automations, and other functions that allow implementation in the form of adoption. However, there is no Dynamics 365 Customer Engagement implementation that does not involve customizations. And as much as we take advantage of native capabilities, and extensions are made with a no-code/low-code approach, such customizations can involve considerable effort not only for the construction but for everything that entails making them follow best practices.

It becomes important then to identify the implications of having a no-code/low-code approach versus a pro-code approach.

When we say that Dynamics 365 Customer Engagement is intrinsically connected to a no-code/low-code application development platform, that primarily means the following:

- It is possible to carry out a project from end to end without the need for custom developments. In other words, no programming knowledge is required to implement and extend a Dynamics 365 Customer Engagement solution.

- The customizations that are carried out are done declaratively or by means of simple tools, such as drag-and-drop designers.

- The maintenance of the solution could be easier compared to custom development.

- Administration of the solution can be performed by business users.

- Time to market will be shorter compared to a solution developed from scratch.

As you can see, there is no correlation between a low-code approach and a low-cost project. However, it's true that if we compare the same scope with a low-code approach and a pro-code approach, in terms of implementation and maintenance costs, the low-code project is more profitable or has a lower cost.

As always, the simplicity of, for example, the maintenance or deployment of a solution, will not only depend on whether the development approach is no-code/low-code versus pro-code. The use of best practices and the selection of the best solution are key factors. As we will see throughout the chapters, on many occasions, the best solution approach might include the use of code. This, far from being detrimental to the overall solution, will contribute to having an optimized solution with a good balance between no-code, low-code, and pro-code capabilities.

However, the cost of the project will depend on two variables: scope and time.

The following diagram represents how the time, cost, and scope of a project are affected when we change any of the conditions:

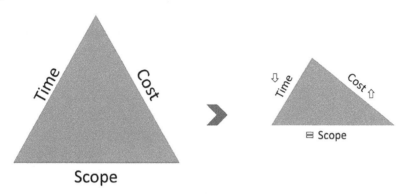

Figure 1.3 – The project management triangle

As we can see, if we maintain the scope and we reduce the time of the project, the cost will increase.

As we have seen, expectation management in relation to a no-code/low-code approach project is important. Note that the type of approach does not change the fact that good practices must be followed to ensure the correct design, construction, and maintenance of the solution, as well as its scalability. This is why it is important to understand that a low-code project does not necessarily imply that it has to be low-cost, but that it will depend on the multiple factors mentioned earlier.

How complex can a no-code/low-code project be?

A solution based on no-code/low-code elements does not guarantee that it will be a simple project. Currently, with the extensive capabilities offered by Dynamics 365 Customer Engagement as standalone applications, along with the possibility of extending them using Power Platform components, we can find ourselves with extremely complex scenarios, and therefore, with a high cost, such as the following:

- Integration with SAP in different business processes, such as the customer registration, at the time of winning a bid, or synchronizing a technician's inventory

- The implementation of a self-management portal for customers with an integrated virtual assistant that resolves queries by referring them to knowledge base articles

- The complete configuration of the Omnichannel Engagement Hub, including multiple streams or mapping rules

- Building an end-to-end process integrated with the organization's business process

In short, the fact that a project or a platform is no-code/low-code does not change the basic principles of any project, among which we find that a project will be as simple or complex as its requirements are.

Selecting the right approach for a solution

With Dynamics 365 Customer Engagement, we have the possibility to choose the best way to solve a requirement, through a simple triage:

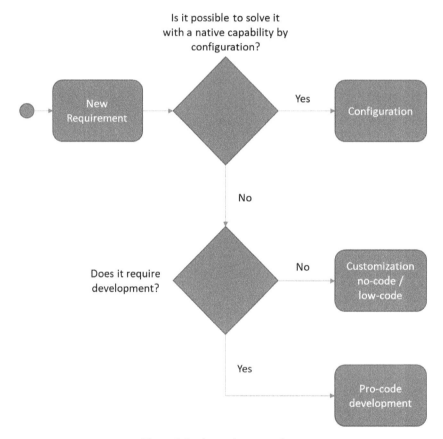

Figure 1.4 – A requirement triage

This way, we can decide whether a requirement will be solved with native Dynamics 365 Customer Engagement capability, whether we will do it through no-code/low-code customization, or whether a pro-code approach is required.

As we have seen, the complexity of a project will depend strictly on its requirements and the possible solutions we can design to meet them.

The triage of the requirements to ensure the correct selection of the best solution approach will give us the size of the project. As a result, the project may be more oriented toward adopting native functionality, or building new functionality through development.

Exploring new opportunities and challenges

Understanding that Dynamics 365 Customer Engagement can be easily extended with Power Platform opens a range of new opportunities and challenges, both when thinking about a solution for a project and when designing our professional path and evolution.

If we focus on the impact that the design of solutions has by being able to use a no-code/low-code approach to extend applications, we find the following:

- We are not limited to the implementation of the business processes defined by Microsoft in its first-party applications, but we can also think about the extension or creation of new business processes that orbit around the native processes.

- We can extend the solution using Power Platform, not only for the creation and extension of applications, but also to build automation and processes, bots, and control panels. We will go deeper into each of these use cases in the later chapters of the book.

- The deployment and maintenance process of the solution can be simplified.

- We have to keep ourselves updated with the constantly evolving capabilities of Power Platform and Dynamic 365 Customer Engagement.

As we will see later, the challenges presented by the constant evolution of the platform are also an opportunity to develop our professional careers.

Developing our careers

On the other hand, from a career development point of view, this paradigm and how both Dynamics 365 Customer Engagement and Power Platform evolve allow us to develop new skills, while we can shape our professional profile by specializing in either a specific Dynamics 365 Customer Engagement application or a non-code type of extension.

To help us enhance the development of our professional careers and to upskill ourselves, Microsoft constantly develops new exams and certifications.

Currently, there are two different types of exams that we can aspire to pass – the MB-XXX and the PL-XXX. The MB-XXX corresponds to the Dynamics 365 exams, both Customer Engagement and other applications, while the PL-XXX exams correspond to Power Platform. Passing these exams will enable us to gain the new certifications of one of its levels – beginner, intermediate, or advanced.

The beginner-level certifications focus on the fundamentals of the platform:

Figure 1.5 – Beginner certifications

The intermediate certifications present more specific specializations, including both functional and technical certifications:

Figure 1.6 – Intermediate certifications

Finally, the advanced certifications are oriented toward architects who will have a wider knowledge and understanding of the platform:

Figure 1.7 – Advanced certifications

As you can see, there are multiple possibilities we have to specialize as Dynamics 365 Customer Engagement professionals, complementing our knowledge of the platform with the capabilities of Power Platform. The multiple exams and certifications allow us to develop a profile that supports our knowledge and experience.

The introduction of Power Platform capabilities for the extension of Dynamics 365 Customer Engagement, which we will discuss in the next chapter, also presents several challenges for architects, consultants, and developers. This is because the new tools force us to step out of our comfort zone so that we can understand why we should use a no-code/low-code tool instead of a custom development.

Summary

In this chapter, we have reviewed basic concepts to understand the extension capabilities of Dynamics 365 Customer Engagement without code. We started from the old concept of XRM to get into what Dataverse is. We discussed why a no-code/low-code project does not necessarily imply a low-cost project, and how to identify the best approach for a solution. Finally, we looked at some of the challenges and opportunities this approach offers us Dynamics 365 Customer Engagement professionals.

In *Chapter 2*, we will focus on understanding the main reasons to extend Dynamics 365 Customer Engagement and what we can achieve with a no-code/low-code approach.

Questions and answers

1. Is Dynamics 365 a no-code/low-code platform?

    Answer: Not precisely. Dynamics 365 Customer Engagement offer us a set of native applications, or first-party applications, with pre-defined processes. However, because Dynamics 365 Customer Engagement applications are built on Dataverse, it has native integration, and extensibility with the Power Platform. As we have learned, Dataverse offers multiple tools to extend and build applications without development. Also, Dataverse integrates natively with Power Apps, Power Automate, Power Pages, Power Virtual Agents, and Power BI, which allows us to build new components to extend our Dynamics 365 Customer Engagement applications, without the use of development.

2. What concepts should I keep in mind when defining what type of solution to propose?

Answer: When we analyze the requirements and start working on the design of the solution, we have to keep several things in mind:

- The first point would be whether the requirement can be covered with some native Dynamics 365 Customer Engagement capability that only requires parameterization or configuration.

- Secondly, it would be to understand whether there is any capability within the platform that allows us to deliver a solution by building without code. For this, we need to know, in greater detail, the no-code/low-code capabilities that Power Platform offers us.

- Finally, it is important to remember that even if a solution is low-code, it might require the help of someone more technical to optimize it or to go that last quarter of a mile. A clear example of this can be seen in the construction of cloud flows, where even though it is a low-code approach, it sometimes requires technical skill.

3. How can I get recognition for my knowledge and experience?

Answer: By taking the official exams and obtaining Microsoft certifications, we can demonstrate our knowledge and experience in a concrete way.

2

Extending Dynamics 365 Customer Engagement with a No-Code/Low-Code Approach

There are multiple reasons to think about extending Dynamics 365 Customer Engagement with a no-code/low-code approach. From automating processes or tasks, facilitating platform governance and management, extending native processes, and enabling a new **user interface** (**UI**) or **user experience** (**UX**), to transforming data into actionable information, we can find multiple use cases for which we can extend Dynamics 365 Customer Engagement without the need for custom code or custom development.

Understanding these common use cases gives us a better understanding of the flexibility Dynamics 365 Customer Engagement has to extend its solutions with Power Platform. This flexibility is undoubtedly one of the reasons why Dynamics 365 Customer Engagement is the platform of choice for many organizations.

It should be noted that the configuration of native functionality, even if it is through parameterizable tools or no-code configuration, will be considered as an implementation of the product out of the box and not as an extension. We will talk about extending with a no-code/low-code approach when we make use of Power Platform capabilities (Dataverse, Power Apps, Power Automate, Power Virtual Agents, Power BI, or AI Builder) to configure a new functionality.

In this chapter, we will discuss and learn about five common use cases when we want to extend Dynamics 365 Customer Engagement, and with which Power Platform tools we will be able to do so:

- Upgrading your platform administration and governance
- Automating tasks
- Business process extension

- Improving the UX/UI
- Transforming data into actionable information

By the end of this chapter, you will know how to describe these common use cases for extending Dynamics 365 Customer Engagement with a no-code/low-code approach and how to build some of these extensions.

Technical requirements

To work with Dynamics 365 Customer Engagement, it is necessary to have an environment with one of the supported licenses. However, the topics covered in this chapter do not require any Dynamics 365 application.

The following is required for this chapter:

- Any Dynamics 365 Customer Engagement license (any of the available ones) with administrator permissions in the environment
- A supported browser

In the following section, we'll gain an understanding of the different scenarios you can extend Dynamics 365 Customer Engagement to incorporate administration and governance tools.

Upgrading your platform administration and governance

The administration and governance of the platform are one of the most relevant aspects for an organization when considering a Dynamics 365 Customer Engagement implementation, and Microsoft offers various tools to facilitate this management. However, the tools and solutions offered by Microsoft as part of the governance and administration of Dynamics 365 Customer Engagement and Power Platform are limited to specific scenarios, and it is common to find reasons to expand them.

From the Power Platform administration portal (`https://admin.powerplatform.microsoft.com/`), we will have access to the tools offered by Microsoft for the governance and administration of Dynamics 365 Customer Engagement and Power Platform environments, as well as resource management (such as storage, Dynamics 365 Customer Engagement applications, or portals), and other governance tools at the tenant level:

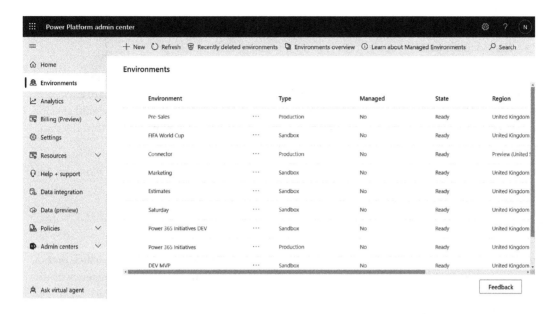

Figure 2.1 – Power Platform Admin Center

In addition to these tools, for administration and governance, Microsoft also offers the **CoE Starter Kit**. The CoE Starter Kit is a set of pre-built tools for governance and management, covering not only the control aspects, but also important processes, such as application or maker onboarding, or internal community-building processes to ensure the correct implementation, use, and adoption of Power Platform.

It is worth mentioning that the CoE Starter Kit is not the focus of this book, so if you are interested, I recommend that you delve deeper into the subject with books or specialized material focused on it. However, given the governance and administration requirements of the platform, it is normal to start by installing the CoE Starter Kit to meet these requirements.

Some of the most recurrent aspects when working with administration and governance requirements are, usually, the following:

- User control and management
- Control of work environments and **application lifecycle management** (**ALM**)
- Platform auditing
- Automation of early warnings
- Usage reporting

- Resource management

- Risk identification

It is common to find governance and management solutions, such as the CoE Starter Kit, implemented in isolated environments where Dynamics 365 Customer Engagement applications are used, and therefore, could not be considered an extension. However, sometimes, it's necessary to build specific solutions or extensions to facilitate or enhance governance and management tools within the same environment where we have our Dynamics 365 Customer Engagement applications.

Next, we'll take a deep dive into different types of task automations we can build for Dynamics 365 Customer Engagement applications.

Automating tasks

One of the most recurring use cases is the automation of repetitive or mundane tasks, which do not add value to the user who must perform them but is important to maintain the consistency of the business process being developed. Examples of this can be found in all Dynamics 365 Customer Engagement applications: Sales, Customer Service, Field Service, Marketing, or Project Operations.

For ease, Dynamics 365 Customer Engagement offers us the option to automate tasks without the need for code. We have the flexibility to use different types of mechanisms or tools to do so and get the type of automation we need in each case.

In the following chapter, we will take a deep dive into some examples of how to automate tasks in Dynamics 365 Customer Engagement.

When understanding a requirement that refers to the automation of a task, it is important to ask ourselves, at the very least, six questions:

- Who is going to execute the automation?

- When will it be executed?

- What will be automated?

- What will it be automated for?

- From where will it be executed?

- How will it be executed?

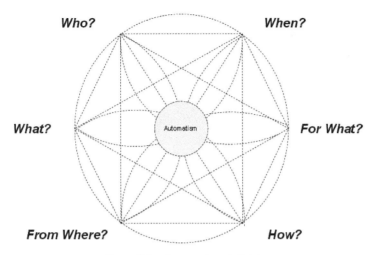

Figure 2.2 – Automation definition

The answers to these basic questions will allow us to triage and understand what type of automation we should design and build. Will it be a real-time automation or will it be a background process? Should it generate a PDF document or update a record? Take a look at the following:

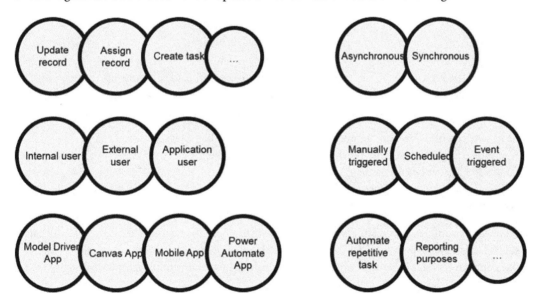

Figure 2.3 – Automation morphology

These questions will allow us to identify limitations or constraints when choosing the type of automation and, thus, offer the most optimal and scalable option.

In addition to the native capabilities (sequences, macros, automatic creation and update rules, routing rules, and more), we will have different capabilities to create automated tasks in Dynamics 365 Customer Engagement, such as Power Automate flows, classic workflows, or business rules.

Power Automate

Power Automate undoubtedly tops the list of tools available to automate tasks in Dynamics 365 Customer Engagement.

With Power Automate, we can build different types of manually executed, scheduled, or event-driven processes and perform different types of background actions with Dynamics 365 Customer Engagement and other applications:

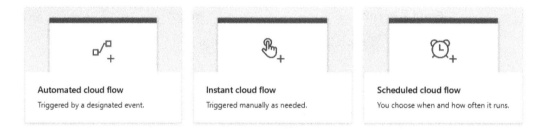

Figure 2.4 – Power Automate flow types

To connect with Dynamics 365 Customer Engagement, we will find different options in Power Automate, although the currently recommended one is the Dataverse connector, which, as discussed in the previous chapter, is the core on which Dynamics 365 Customer Engagement is built.

Currently, we can find different connectors in Power Platform that refer to Dataverse and Dynamics 365 Customer Engagement. These include Microsoft Dataverse, Microsoft Dataverse (legacy), and Dynamics 365 Customer Engagement. However, both Dataverse (legacy) and Dynamics 365 Customer Engagement connectors are deprecated, and Microsoft's recommendation is not to use them in new flows or applications that we are going to build.

However, we can still find interesting templates when we filter out the deprecated connectors. We can get several ideas about processes that we can build using the templates that were originally designed for this connector as an example. The following screenshot shows some of the templates designed for the Dynamics 365 Customer Engagement connector:

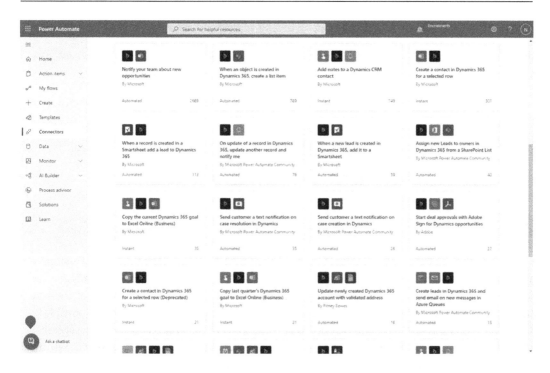

Figure 2.5 – Dynamics 365 Customer Engagement Deprecated Connector's templates

As we can see in the preceding screenshot, some of the actions we have detailed in the templates include integration with Microsoft Teams, Microsoft Excel, Microsoft SharePoint Online, Smartsheets, Office 365, and Azure Queues, among others. They serve to automate tasks that we could group as follows:

- Notifications

- Data validation

- Records creation, update, and delete operations

- Sending messages

- Migration/copy of data between systems

- Approval flows and digital signature

Any of the existing templates for the Dynamics 365 Customer Engagement connector can be modified and adapted to use the new Dataverse connector to ensure the correct functioning of the automated process.

Beyond templates, it is always possible to create a workflow from scratch. Some of the most commonly used connectors in the context of Dynamics 365 Customer Engagement are Approvals, SharePoint, Booking, and Microsoft Teams.

Approvals

Using the native functionality of approval flows nicely complements the native Dynamics 365 Customer Engagement processes. Among other benefits, we can use these to do the following:

- Dynamics 365 Sales scenario – Approve discounts on offers before this is delivered to the customer
- Dynamics 365 Customer Service scenario – Approve new or changed knowledge base articles
- Dynamics 365 Project Operations scenario – The approval of project hours allocation
- Dynamics 365 Field Service scenario – The approval of fieldwork parts
- Dynamics 365 Marketing scenario – The approval of social media postings

SharePoint

Beyond the existence of a native integration between SharePoint and Dynamics 365 Customer Engagement, sometimes, for security reasons, we might want to synchronize access permissions to documents between the two platforms (something that is not offered natively by the out-of-the-box integration between SharePoint and Dynamics 365 Customer Engagement). To do this, it is possible to establish synchronization between the members that are part of a Dynamics 365 Customer Engagement access team and the users with whom access to the folder where the files are stored is shared. We can do this by building a custom solution or implementing third-party solutions.

Booking

For both sales and customer service scenarios, often, we need to offer customers the possibility to self-manage appointments with Dynamics 365 Customer Engagement users. By integrating Dynamics 365 Customer Engagement, Outlook, and Booking, it is possible to set up automated message processes that are sent to prospects or customers with the corresponding Booking calendar link. This will help ensure that they can easily book the required service or resource.

Microsoft Teams

The integration scenarios between Dynamics 365 Customer Engagement and Microsoft Teams as processes that extend the native integration capabilities are multiple. We could try to summarize them among the following:

- **Notifications**: Manage notifications to users or channels when an event occurs in Dynamics 365 Customer Engagement that needs to be communicated
- **Create records**: Enable the creation of records in Dynamics 365 Customer Engagement (leads, contacts, opportunities, and more) from a Microsoft Teams message

> **Note**
>
> It is important to validate that workflows built with Power Automate meet the licensing conditions according to the criteria established by Microsoft in the Power Platform and Dynamics 365 licensing guides.

Classic workflows

Before the existence of Power Automate, Dynamics 365 already offered the option to create automations thanks to classic workflows. There are two types of classic workflows: **synchronous** and **asynchronous**. To build asynchronous workflows today, it is advisable to use Power Automate, not only because it allows us to incorporate more actions, data transformations, and even integrations with other systems, but also because it does not run on Dynamics 365 Customer Engagement and does not use the platform's resources.

However, for synchronous workflows, there is still no no-code/low-code replacement within the Power platform that we can use. Synchronous workflows, as the name suggests, happen in real time, so we must be very careful when designing them so as not to affect the performance of the platform or the experience of the user who, once executed, waits for it to finish executing.

The option to create a classic workflow in a solution can be found in the **Process** section, under the **Automation** category, as shown in the following screenshot:

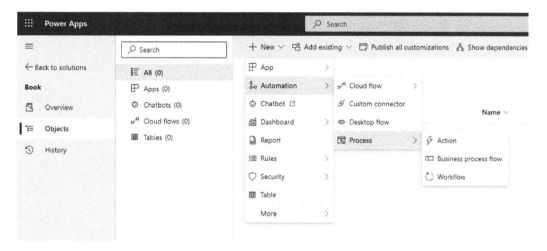

Figure 2.6 – Classic workflows in Dataverse solutions

When building a workflow, we must establish certain conditions such as in which table it will be executed, whether it will be in the background (asynchronous), and whether it will be built from a template or from scratch. Once all this has been defined, we can build the flow itself.

Business rules

Finally, business rules are the third type of object we can use for task automation as an extension of Dynamics 365 Customer Engagement. Like classic workflows, business rules are Dataverse objects and have been available since before the existence of Power Automate.

Although the most common use of business rules is data validation, they can also be used to set values to columns in a row of a Dynamics 365 Customer Engagement table:

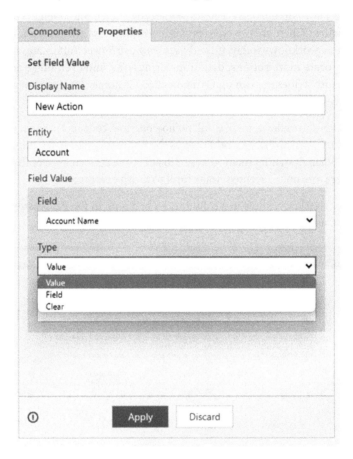

Figure 2.7 – The Set Field Value step

In *Chapter 3*, we will discuss the business rules in more detail.

Business process extensions

Dynamics 365 Customer Engagement includes multiple business processes that have already been defined, such as **Lead to Opportunity**, **Call to Case**, **Case to Work Order**, **Event Management**, and more. These processes are composed of an easily recognizable visual component, such as the **business process flow** (**BPF**), and the definition of a data model that accompanies the process.

The business process flow is composed of a series of stages, conditions, workflows, and steps. When implementing Dynamics 365 Customer Engagement, we can choose to adopt the native processes or extend them:

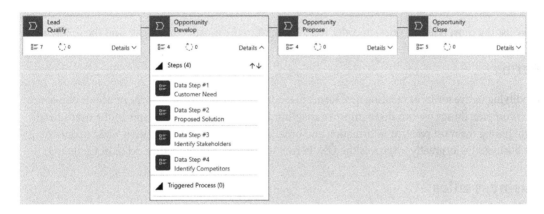

Figure 2.8 – The native lead to opportunity sales process

Among the actions we will be able to perform, we can include the following:

- Creating another business process that applies under certain conditions on demand
- Establishing conditions in the flow of the business process that end up implying branches to the initial process
- Adding or removing stages
- Adding or removing steps
- Adding workflows that are executed when entering or exiting a stage of the business process flow

In *Chapter 7*, we will go into further detail about how we can empower users when working with business process flows.

Next, we will discover the fundamental aspects that we can work on in terms of UI and UX without the need for development.

Improving the UX/UI

Dynamics 365 Customer Engagement applications correspond to model-driven apps, which means that the overall design corresponds to the same framework as any other model-driven app, with the exception of workspace or omnichannel engagement hub applications that present a multi-session experience, overriding the sitemap on the left-hand side of the screen.

It is true that for many UX or UI enhancements, we will need to make use of custom code or development, whether for **Power Apps component framework** (**PCF**), web resources, or JavaScript components. However, the platform also allows us to substantially improve the UX and UI of applications in several ways.

If we list the most relevant ones, in order from the least to the most complex, we find the following.

Forms

Modifying native forms or creating new forms that adapt to the needs of each type of user is one of the least complex things we can do to improve usability and UX. A form that adapts to the user's needs, highlighting the most relevant information and ordering the rest of the information while maintaining the business logic, greatly improves the UX. Forms will be covered in further detail in *Chapter 3*.

Business rules

We have already mentioned business rules in the context of automating some actions. However, that is not the only type of action we can configure in a business rule:

Figure 2.9 – Business rule actions

Business rules will allow us to improve the UX by incorporating visual alerts, modifying the visibility and applicability of form attributes based on conditions evaluated in real time, defining values to attributes, or locking/unlocking fields. Business rules will be covered in more detail in *Chapter 3*.

Views

Like forms, modifying native views or creating new views to adapt them to the user's needs is a low-complexity task, but being one of the most used components by users will have a great impact on the UX. Views will be covered in more detail in *Chapter 3*.

Charts

Charts are the first resource users have for data exploitation and exploration:

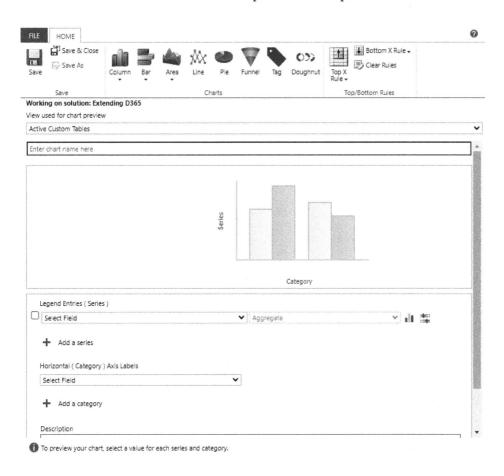

Figure 2.10 – Chart definition

With an Excel-like complexity definition, we can easily create charts and use them as part of dashboards or when working with views.

Native components

Dynamics 365 Customer Engagement offers us a wide variety of native components (PCF) to change the usability of views or add forms:

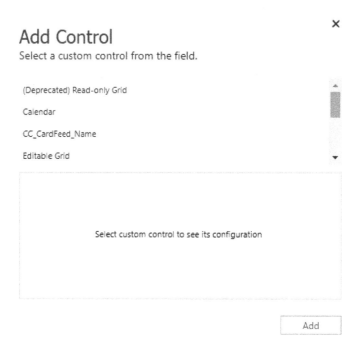

Figure 2.11 – Native controls in the table settings

These components do not require development or advanced configuration and allow us to have an enhanced UX with an advanced UI. They can be enabled from the table settings, or for the form when we are editing it in the form designer. Some examples of these components are the Business Card Reader component or the Kanban view for opportunities.

Dashboards

Often, dashboards will be a user's entry point to the application: they will be the first thing they see when they enter, and if we offer them a dashboard targeted to their needs, then it will be one of the most important working tools they will have.

Depending on the user's role, we can make use of classic dashboards, interactive dashboards, or Power BI dashboards. Dashboards will be covered in greater detail in *Chapter 3*.

Sitemap

The sitemap defines how an application will be navigated. Although Dynamics 365 Customer Engagement applications come with a defined sitemap, it is possible to modify and adapt it to meet the specific needs of users.

Business process flows

As we already discussed, business process flows serve as a visual guide to the process being developed. By using Dynamics 365, we will be able to modify native processes or create new ones.

Embedded artificial intelligence

Dynamics 365 Customer Engagement offers several artificial intelligence capabilities natively. However, we will be able to extend these capabilities to offer more elaborate insights, predictions, or suggestions based on historical data, without the need to develop artificial intelligence models.

Custom pages and embedded canvas apps

Custom pages and embedded canvas apps are two ways in which to enable a canvas app experience in the context of a Dynamics 365 application. In *Chapter 5*, we will delve into the detail of how we can make use of these components.

Transforming data into actionable information

Last but not least, when working with Dynamics 365 Customer Engagement, users will constantly generate data, either because they manage opportunities, customer journeys, cases, or work orders. Regardless of the application or applications that have been installed, the use of the platform itself will lead us to have a considerable database that we must be able to exploit to draw conclusions and, thus, help our business.

As we already mentioned, Dynamics 365 offers multiple capabilities for data extraction, among which we can find views, graphs, dashboards, reports, or templates. To help users work smarter on the data stored and managed in Dynamics 365 Customer Engagement, we can create any of these objects without development.

However, if we need advanced capabilities, we can make use of Power BI to build custom reports and dashboards. These reports and dashboards can be used decoupled from Dynamics 365 Customer Engagement, or as part of a platform unification strategy, and both reports and dashboards can be consumed from Dynamics 365 Customer Engagement. We will cover this topic in depth in Part Five of the book, in *Chapter 12* and in *Chapter 13*.

Summary

In this chapter, we have identified the most common use cases for extending Dynamics 365 Customer Engagement without development and have developed a high-level understanding of the scope of each.

By understanding the options the platform offers to quickly extend Dynamics 365 Customer Engagement applications, we can design the applications to fit the organisation's business processes. At the same time, we can empower users by automating repetitive mundane tasks, provide more consistency by automating system processes, and even define the experience that each type of user will have in the application.

In short, by exploring these issues, you will be able to demonstrate the value of the platform in no time, which means a quick and unquestionable win for the organization.

In *Chapter 3*, we will begin to dive deeper into each of these topics, focusing on those capabilities we have to extend native capabilities and describe the most important concepts around creating forms, business rules, views, charts, graphs, components, and navigational aspects such as the sitemap and ribbon.

Questions and answers

1. Which are the most common use cases for extending Dynamics 365 Customer Engagement?

    Answer: Some of the most common scenarios for extending Dynamics 365 Customer Engagement Apps are:

    -   Upgrade the administration and governance capabilities with custom applications, processes, automations, or internal bots

    -   Automate tasks, both the system and user tasks, that could happen in real time or as a background process

    -   Extend the business processes to adapt the platform to their specific processes

    -   Improve the UX by adjusting the UI

    -   Develop custom reporting components in order to transform the data the organization generates into actionable information

2. Which type of automations can we build with a no-code/low-code approach?

    Answer: The three most important no-code/low-code automation capabilities we have available when working with Dynamics 365 Customer Engagement are the Power Automate flows, classic workflows, and business rules.

Part 2: Extending Dynamics 365 Customer Engagement Applications

In addition to creating a custom application, thanks to Power Apps, we can extend the user experience (both internal and external) by incorporating embedded applications as components, extending the command bar with Power Fx, or enabling a web portal with Power Pages.

This part will help you understand what tools or features are used to extend Dynamics 365 Customer Engagement applications in the most common scenarios and use cases.

This part has the following chapters:

- *Chapter 3, Extending Dynamics 365 Customer Engagement Native Applications*
- *Chapter 4, Building Applications with Dynamics 365 Customer Engagement*
- *Chapter 5, Dynamics 365 Customer Engagement with Custom Embedded Applications*
- *Chapter 6, Extending Your Apps with AI and Mixed Reality*

3
Extending Dynamics 365 Customer Engagement Native Applications

Within the platform of Microsoft business applications, we find Dynamics 365 and Power Platform. Dynamics 365 corresponds to the business applications designed, built, and marketed by Microsoft, also known as first-party applications, while Power Platform corresponds to the set of tools that Microsoft offers us so that we can design our own applications, processes, bots, and dashboards.

In turn, Dynamics 365 has multiple products that we can implement with an adoption approach, but also adapting the out-of-the-box processes, by extending and customizing the applications. We can broadly categorize them as applications focused on the customer relationship (Customer Engagement) and applications focused on operations and finance (Finance & Supply Chain Management, Business Central, and more).

In this chapter, we will see some of the most common scenarios for extending native Dynamics 365 Customer Engagement applications through extensions or customizations of the applications. In the following chapters, we will be exploring how to extend processes, bots or dashboards, and reports. It should be noted that Dynamics 365 Customer Engagement allows us to adapt or extend its applications both with a no-code/low-code approach and by introducing custom developments. In this book, we focus exclusively on the no-code/low-code capabilities, and we will not cover how we can extend Dynamics 365 Customer Engagement with a pro-code (development) approach.

By the end of this chapter, you will understand how to adapt native Dynamics 365 Customer Engagement applications, extend the data model, adjust the user interface according to the business requirements, and implement the processes. In this chapter, we will cover how to extend the following:

- Dynamics 365 Customer Engagement data model
- Forms and business rules

- Views and dashboards
- The sitemap and command bar

Technical requirements

To work with Dynamics 365 Customer Engagement, it is necessary to have an environment with one of the supported licenses. However, the topics covered in this chapter do not require any Dynamics 365 application.

The following is required for this chapter:

- Any Dynamics 365 Customer Engagement License (any of the available ones) with administrator permissions in an environment
- A supported browser

Understanding the Dynamics 365 Customer Engagement data model

When implementing Dynamics 365 Customer Engagement, one of the first things we will do is to understand the data model that comes with the platform and contrast it with the data model we need to respond to business requirements. As discussed in *Chapter 1*, Dynamics 365 Customer Engagement applications are built on Dataverse, which implies that there is a set of pre-built objects even before we install any Dynamics 365 Customer Engagement application. Dataverse includes a set of tables under the **Common Data Model** (**CDM**) data schema. On top of this set of common tables, each Dynamics 365 Customer Engagement application introduces another subset of tables specific to every business model.

Together, let's explore what the CDM is, why it is important for Dynamics 365 Customer Engagement Apps, and how can we work with tables in Dataverse.

What is the CDM?

If we are going to work with Dataverse, whether we work with Dynamics 365 Customer Engagement or not, first, we must understand what the CDM is, how it will affect us in the design of our applications, and finally, what the most relevant recommendations are when designing our applications.

The **CDM** is the product of an initiative led by Microsoft to facilitate data integration between applications built by different vendors through the definition of a metadata system and a set of standardized and extensible data schemas, including entities/tables, attributes/columns, semantic metadata, and relationships. The definition of these schemas will allow us to work with common concepts between applications such as Accounts, Contacts, or Phone Calls, thus simplifying the creation, transformation, and analysis of data.

As you can see in the following diagram, the CDM serves to standardize and share data, allows the construction of applications by multiple developers working independently, and facilitates integration and deployment between applications:

Figure 3.1 – The essence of the CDM

The data model included in the CDM covers the aspects common to all Dynamics 365 Customer Engagement applications, thus allowing rapid and consistent deployment of these applications in a Dataverse environment. Accounts, Contacts, Activities, Currency, Goals, and Products are some of the tables in the CDM; therefore, they will be found in all Dataverse and Dynamics 365 Customer Engagement environments. On top of this base, each Dynamics 365 Customer Engagement application incorporates a set of additional tables specific to its business processes. For example, consider the following:

- *Sales*: Includes Opportunity, Lead, Quotation, Order, Invoice, and more

- *Marketing*: Includes Email Message, Event, and more

- *Customer Service*: Includes Case, Entitlement, Service, and more

- *Field Service*: Includes Work Order, Agreement, Asset, and more

- *Project Operations*: Includes Project, Project Task, Project Task Member, and more.

There are also tables specific to Dynamics 365 Customer Engagement but shared between applications, such as Case or Resource.

The following diagram is a representation of how the CDM schema groups the Core, the Dynamics 365 Customer Engagement, and Dynamics 365 Industry Accelerators tables:

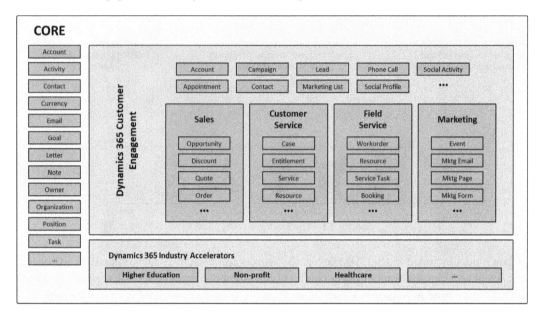

Figure 3.2 – The CDM scheme

Although it is not the subject of this book, it is worth mentioning that even if an environment has certain Dynamics 365 Customer Engagement application tables enabled, the access or use of these tables by users is defined by the licenses that the user has associated with them.

Working with tables/entities

When working with data in Dynamics 365 Customer Engagement, we have two options to extend the data model – modify an existing entity/table or create a new entity/table.

When creating a new table, we will have to select some properties that define the behavior and affect the security model for the table, such as table type and owner type. These characteristics cannot be modified once the table/entity has been created, so it is advisable to take the necessary time to design them correctly. Understanding not only the immediate requirements of the business but also the scalability and evolution of it is critical to ensuring the correct configuration of the table.

Understanding each table/entity type in Dynamics 365 Customer Engagement

A new table in Dynamics 365 Customer Engagement can be of three types – standard, activity, or virtual:

- **Standard tables** are those that allow you to manage data within Dataverse/Dynamics 365 Customer Engagement and do not have to have the behavior of an activity. Natively, the vast majority of tables are of the standard type, such as accounts or opportunities.

- **Activity-type tables** have special behavior and have some shared field/column definitions in Dataverse/Dynamics 365 Customer Engagement. Activities have time dimensions to indicate the start and end date and time, both actual and expected, and the duration of the activity. Activities allow us to identify in which other table the activity occurs (for example, whether it is opportunity- or case-related), and the participants in the activity. Activity-type tables are displayed together in Dynamics 365 Customer Engagement and are part of the timeline and have common permission settings.

- **Virtual tables** are custom tables whose structure includes column definitions but whose data is stored in another system. For the end user, there will be no difference between the appearance of virtual tables and other types of tables, although they will have some restricted actions when they want to work with this data. These tables are ideal for scenarios where we need to access data that is managed in another system (for example SAP), from Dynamics 365 Customer Engagement. This approach avoids data duplication and complex integrations while allowing users to work with data external to Dynamics 365 Customer Engagement in their applications. However, it's important to consider the current limitations at the time of evaluation of a virtual table as a data integration approach.

Now that we have gained a basic understanding of tables/entities in Dynamics 365 Customer Engagement, let's learn how to create a new table.

Creating a new table

We can create a table from inside or outside a custom **solution**. A solution is a way Dynamics 365 Customer Engagement, such as Dataverse, packages the customizations for better **application lifecycle management** (**ALM**). Every Dataverse environment will have a Default Solution that will include every object that we could build in the environment, regardless of whether we created it in a custom solution or outside a custom solution. The recommendation is to always work with solutions, as it allows us to package all the customizations. To create a new table from a solution, follow these steps:

1. Go to `https://make.powerapps.com`.

2. Select the working environment where the Dynamics 365 Customer Engagement applications are installed (it is recommended that you work in the development environment):

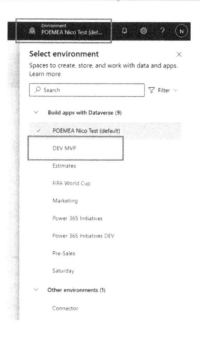

Figure 3.3 – Selecting the working environment

3.   Navigate to the **Solutions** section:

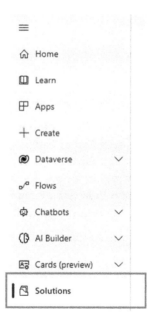

Figure 3.4 – Go to the Solutions section

4. Select the **solution** you want to work on (or create a new one if none exists yet):

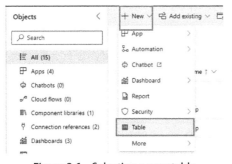

Figure 3.5 – Selecting a solution

5. In the command bar, select **+ New | Table**:

Figure 3.6 – Selecting a new table

6. Fill in the properties and information for the new table, including **Display name**, **Plural name**, and **Description**, as well as **Advanced options** and the **Primary column definition**:

New table

Use tables to hold and organize your data. Previously called entities
Learn more

Properties   Primary column

Display name *

Plural name *

Description

☐ Enable attachments (including notes and files) [1]

Advanced options ⌄

Figure 3.7 – New table form

The properties that can be defined in a table are as follows:

Property	Details
Display name	Corresponds to the singular name of the table that will appear in the application. For example, Account.
Plural name	Corresponds to the plural name of the table that will appear in the application. For example, Accounts. The system will suggest the plural name automatically.
Description	Additional information to describe the use of the table.
Enable Attachments	Enable the table to have attachments, including notes and documents. This feature cannot be reversed once selected.

Table 3.1 – Table base properties

It is also possible to define advanced properties for the table, such as the following:

Property	Details
Schema name	It represents the internal name (schema name) of the table, composed of the **Publisher** prefix of the solution and the table name. This data is suggested by the system but can be modified.
Type	**Standard**, **Activity**, or **Virtual** can be selected
Record Ownership	You can select a user or team, or organization. If a table is an organization table, its records cannot be assigned to a user or team, and therefore the security model will define whether it has access to all records or none. Whereas a user or team implies that the records can have a specific owner and the security model can look at the owner and the business unit where the owner is located to define the level of access allowed. Usually, you'll choose a user or team when you need to apply a security model with five levels of granularity (none, own, business unit, parent business unit, and organization). If the requirement is not clear, it's recommended that you choose a user or team, as this option cannot be changed after the table is created.
Image	Allows you to select a custom image that will appear in different places in the application, such as the site map.

Table 3.2 – Table advanced properties

Finally, there are three properties groups defined in an easy-to-understand manner, as **For this table…** properties, **Make this table an option when…** properties, and **Rows in this table..** properties.

We can enable the following properties for the table:

Property	Details
Apply duplicate detection rules	This option is selected by default and allows you to create duplicate detection rules for this table.
Track changes	This option enables data synchronization with external systems and enables offline capabilities.
Custom help	This allows you to define the help URL for the table.
Audit changes	This enables audit logs in the table. Auditing must be configured at all levels for the audit log to be effective.
Quick create form	This enables the table to have quick creation forms.

Table 3.3 – Table properties to apply for the table

We can define the following properties to make the table an option when performing the following actions:

Property	Details
Activities	Only by enabling this option will it be possible to associate activities with the record, through the native **regarding** field. This feature cannot be reversed once selected.
Mail Merge	Enables users to use Word templates on this table
SharePoint	Enables the table to manage documents in SharePoint libraries.

Table 3.4 – Table properties to enable the table an option when performing different actions

We can define the following properties for the table rows:

Property	Details
Connections	This enables the table to have connections to other tables that are enabled. This feature cannot be reversed once selected.
Email	This enables users to send emails to an email address set as a column in the table. This function cannot be overridden once selected.
Access Teams	This enables the creation of equipment templates associated with the table.
Feedback	This enables customers to write comments associated with the record. This function cannot be canceled once selected.
Queues	This enables you to manage the table records in the work queues as queue items, together with other queue items corresponding to other tables. This function cannot be reversed once selected.
Search results	This enables Dataverse search for the table.
Offline	This enables the table to be configured in offline profiles.

Table 3.5 – Table properties to apply to the rows of the table

In addition to the table properties, we can define some primary column properties:

Property	Details
Primary column display name	This corresponds to the column label
Primary column description	This corresponds to the column description
Primary column schema name	This corresponds to the internal or schematic name of the column
Primary column requirement level	This allows you to define whether the column will be required by the system, recommended, or optional
Primary column configuration	As the primary column is always a string, it's possible to define the maximum length of the column content

Table 3.6 – Table primary column properties

7. Select **Save**.

After you save the form, the system will create the table based on the selected properties. This will include several out-of-the-box fields, forms, and views.

Data type

When working with a table/entity, there are many things that we can extend, such as columns, forms, views, business rules, relationships, dashboards, charts, and more.

To create a column, simply perform the following steps:

1. Select the table:

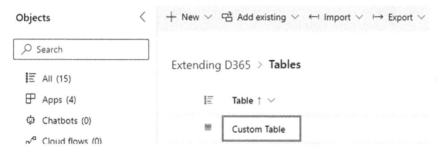

Figure 3.8 – Selecting the table

2. In the command bar, select + **New** | **Column**:

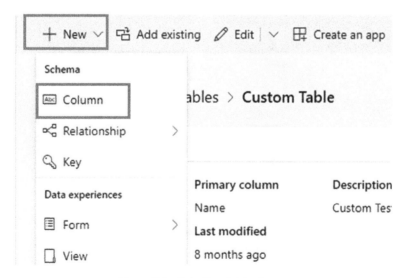

Figure 3.9 – Selecting Add column

3.   Fill in the details in the **Column properties** form:

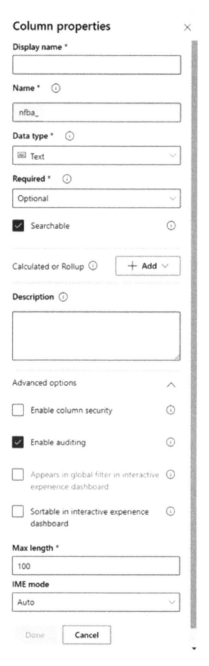

Figure 3.10 – New column form

Let's take a look at what these field properties are:

Property	Details
Display name	This corresponds to the column label. This label will appear in forms, views, and other components where the column is referenced.
Name	This is the internal or outline name of the column.
Data type	This corresponds to the data type of the column, which could be **Text line**, **Date time**, **Whole number**, **Floating point number**, **Decimal number**, **Lookup**, **Customer**, **Choice/Option**, **Choices/Options**, **Currency**, **File**, **Image**, **Multiple text line or Boolean/Yes-No**. In turn, some of these categories have subcategories that will condition the behavior of the column.
Required level	This allows you to define the required level of the column.
Searchable	This allows you to define whether the column will appear in the advanced search of the Dynamics 365 Customer Engagement Apps and any other model-driven apps and whether it will be available to customize views.
Calculated or Rollup definition	This allows you to define the characteristics of the calculated and rollup columns. The calculated columns will be automatically calculated from a formula.
Description	This allows you to define the usage instructions for a column. This description will appear when working with the column in a form as a tooltip.
Security	This allows you to enable the column security level for the column.
Audit	This allows you to enable audit tracking for this column.
Global filter	This allows you to define whether the column will appear as an available filter when using interactive experiences dashboards.
Sortable in interactive dashboard	This allows you to define whether data can be sorted by this column when using interactive experiences dashboards.
Data type-specific properties	Each data type will have specific properties to complete.

Table 3.7 – Column properties

4. Select **Save**.

Calculated and rollup columns

Calculated and consolidated columns are column types that allow us to add logic to your definition. The value of these columns will be defined by the formulas we define in them.

In the case of calculated columns, they can take data from the record where they are located, and from records related to a many-to-one relationship. Depending on the type of data contained in the column (for instance, text, integer, currency, date, etc.), we will use one or another formula. For example, we can perform a concatenation of texts, add or subtract dates, or multiply numbers, among many other possibilities.

On the other hand, the consolidated columns will use the data from the one-to-many relationships. With these types of columns, we will be able to make calculations or count the child records. For example, we can take averages, obtain a sum of values, or count the records.

Global versus local option sets

In Dataverse, there are two different types of lists that we can define to use in the choice and choices columns. They are the global option set and the local option set.

Global option sets are defined at the environment level and are available for use in any table. This means that if you change a global option set, it will affect all of the tables used.

Local option sets are defined at the table level and are not shared between tables. This means that if you change the local option set, it will only affect the table in which it was created.

Once the data model has been extended, it is necessary to adapt the other components of a table that users will work with. Let's start by understanding how to extend and work with forms and business rules.

Extending and working with forms and business rules

Dynamics 365 Customer Engagement applications include several types of forms that can be used for different purposes. We will use forms when we want to access a specific record and find its data, including the relationships and data of the record itself. It will also be the component we will use to create a new record from scratch.

Extending a native form or creating a new one is another way to extend native Dynamics 365 Customer Engagement applications without the need to use developments or custom code.

Main forms

All tables can have one or more main forms. We will use a main form to create, view, or modify an entire record.

Having more than one main form can help organizations work with records in a specific way – have different forms for different applications and/or assign roles to the forms and, thus, define the experiences of users when working with a particular record.

The main form is composed of tabs, sections, and components. A form can have one or more tabs. A tab can contain one or more sections. And a section can contain one or more components. A few examples of components are fields (table columns), sub-grids, timelines, **Power Apps Component Framework** (**PCF**) components, quick view forms, web resources, IFRAMES, and an embedded canvas app, among others. Depending on the license we have, we can make use of other specific components such as the relationship wizard:

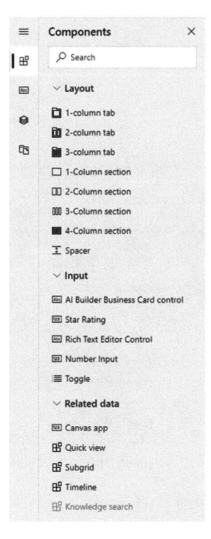

Figure 3.11 – Form components

Each of the different types of components, as well as tabs and sections, will have its own properties.

In the following example, we can identify a two-tab form. The first tab has three columns, with one section in each:

Figure 3.12 – Main form example – Account for interactive experience form

To create a new main form, simply follow these steps:

1. Select the solution we are going to work on (or create a new one if it does not exist yet):

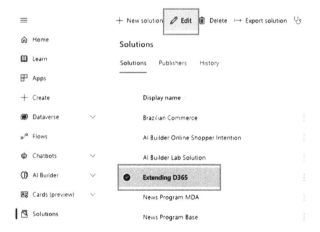

Figure 3.13 – Selecting the solution

2. Select the table on which we want to modify or create a form and go to the **Forms** section:

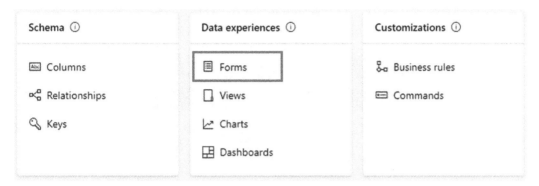

Figure 3.14 – Selecting the table

3. Select the form we want to modify or create a new one by selecting + **New form**, and then + **Main Form**:

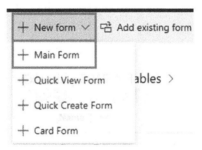

Figure 3.15 – Adding a form

After that, the form designer will open and you'll be able to edit the main form, by adding tabs, sections, and other components.

However, main forms are not the only type of forms. Let's continue with the quick create form, to understand it in more detail.

Quick create form

The quick creation form is a tool that is used less than it should be. It allows us to quickly create a record without having to navigate from the screen, as shown in the following screenshot:

Figure 3.16 – The Quick Create option

With a form that appears on the right-hand side of the screen, we can quickly create a record with the most important data and continue working. It is a very useful element to have for records that need to be created unrelated to a previous one, from any screen, or from a sub-grid in a form when it is a child record that we need to create. The following screenshot is the native, out-of-the-box, quick create form for contacts:

Figure 3.17 – An example of a contact quick create form

Unlike the main form, a quick creation form is limited to having a single column with three sections and having attributes (columns) or controls. It is important to remember that to make use of the quick creation forms, the table must be enabled to support them.

In addition to **main forms** and **quick create forms**, Dynamics 365 Customer Engagement also has **quick view forms**.

Quick view forms

The **quick view forms** option allows us to have a form of record type A inside a form of record type B, between which there must be a relationship. Essentially, the quick view form allows us to see more information about a linked record. For example, in a case form, we can see more details of the client and other cases they have recently had. This allows users to access the related record without having to navigate between records.

To add a quick view form for a form, just select this option in the form editor, choose the relationship on which the component will be added, and the form you want to display, as shown in the following screenshot:

Figure 3.18 – Quick view component in the form designer

Finally, we can add business logic to our forms and tables without any development, by creating **business rules**.

Other considerations with forms

When working with main forms, we also have to consider four important aspects: role security, form ordering, fallback forms, and the form access checker.

Role security allows us to define for which security roles a form will be available. This allows us to easily define very different user experiences for a user with role A and a user with role B (for example, a salesperson and a customer service agent).

The form order allows us to define the order in which the available forms will appear for a user when more than one form is available.

The fallback form defines the form(s) that, by default, will be available to all users. It is important to consider fallback forms when implementing role-based security for forms.

Finally, we can use the form access checker to validate which forms a user with a specific security role will see when using a particular application:

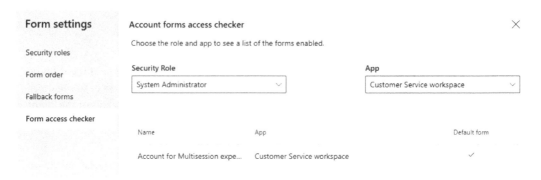

Figure 3.19 – Form access checker

As we can see in the previous screenshot, the form access checker asks us to select a role and an application and shows us the list of forms that a user in those conditions will see.

Business rules

We have already seen the basics of extending the Dynamics 365 Customer Engagement data model and forms. Now, let's get into the details of the business logic that we can extend without the need for code or custom development, and how we can define its scope to affect only one form or have a broader scope.

We will use business rules to define the business logic that allows us to establish a consistent business process. The first thing to keep in mind is that a business rule will apply to a single table (opportunities, cases, and more) and that it has multiple components to consider:

Component	Detail	Screenshot
Scope	The scope of a business rule defines where the business rule will be applied. The scope can be the entire table (i.e., the logic will be applied to all forms and at the server level), to all forms, or to a specific form.	
Condition	This defines when, or under which conditions, the business rule is executed.	
Action	This corresponds to the action that will be executed as part of the business rule. It can be as follows: • Make a recommendation: displays a recommendation or a message in a field. • Lock or unlock: allows you to set a field as locked or unlocked in the form. • Show error message: allows you to set an error message on the screen. • Set column/field value: this allows you to set the value of a field at the time of the rule execution. • Set default value: this allows you to set the default value of a field that will always be updated in the record when it is loaded. • Set as system required: this allows you to change the system required or optional status of a field. • Set visibility: this allows you to show or hide fields in the form.	

Table 3.8 – Business Rules components

By now, we should be able not only to work with tables and extend the data model but also to customize the user experience with main forms, quick create forms, and quick view forms, and to add business logic through the business rules. Now, let's discuss how we can work with data with views and dashboards.

Extending and working with views and dashboards

Views and dashboards are other components in Dynamics 365 Customer Engagement that we can customize and extend without code. Natively, Dynamics 365 Customer Engagement includes a series of views and panels tailored to the business processes offered by each of its applications (Sales, Customer Service, Marketing, Field Service, and Project Operations). However, when implementing Dynamics 365 Customer Engagement, we do not have to limit ourselves only to the adoption of these. We can create the views and dashboards our organization requires.

In Dynamics 365 Customer Engagement, views are lists of records composed of the following:

- The definition of which table the records are to be viewed; for example, Accounts.

- The definition of the filtering criteria that is to be set in the view; for example, Accounts with an Active status.

- The definition of the columns you want to display in the view, including the order, size, and data sorting criteria.

Therefore, views are only a definition and not the set of records that will be shown. The records each user can see in a view depend on the security model that is implemented and the privileges that each user has for each table. That is, two users with different conditions in the security model will be able to see different records in the same view.

There are different types of views and different places from where we can access them:

Type	Details
Personal View	These are the views created by each user and are only visible to their creator unless they are shared with other users.
System View	These are the views that an administrator or customizer created to incorporate into the application. Within them, we find the following: • **Quick Search**: This is the default search that is used in the searches when using the quick search. This view also defines the columns that are searched when using the quick search and the searches. • **Advanced Search**: This is the default view when using the advanced search. This view also defines the columns that are used when creating a new public or personal view. • **Associated**: This corresponds to the default view when displaying the related tables. • **Search**: This is the default view that is displayed in a search field.
Public View	These are views that can be customized as they are used. All users can access these views when they are available. Public views are used in sub-grids and dashboards. By default, Dynamics 365 Customer Engagement includes several public views. Note that public views can be created and deleted if they are in unmanaged solutions. However, system-defined public views cannot be deleted.

Table 3.9 – Types of views

In the following screenshot, we can see the native view from the Account table, each one with the specific **View type** values:

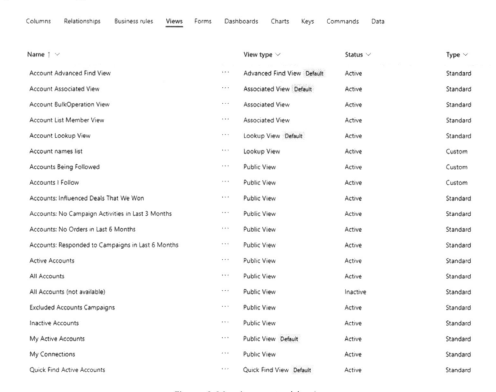

| Columns | Relationships | Business rules | Views | Forms | Dashboards | Charts | Keys | Commands | Data |

Name ↑ ⌄		View type ⌄	Status ⌄	Type ⌄
Account Advanced Find View	⋯	Advanced Find View Default	Active	Standard
Account Associated View	⋯	Associated View Default	Active	Standard
Account BulkOperation View	⋯	Associated View	Active	Standard
Account List Member View	⋯	Associated View	Active	Standard
Account Lookup View	⋯	Lookup View Default	Active	Standard
Account names list	⋯	Lookup View	Active	Custom
Accounts Being Followed	⋯	Public View	Active	Custom
Accounts I Follow	⋯	Public View	Active	Custom
Accounts: Influenced Deals That We Won	⋯	Public View	Active	Standard
Accounts: No Campaign Activities in Last 3 Months	⋯	Public View	Active	Standard
Accounts: No Orders in Last 6 Months	⋯	Public View	Active	Standard
Accounts: Responded to Campaigns in Last 6 Months	⋯	Public View	Active	Standard
Active Accounts	⋯	Public View	Active	Standard
All Accounts	⋯	Public View	Active	Standard
All Accounts (not available)	⋯	Public View	Inactive	Standard
Excluded Accounts Campaigns	⋯	Public View	Active	Standard
Inactive Accounts	⋯	Public View	Active	Standard
My Active Accounts	⋯	Public View Default	Active	Standard
My Connections	⋯	Public View	Active	Standard
Quick Find Active Accounts	⋯	Quick Find View Default	Active	Standard

Figure 3.20 – Account table views

It is possible to change the native behavior of read-only views by different components available in Dynamics 365 Customer Engagement, including the following:

- An editable grid that allows line editing

- Special components that are PCF components that alter the behavior of the view, such as a Kanban board or a calendar

Currently, it's not possible to change the native behavior of the read-only view for a canvas application. However, if we want to have an embedded Canvas App instead of the view, we can replace the object in the form.

When implementing Dynamics 365 Customer Engagement, it is very important to consider the organization's processes to extend, create, or modify views and, thus, offer the best solution to users. Correctly designing views can facilitate customer management, making customer information available in an orderly fashion, avoiding unnecessary clicks to access it, or offering inline editing behavior.

However, it's important to review the limitations of each component when we are considering how to use them.

In addition to views, Dynamics 365 Customer Engagement provides us with dashboards to work with data at both executive and operational levels. The system supports two types of dashboards – classic or standard dashboards and interactive dashboards. Dashboards can be personal (or user) or system dashboards.

Classic or standard dashboards support multiple types of components, such as the following:

- Views
- Charts
- Web resources
- Timelines
- IFRAMES
- Relationship Assistant

Interactive dashboards can be multi-stream or single-stream. Multi-stream dashboards will display real-time information arranged in multiple streams, with no maximum number of streams per dashboard that can be configured. Each stream can display data from a single table, and different streams of the same dashboard can display data from different tables. On the other hand, single-stream panes display data from a single table from one or multiple views/queues (except table panes that have special behavior).

In the following screenshots, you can see the differences between the design of a multi-stream and a single-stream interactive panel:

Figure 3.21 – Multi-stream dashboard - Dashboard designer

As you can see in the preceding example, the interactive knowledge management dashboard presents graphs at the top of the dashboard and multiple streams at the bottom:

Figure 3.22 – Single-stream interactive dashboard - Dashboard designer

In this second example, we have a single stream on the left-hand side of the panel, and multiple graphics within the rest of the panel.

Both multi-flow and single-flow panels contain interactive charts that act as visual filters for the panel listings.

Now that we have seen how to work with tables, forms, views, and panels, we need to go deeper into how to improve the navigation of the application by working with its site map and command bar.

Extending and working with sitemap and command bar

Finally, among the first things we can customize to extend to Dynamics 365 Customer Engagement applications are the sitemap and ribbon.

But before we go into detail about how we can extend it, let's understand what it is and what the importance of working with the sitemap in a Dynamics 365 Customer Engagement application is.

The sitemap defines how users will navigate through an application. The sitemap will define the areas enabled to be accessed by the user interface, becoming a fundamental aspect of the user experience when working with the application. The sitemap structure has three levels:

- **Areas**: Dynamics 365 Customer Engagement applications can have one or multiple areas. Areas separate the application into sections containing groups and sub-areas.

- **Groups**: Groups are part of areas and serve to group subtasks in a logical and convenient way for users.

- **Subareas**: Sub-areas correspond to the actionable components of the site map, which can be tables, custom pages, panels, or other types of components.

A good sitemap facilitates the adoption of an application and makes it easier for users to work while a bad sitemap can be detrimental to the use and adoption of the application.

Every model-driven app has a sitemap, which may be unique to that app or may be shared between different apps.

Currently, there are two ways to modify a sitemap – with the classic editor and with the modern editor. To do this you need to do the following:

1. Select the application on which you want to work (or create a new one if none exists yet):

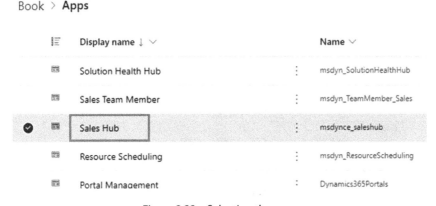

Figure 3.23 – Selecting the app

2.   Select to edit in the same tab or in a new tab:

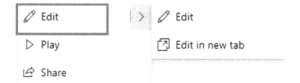

Figure 3.24 – Editing the app

You'll enter the editor by selecting **Edit**, while you'll open the editor in a new tab by selecting **Edit in a new tab**.

In the following screenshot, we can see the different ways to configure the site map, or navigation, depending on the type of editor:

Figure 3.25 – Modern versus classic app editor

As we can see in the preceding screenshot, the new application editor offers a **What You See Is What You Get (WYSIWYG) experience**, unlike the classic editor.

Now, let's see how we can customize the user experience in terms of the command bar and the actions in it.

Modifying the command bar without code

Dynamics 365 Customer Engagement applications organize action commands in different ways depending on where they appear and which customer is being used. The command bar groups the series of commands available for a table in a particular context, and they form one of the fundamental usability elements of Dynamics 365 Customer Engagement.

In the following screenshots, you'll identify different ways the command bar appears in the application:

Figure 3.26 – Command bar in a form

In a form, the command bar appears at the top of it, while in a sub-grid the command bar is accessible from the ellipses button on it:

Figure 3.27 – Command bar in a sub-grid

The command bar will show users the actions available to perform on the record in which it appears. Sometimes, it will be necessary to modify the visibility of the commands depending on the user's role or status.

To modify the command bar, it is necessary to edit a Dynamics 365 Customer Engagement application (or any model-driven app) using the modern editor. Once the editor is open, select the table in which you want to edit the command bar and select the option, as shown in the following screenshot:

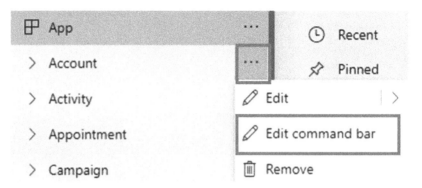

Figure 3.28 – Edit command bar option in the modern app editor

This will open the command editor, and the first thing to select is the type of **command bar** we want to modify, as shown in the following screenshot:

Figure 3.29 – Command bar selector

Once selected, we can create new commands or modify the ones we have already created, selecting whether we want a no-code/low-code approach, using **Power Fx**, or whether we prefer a **pro-code** option, using JavaScript.

In the new command, we will be able to do the following:

- Define the label and icon
- Set the formula we want to be executed
- Define the visibility by formula or predefine it
- Set the help text and accessibility

By customizing and extending the command bar, we can ensure that each user finds the most optimal way to work with Dynamics 365 Customer Engagement records.

Summary

In this chapter, we learned how we can start extending Dynamics 365 Customer Engagement applications. We started by understanding how the data model is composed and how we can extend it, and then identified the main components that are part of an application and how we can work with them: forms, business rules, views, dashboards, the sitemap, and command bars.

In the next chapter, we will go into detail about how we can build custom applications based on the applications and processes offered by Dynamics 365 Customer Engagement. We will identify the different types of applications and how we can leverage each of these for the benefit of the users.

Questions and answers

1. What is the name of the data schema used by Dataverse that includes the definition of master tables such as Account and Contact?

    Answer: The data schema used by Dataverse is the CDM.

2. Why is it advisable to design the data model correctly before starting to build custom tables?

    Answer: It is advisable to design the data model correctly before starting to build custom tables because, on the one hand, it is possible that there is a native table that fulfills the function we are looking for. And on the other hand, if it is necessary to create a custom table, it is important to understand what properties it must have since some of the properties cannot be modified once the table is created.

3. How many types of dashboards are available and when can I use each one?

    Answer: There are two types of dashboards: classic and interactive. Classic dashboards are used for non-real-time data and can include several types of components, including AI-driven components such as Relationship Assistant. Interactive dashboards are near-real-time data and are ideal when users need to interact with data directly from the dashboard.

4. Why is it important to have a good site map design?

    Answer: A good sitemap facilitates the adoption of an application and makes it easier for users to work, while a bad sitemap can be detrimental to the use and adoption of the application.

4

Building Applications with Dynamics 365 Customer Engagement

Dynamics 365 Customer Engagement offers us multiple applications built by Microsoft such as Sales, Customer Service, Marketing, and Field Service, to mention the best known. These applications were designed to cover specific business processes; we saw how we can extend them in the previous chapter. However, we may encounter the requirement to have an application that is customized and designed entirely on **user experience** (**UX**) requirements different from those offered by native applications. This may be because there are requirements for a specific group of users. After all, we may want to narrow an application to one or a limited set of use cases, or because there is an external user type that must be part of the Dynamics 365 Customer Engagement processes.

In this chapter, we will learn why we could build new, fully customized applications on top of Dynamics 365 Customer Engagement applications while leveraging the capabilities of Power Apps and Power Pages (formerly Power Apps portals). We will work through several examples of real implementations where it was necessary to have a standalone application built on top of one of the Dynamics 365 Customer Engagement applications and processes. However, before we dive into how to build these applications, we will review some tricks to quickly and easily identify when a new application may be needed.

By the end of this chapter, you will have learned why and how to create new applications around Dynamics 365 Customer Engagement, including Canvas apps, model-driven apps, and portals, with Power Apps and Power Pages, respectively.

In this chapter, we will cover how and why to build the following:

- A Canvas app as a standalone application on Dynamics 365 Customer Engagement
- A model-driven app as a standalone application on Dynamics 365 Customer Engagement
- A portal with Power Pages (formerly Power Apps portals) as a standalone application on top of Dynamics 365 Customer Engagement

Technical requirements

To work with Dynamics 365 Customer Engagement, it is necessary to have an environment with one of the supported licenses.

The following are required for this chapter:

- Any Dynamics 365 Customer Engagement license (any of the available ones) with administrator permissions in an environment
- A supported browser

Designing a custom application

The first thing we have to understand is that we are not necessarily going to build a custom application on Dynamics 365 Customer Engagement, and even sometimes, it is not the recommended option because we could lose the native functionality that Microsoft has designed and built for the native application.

We also have to remember that we can customize the experience of different users of an application by incorporating role-based restrictions to different components, such as forms or business process flows.

So, how can we identify if we need a customized application?

Among some of the arguments or requirements that we can find to think that we need a customized application, we have the following:

- We need external users to intervene in a process or access certain information
- We need a simpler interface
- We need to limit the use cases of the application
- We need to have two versions of the same application, but in one of them, we want to limit the available system views

In general, the requirements will be surrounding how users will access the date or the UX. Sometimes, there won't be an explicit requirement but an implicit one on the security or usability requirements. Our job, as architects or consultants, is to identify those requirements and to propose the best solution, which could be adopting the Dynamics 365 Customer Engagement applications or extending them.

In the next few sections, we will go into detail about what decisions we can make when a user presents us with any of these requirements.

Building Power apps for Dynamics 365 Customer Engagement

To build a new application in a Dataverse environment, we have to consider two things:

- **Technical feasibility**: The technical feasibility discussion is the easiest one because as we already mentioned in *Chapter 1*, when we implement a Dynamics 365 Customer Engagement solution, underneath, we have a Dataverse environment with all the capabilities that Power Platform offers us. It is important to remember that a detailed analysis of the requirements is always necessary to correctly understand the technical solution to be implemented.

- **Licenses required to use the application**: The analysis of the licenses required to use the application must be done while considering the licensing model in force at the time of the analysis. The objective of this book is not to detail the Dynamics 365 Customer Engagement or Power Platform licensing model, mainly because it is a dynamic model that changes regularly. The following reference to the current licensing can only be considered as an example of the analysis we should do on each project.

Types of applications

When we think about building a custom application, we have three options:

- Build a model-driven app
- Build a Canvas app
- Build a web portal

To decide which is the best option to meet the requirements we have, we have to understand when it applies to use a model-driven app, a Canvas app, or a portal.

Model-driven apps are the type of applications recommended for the implementation of process-driven apps, which manage a large amount of data, and in which users need flexibility and agility in moving between different related records. Model-driven apps offer a predefined user interface and make use of Dataverse's forms, views, charts, and table panels, making them relatively simple and fast to build. Model-driven apps can contain multiple complex processes, and their main data source will be Dataverse. Model-driven apps are ideal for when we have to implement an end-to-end process or a complex process.

Canvas apps, on the other hand, are more flexible applications in terms of the user interface since we will have total freedom to design each of the screens, validations, and behavior of each component. Canvas apps connect easily with Dataverse, but can also use the 700+ Power Platform connectors as data sources. Canvas apps are ideal for extending the last quarter mile in a process or complementing a process with a fully customized application.

Finally, portals, unlike model-driven apps and Canvas apps, are ready to be used by both internal and external users. They are natively integrated with Dataverse, using Dataverse as the main data source, and use the table views and forms to define the portal lists and forms. Portals are ideal for when we have to implement a website to be accessed by internal people but also externally by the organization.

Licensing considerations

Under the current licensing model, we can group Dynamics 365 Customer Engagement license types into Enterprise (or higher) and non-Enterprise licenses. Enterprise licenses give us the right to build standalone Power apps within the same environment where we have Dynamics 365 Customer Engagement, while non-Enterprise licenses will not give us that right, as shown in the following figure:

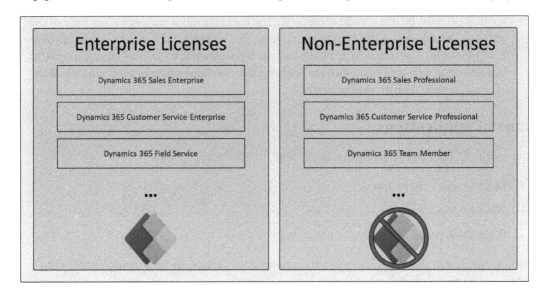

Figure 4.1 – Power Apps rights in Dynamics 365 licenses

In addition to Dynamics 365 Customer Engagement licenses, we can build custom applications for users with Power Apps licenses as they have read rights to all Dynamics 365 Customer Engagement restricted tables and **create, read, update, and delete** (**CRUD**) rights to the rest of the tables in the environment:

	Power Apps Licenses	Dynamics 365 Enterprise Licenses	Dynamics 365 Non-Enterprise Licenses
Dynamics 365 Applications	Not entitled to it	Within the privileges of the assigned licenses.	Within the privileges of the assigned licenses
Custom Applications	Entitled to one or more, depending on the license	Entitled only in the context of the license.	Not entitled to it
Non-Restricted Tables	Entitled to CRUD privileges	Entitled to CRUD privileges.	Limited privileges
Restricted Tables	Entitled to read privileges only	If the user has the required license, he/she will have CRUD privileges. Otherwise, only read privileges.	Limited privileges

Table 4.1 – Dynamics 365 and Power Apps licenses considerations

In the preceding table, we can see the rights that are granted by the different Dynamics 365 and Power Apps licenses on native and custom applications, as well as Dataverse tables.

I recommend verifying which tables are restricted before making a design or licensing decision to verify compliance with licensing policies, as well as the latest versions of the Dynamics 365 and Power Apps licensing guides.

Licensing guides and restricted tables definition

Dynamics 365 Customer Engagement Licensing Guide: `https://go.microsoft.com/fwlink/p/?LinkId=866544`

Power Apps and Power Automate Licensing Guide: `https://go.microsoft.com/fwlink/p/?linkid=2085130`

Restricted tables: `https://docs.microsoft.com/en-us/power-apps/maker/data-platform/data-platform-restricted-entities`

Now that we know what to consider before thinking about building a standalone application, let's analyze model-driven app scenarios.

Building a model-driven app

Building a custom model-driven app can be the right approach in certain scenarios. In this section, we will discuss some of these scenarios from actual Dynamics 365 Customer Engagement deployments.

Power Apps licensed users

In general, and regardless of the Dynamics 365 Customer Engagement processes that we have implemented, it is possible that there are licensed users with Power Apps licenses that should be part of these processes. Power Apps users may have restrictions for both restricted tables and complex tables, and it is important to have an adequate security model to prevent any non-compliant use of those tables.

Likewise, Power Apps users will most likely not need to access processes in the same way as a Dynamics 365 Customer Engagement licensed user, as their impact on the process is likely to be ad hoc. In these cases, having an application designed for their specific use cases can help with platform adoption.

Back-office users

When we implement a customer service solution, there are usually several types of users involved, and for each of these, we have to ensure the best experience and ease of adoption.

Here is a breakdown of some of the user types we will encounter:

User Type	Details	Possible App To Use
Agent, Advisors	These users are responsible for the first level of support. They interact directly with customers through various channels. In general, they need to work with work queues, and their vision of the business is based on operational aspects.	Customer Service Hub Customer Service Workspace Omnichannel Engagement hub
Supervisors, Team Leaders	These users are responsible for the performance of the agents and usually have one or more teams in charge. They are usually responsible for managing resources and queues, to ensure that the best KPIs are obtained.	Customer Service Hub Customer Service Workspace Omnichannel Engagement hub

Back-Office User	These are users who perform offline tasks related to an incident. They do not usually interact with customers in online channels but through offline communications such as emails or publications in a self-management portal. They can also develop the work and leave the conclusions associated with the incidents without interceding directly on them, being a front-office agent responsible for contacting the customer with the response.	Customer Service Hub Customer Service Workspace Custom Power App

Table 4.2 – Example of different types of users and their applications

In this scenario, we can identify that back-office agents could use any of the applications included within Dynamics 365 Customer Service, both the Customer Service Hub and Workspace, to take advantage of the multi-session experience and the inbox capacity. They could also use the Customer Service Team Member application, or benefit from a custom application built on the Dynamics 365 Customer Service model, which would focus on their task management associated with the cases. This model-driven app could consist of the following:

- An interactive dashboard to manage the flow of tasks to the back-office team

- A classic or Power BI dashboard for the back-office team supervisor to keep track of the most important KPIs

- A task form designed for the back-office function, with a quick case view form and, potentially, a Canvas app or Power Apps Component Framework to improve usability

Indeed, some capabilities of the Workspace application cannot be replicated in a customized model-driven app, so it will be necessary to properly evaluate the requirements to understand if it is necessary.

Dispatchers/task scheduling

Dynamics 365 Universal Resource Scheduling allows us to manage and schedule tasks of different types (project tasks, work orders, service tasks, and other custom activities), ensuring that the best resource is assigned. The implementation scenarios of Universal Resource Scheduling are wide and varied, being able to be some of the native processes that Dynamics 365 Customer Engagement proposes, such as scheduling custom task types. In any case, we will have different user profiles working with resource scheduling, and even though Dynamics 365 offers different applications, sometimes, having a customized application will be necessary. Consider, for example, the case of the dispatcher that has a Dynamics 365 Field Service license.

The dispatcher can use the Dynamics 365 Field Service application to make use of the scheduling dashboard to manage resources, bookings, and work orders pending to be scheduled. For a simplified experience, the dispatcher can use the Universal Resource Scheduling resource management application, which limits their site map to specific areas of resource management, including the scheduling dashboard.

Thus, as shown in the following diagram, for the dispatcher, we would have at least these three options to use the same functionalities:

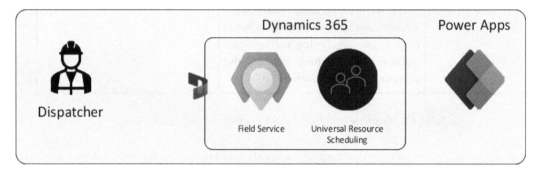

Figure 4.2 – Possible app approaches for a dispatcher

For this example, we will have to consider all of the requirements and user stories for that type of user. In this way, we will be able to make the best design decisions for the solution we will propose.

Agenda management

Sometimes, we encounter very simple use cases, in which any of the first-party model-driven apps become too complex. The contact and agenda management scenario is a clear example of this, and a really common use case in sales. In different industries and sectors, we find users who need to have limited access to customers and activities, either because they are users of a front desk, or because they manage appointments in a health center. For these scenarios, even if there are Team Member user applications that are simple in themselves, it is sometimes convenient to build a specific model-driven app optimized for these specific use cases.

App for a customized process linked to a native one from Dynamics 365

It is normal that, in a Dynamics 365 Customer Engagement project, in addition to involving the native processes of its applications (opportunity management, work order management, and so on), other related processes are designed and built, but they are managed by other users who do not need to interact with Dynamics 365 Customer Engagement applications.

Let's check out the following examples.

Resources management

When we implement a process that includes resource management, whether Customer Service, Field Service, or Project Operations, there are multiple processes related to the resource that are not covered by Dynamics 365 Customer Engagement. It is possible that the organization already has a system in which it manages resources and they need to be integrated, but on other occasions, organizations will not have a specific system or prefer to unify the operational management of resources in a single platform. Some examples of this may be the management of continuous training or upskilling of resources or the management of onboarding.

For these cases, we will be able to design and build these processes and enable a model-driven app for their management. As they are resource-based processes, we will be able to build a 360-degree view of the extended resource, extending the native model to include processes to ensure that the initial setup of resources is validated and ensure the knowledge and skills that will later be considered for scheduling or case routing, establish automated periodic performance reviews, establish annual training and upskilling plans and eventual training.

Case management process

When we implement customized processes where there is a stakeholder that interacts (it can be a customer, a citizen, or an internal user of the organization), it is very common to implement a Customer Service process/user service/citizen service on the native process of Dynamics 365 Customer Service. This means that the main process is not the one defined by Dynamics 365 Customer Service, but it simply supports the main process.

How to start with a new model-driven app

To create a model-driven app, you need to do the following:

1. Go to `https://make.powerapps.com`.
2. Go to **Solutions** and enter a solution:

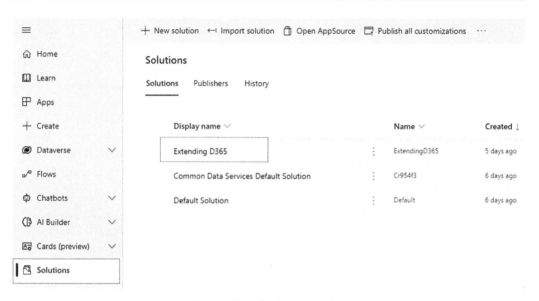

Figure 4.3 – Selecting a solution

3. Click on +**New**, then **Model-driven app**, in the **Apps** section:

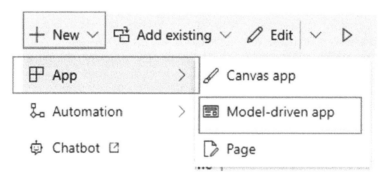

Figure 4.4 – Creating a model-driven app

4. That will open the app designer. Define the name and click on **Create**:

Figure 4.5 – Defining the app's name

5. Then, you can start adding pages to the app and define the app settings:

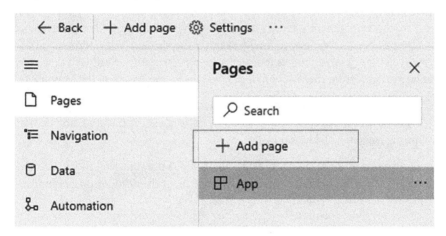

Figure 4.6 – Adding a new page to the model-driven app

Now that we've covered model-driven apps, let's discuss Canvas apps.

Building a standalone Canvas app

As we have already seen, model-driven apps are useful for designing custom applications when we have a particular process or use cases, and for which native Dynamics 365 Customer Engagement applications are not the best option. However, we don't just have the option to build model-driven apps on top of Dynamics 365 Customer Engagement processes –we can also build Canvas apps.

In this section, we will discuss some common scenarios for which a standalone Canvas app is a viable option as a solution.

Visit management

Activity management is one of the central axes of Dynamics 365 Customer Engagement as it allows us to track the interactions in the different points of contact we have with our customers. (Understanding customers is a generic term that may vary, depending on the industry or sector; for example, in the public sector, this would be citizens and not customers.)

It is common to use meetings to schedule visits to a location, whether the location is a company's own business, a client's premises, or a public space. Organizations that have physical points of sale, both their own and under a franchise model, usually make visits with a pre-defined structure where different aspects must be taken note of to finally evaluate the visit and take follow-up actions. This type of use case is also frequent in models in which sales representatives must visit prescribers since they must capture insights from the visit and then schedule actions based on the responses.

For these types of scenarios, it is common to find the need for mobile applications (for tablet or mobile) that allow the user to schedule visits, define the type of visit that will be, and then make the visit while capturing insights quickly and easily.

In these cases, both because of the flexibility of the application's user interface design and the ease of supporting complex forms and advanced business rules without the need for programming (simply using **Power Fx**), a Canvas app is often the design choice.

Some of the key capabilities that can be considered for the application are as follows:

- Calendar view with a summary of scheduled visits
- Inbox section or alerts on recommended visits
- Quick form to schedule a visit
- Ability to send emails to the people scheduled
- Dynamic form that adjusts to the type of visit for capturing insights
- Capture photos and other multimedia formats
- Capture business cards

In this way, we can offer another type of mobile experience, more personalized and adjusted to the needs that arise from the realization of visits where the priority is to have an application designed specifically for this use case.

Meeting Capture

In the same way that when a visit takes place, information related to the visit must be captured when meetings take place. To understand this use case, we can take the Meeting Capture template, built by Microsoft, as an example.

This Canvas app template uses connectors with Outlook, Planner, and OneNote to offer us an advanced productivity tool in which we can take notes, schedule a new meeting, and define follow-up tasks.

The following screenshot shows how the different features can be combined on the same screen, enabling the users to write notes, create new tasks, and track the remaining time for the meeting:

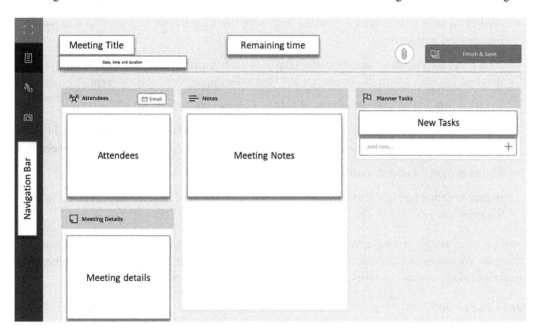

Figure 4.7 – Microsoft's Meeting Capture template

If we connect this use case with Dynamics 365 Customer Engagement, the result is obvious. Instead of taking appointments from the Outlook calendar, we can do so from Dynamics 365 Customer Engagement and offer an enhanced experience when managing the meeting, including the following:

- Calendar display and suggested meeting to take notes on
- Meeting management with contextual information about the context of the meeting – for example, information on the opportunity, case, project, customer, or custom process on which the meeting is scheduled
- Ability to schedule a follow-up meeting
- Ability to contact all invitees to a meeting
- Ability to contact the organizer of a meeting
- Ability to create a Teams chat with a subset of the meeting invitees
- Ability to take notes from a meeting and save them in the Dynamics 365 Customer Engagement appointment
- Ability to take photos or sketches, and save the attachments to SharePoint or OneDrive for Business associated with the Dynamics 365 Customer Engagement appointment
- Ability to edit a scheduled appointment, add or remove people, and add a Teams link
- Ability to define follow-up tasks and create them in Dynamics 365 Customer Engagement and/or Planner, either as a task assigned to a user or as a customer/attendee engagement of the meeting
- Ability to attach and distribute links and files pre- and post-meeting
- Ability to define and distribute meeting notes and minutes to all or some attendees, as well as to non-attendees

As we can see, a simple use case such as taking meeting notes does not have to involve a simple application. We can extend the capabilities of Dynamics 365 Customer Engagement concerning the management of appointments, offering a work hub around appointments.

Events check-in

One of the features offered by Dynamics 365 Marketing is the management of events, both online, as well as face-to-face, and hybrid. When we have a face-to-face event where the capacity is limited, it is important to manage the check-in to the event – even more so if, among the guests, there are prominent personalities or if, due to absences, it is necessary to make changes to the logistics of the event in real time.

Although we could use Dynamics 365 Marketing from the native application for mobile or tablet, being a specific use case is an excellent example of how we can improve the UX, and at the same time optimize the process, with a customized Canvas app.

We can provide users with an app that allows them to do the following:

- View the list of guests/registrants and perform quick searches on them
- Check in manually or by scanning the QR code
- Identify the percentage of attendees who have checked in and those who have not yet arrived
- Have all the information about the logistics of the event
- Receive push notifications
- Manually create alerts

In this way, we can extend not only the functionality of Dynamics 365 Marketing but also offer a UX designed for on-site work.

Field Service warehouse management

When we implement Dynamics 365 Field Service, we have many functionalities that include fully defined end-to-end processes. However, there are some that, in a standalone implementation, are often improved and adapted to the needs and requirements of each organization.

Warehouse management allows us to have control over tracking stock and moving equipment and supplies. However, this module is designed to be integrated with the organization's ERP. In these implementations, regardless of whether or not we have an ERP where inventory is managed, we can create a Canvas app for warehouse managers, to facilitate, among other things:

- Inventory management
- Stock movement management
- Stock reservations
- Management of early warnings

The importance of this type of app is that it can be designed for warehouse employees, regardless of their level of technical knowledge. So, we can offer a simplified interface with information that's easy and quick to find, as well as well-defined action buttons:

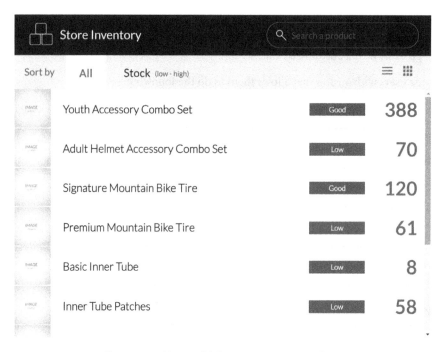

Figure 4.8 – Microsoft's Store Inventory template

The preceding screenshot corresponds to the inventory management application template. In it, we can see a quick and easy way to present a new interface to users who need to work with inventory.

Time-off request

Dynamics 365 Customer Engagement allows us to manage our resources and, therefore, their calendars and working days. It natively offers a time-off request process. However, it is very common to extend Dynamics 365 by constructing a custom application to make these requests and have a global view of the balance of days off or remaining vacation.

As an example, we can take (and even as a template when building the application) the template that Microsoft offers us for this purpose – the Leave Request template.

This template can be found among the rest of the templates at https://make.powerapps.com, as shown here:

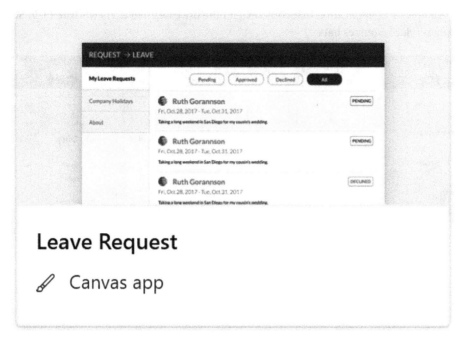

Figure 4.9 – Microsoft's Leave Request template

As we can see, this template only uses Outlook 365 and Office 365 connectors, but it can be adapted so that it supports the Dynamics 365 Customer Engagement model and process, allowing us to do the following:

- Request time off
- Approve or reject time off
- Have access to request history
- Have control of the balance of available days
- Have information about the organization's calendar

This is an example of an application that could extend the use cases that users who are Field Service or Customer Service resources have:

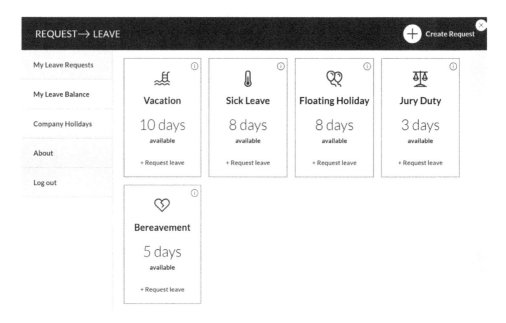

Figure 4.10 – Microsoft's Leave Request template's My Leave Balance screen

By connecting this process with the native time-off process, you can offer an immersive experience in Teams or as a standalone application for managing these types of requests.

Customer 360-degree view

The 360-degree view of the customer is one of the most important components of any Dynamics 365 Customer Engagement implementation. Whether it's a B2B or B2C model implementation, having a holistic view of our customers allows us to make informed decisions and ensure we have the best possible customer management. For many years, we have tried to consolidate in Dynamics CRM/Dynamics 365 Customer Engagement all customer information to achieve that 360-degree view. However, with the advancement of the platform, Microsoft has given us the option to have that consolidated view of our customers with a **Customer Data Platform** (CDP), such as Customer Insights.

However, regardless of whether or not we have Customer Insights implemented, having a 360-degree view of our customers is not the same as having a 360-degree view of the customers available. Again, building a customized application will allow us to establish a completely user-friendly UX, with simple use cases, such as simply having the complete information of our customers in a consolidated way from different systems (Dynamics 365 Customer Engagement, Dynamics 365 F&SCM, SAP, and so on).

Let's use the Customer Success template again as an example. Here, we can see a clear example of an application designed and built to provide a specific view of our customer, focusing on the health of the relationship and the consolidation of information that we can have disaggregated by multiple systems. The following screenshot shows the template offered by Microsoft:

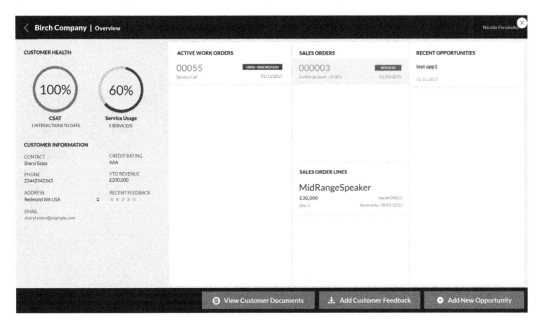

Figure 4.11 – Microsoft's Customer Success template

We can see how this application also allows us to capture information from our customers, such as feedback, and even initiate new management, such as a new opportunity.

Project tasks

Project Service Finder, or Project Service by Dynamics 365, was an application that enabled workers to find available project work and sign up for work. In addition to that, it allowed users to manage their profiles. This application was a native mobile application for Dynamics 365 Project Service Automation.

This application, as shown in the following screenshot, cannot be found in the app stores anymore:

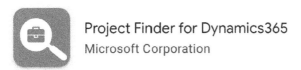

Figure 4.12 – Microsoft's Project Finder for Dynamics 365 in Google Play Store

As part of the migration from Project Service Automation to Project Operations, this application was deprecated. Users only have the option to use the native Dynamics 365 mobile application, which executes the same application on the mobile as on a web browser.

The following figure shows screenshots of what was available on the app stores:

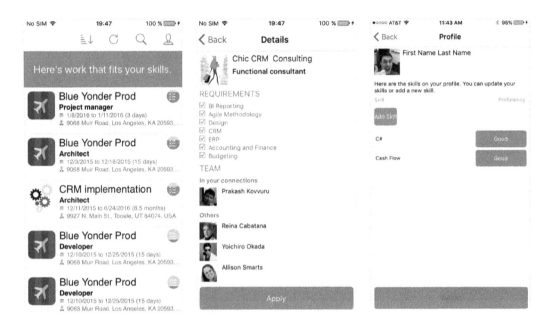

Figure 4.13 – Microsoft's Project Finder for Dynamics 365 screenshots in Apple Store

Since the application has been deprecated, if we want to offer an application that allows us to expose projects available for Dynamics 365 Project Operations resources, we can do so by building a custom Canvas app. This application can be used to allow us to:

- List projects where there is a resource requirement for which we qualify, considering skills and rating levels
- See the details of the tasks to which we could apply for
- Enable a process to apply for tasks
- View a summary of the tasks requested, and the status of the request
- Receive notifications when a task has been assigned or rejected
- List the tasks assigned to the logged-in user

As with the previous examples, this application will not apply to all clients with Project Operations, and an individual assessment of each project's needs is recommended.

Product Showcase and Product Visualize

The sales force needs powerful tools to build trust with customers and potential customers. When an organization sells products, whether they are large volume products for factories, furniture, or any other type of product, it is unlikely that the salesperson will always have a catalog of products to show the customer and convince them. That is why, with the help of technology, we need to empower salespeople with innovative solutions that allow them to record sales activities without this being a problem when adopting the solution.

In the following figure, we can see an example of a Canvas app template developed by Microsoft that allows us to explore product features and resources to present them to a customer:

Figure 4.14 – Microsoft's Product Showcase template

Building a digital product catalog with Canvas apps allows us not only to add technical or commercial details of the product but also to add material associated with the product and modern tools. For example, we could include the following:

- Link sales literature and multimedia material associated with the product

  Additional supporting material, such as brochures, promotional videos, or photos will be a valuable tool for the salesperson when discussing a product with a customer.

- A barcode scanner to quickly search for a product

  Adding the option to scan the barcode will make it easier for users to search for a product in the catalog.

- Adding mixed reality capabilities

  Microsoft released the Dynamics 365 Product Visualize application in preview. This application allowed you to access 3D models of products and view them in a real context, thanks to mixed reality technology. With the addition of mixed reality capabilities to the Canvas app, Microsoft has opted to deprecate this application. This leaves us with the option to build a custom app that allows us to:

  - Select a product from the catalog and the associated 3D model to view it using mixed reality
  - Take notes of the 3D model to share with the production team on specifications requested by the customer

In this type of application, not only the internal UX (the salesperson) is important, but also the external UX (the customer) since it will be used by both simultaneously.

In these examples, we have been able to identify how and why we may find ourselves in the position of having to build a Power Apps application independent of the Dynamics 365 Customer Engagement applications, but interacting with the processes defined by them.

Next, we will look at the most common scenarios for implementing Power Pages (formerly Power Apps portals).

How to start with a new Canvas app

To create a Canvas app in a solution, you need to do the following:

1. Go to `https://make.powerapps.com`.
2. Go to **Solutions** and enter a solution:

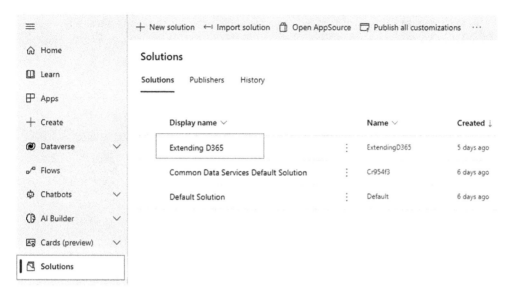

Figure 4.15 – Selecting a solution

3.   Click on +**New**, and then **Canvas app** in the **Apps** section:

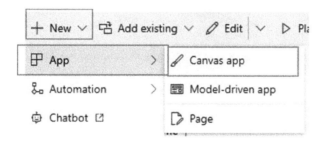

Figure 4.16 – Creating a Canvas app

4. This will open the **Canvas app** wizard, where you'll have to define an **App name** and a **Format** (**Tablet** or **Phone**). Then, click on **Create**:

Figure 4.17 – Defining a Canvas app name and format

5. Then, you can start inserting screens and different objects:

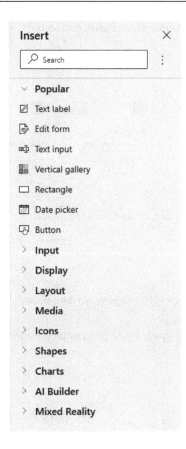

Figure 4.18 – Power Apps studio – the Insert tab

However, you can start a new Canvas app from a template, an image, or a data source. To create one from a data source, follow these steps:

1. Go to `https://make.powerapps.com`.

2. Select + **Create** to navigate to that area.

3.   Click on a data source (**Dataverse**, **SharePoint**, and so on):

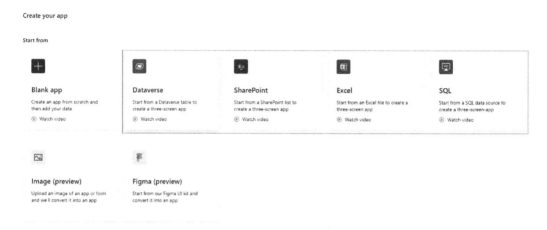

Figure 4.19 – Selecting a data source

4.   The **Connections** screen will open. From here, you can select or create the connection and select a table, site, list, or file:

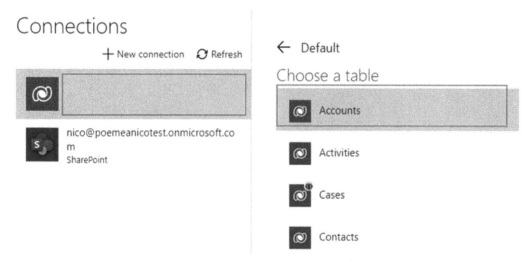

Figure 4.20 – Selecting a connection and table/site/file

5.   Power Apps Studio will open with some pre-built screens:

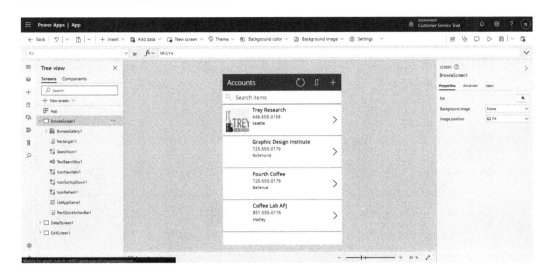

Figure 4.21 – Pre-built screens

To create a Canvas app from an image, you need to do the following:

1. Go to `https://make.powerapps.com`.

2. Select **+ Create** to navigate to that area.

3. Select **Image (preview)**.

4. The **Convert an image into an app (preview)** dialog appear. From here, click on **Next**:

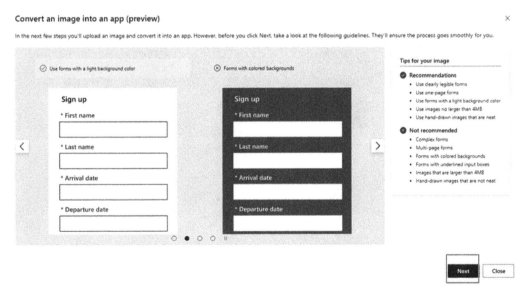

Figure 4.22 – Converting an image into an app dialog

5.   Define a name, select the image and the format, and click on **Next**:

Upload an image or a screenshot of an existing form. Or, start with our sample image to get an idea of how the process works.

Name *

New Image App

Image

⦿ Upload my own

◯ Start with a sample image

Upload my own *

Choose file   Maximum file size: 4MB

JPG and PNG files are supported.

Format

⦿ Tablet

◯ Phone

Figure 4.23 – App configuration

6.   The system will identify the components and will show you the result. You can click on each component and adjust it, or even define new components. When you're finished, click **Next**:

Figure 4.24 – Components mapping

7.   You can choose to create a new table in **Dataverse** or not:

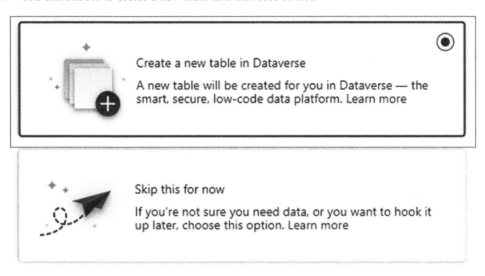

Figure 4.25 – App data configuration

8.   If you wish to create a new table, then you'll have the chance to define the columns in the table (optional):

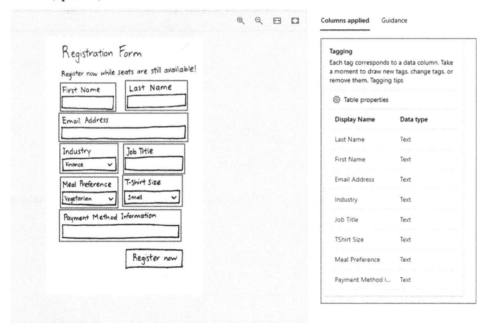

Figure 4.26 – Defining the columns

9. The last step will be to review the table. You'll have the option to edit the table properties before you create the app:

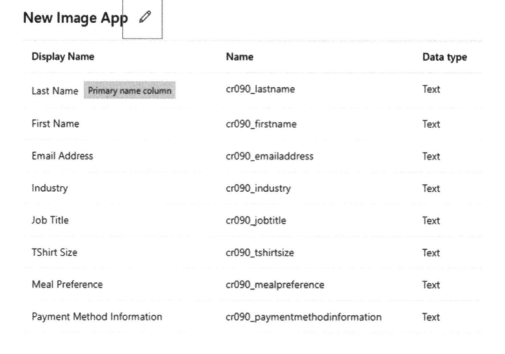

Display Name	Name	Data type
Last Name Primary name column	cr090_lastname	Text
First Name	cr090_firstname	Text
Email Address	cr090_emailaddress	Text
Industry	cr090_industry	Text
Job Title	cr090_jobtitle	Text
TShirt Size	cr090_tshirtsize	Text
Meal Preference	cr090_mealpreference	Text
Payment Method Information	cr090_paymentmethodinformation	Text

Figure 4.27 – Data review

10. After the system has finished processing this information, your app will be created from the image:

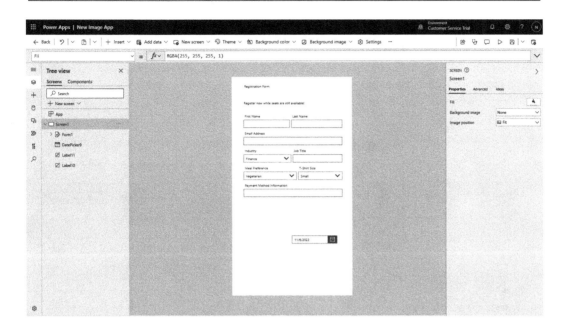

Figure 4.28 – App built from an image

If you want to create a Canvas app from Figma, you need to do the following:

1. Go to `https://make.powerapps.com`.

2. Select + **Create** to navigate to that area.

3. Select **Figma (preview)**:

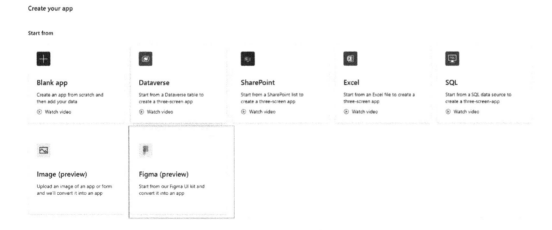

Figure 4.29 – The Figma (preview) option

4. You need to enter details for **App name**, **Link to Figma page or frame**, and **Figma personal access token**, and define the app's format:

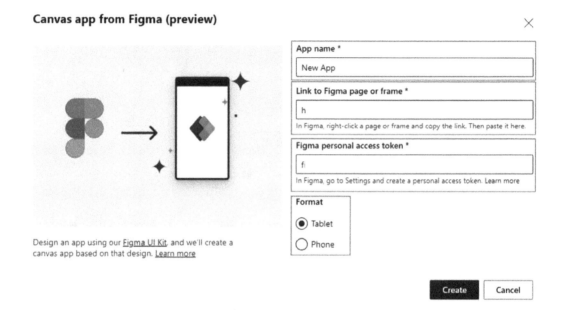

Figure 4.30 – Canvas app from Figma wizard

5. After the system processes this information, your app will be created via Figma.

Finally, to create a Canvas app from a template, you need to do the following:

1. Go to `https://make.powerapps.com`.
2. Select + Create to navigate to that area.
3. Scroll down and select the template you wish to use:

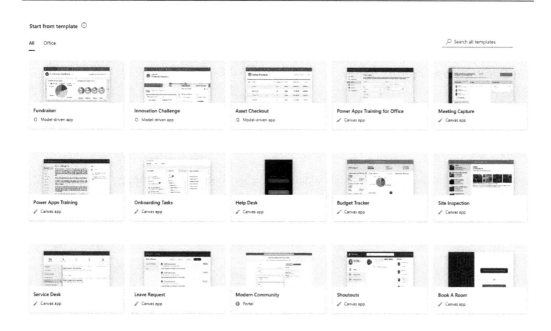

Figure 4.31 – Power Apps templates

4.   In the dialog, you need to define an **App name** and click on **Create**:

Figure 4.32 – Power Apps template dialog

Now that we discussed the different ways we can create a Canvas app, let's quickly review the main Canvas apps components.

Main Canvas apps components

When working with Canvas apps, we use different components. Let's look at the main components you'll find in Power Apps Studio.

Screens

The screen is the main UI component and contains the other components in the app. Every app will have at least one screen. Commonly, apps are multi-screen apps.

You can add screens with predefined layouts or scenarios:

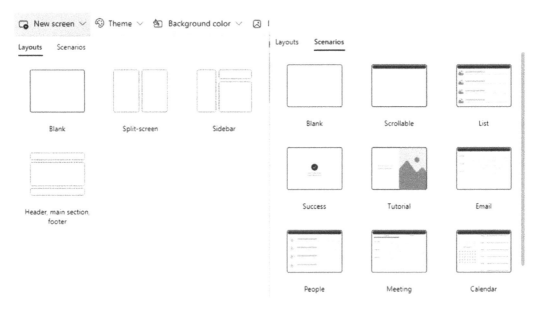

Figure 4.33 – Power Apps – New screen layouts and scenarios

The preceding screenshot shows the options available when creating a new screen.

Galleries

A gallery allows you to present a set of data. This gallery can be connected to a collection or any other data source:

Figure 4.34 – Canvas app gallery

As we can see, galleries can contain different types of components, such as images, text, or icons.

Forms

Forms allow you to create, edit, or just display data from a data source. Forms in Canvas apps are not related to the forms in Dataverse.

Containers

Containers help you design your interface by grouping different controls easily and flexibly. In addition to these controls, containers have properties that help you define the layout of your screen:

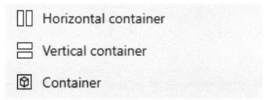

Figure 4.35 – Types of containers

As we can see, we can select vertical containers, horizontal containers, or containers. Depending on the container we choose, the components in it will be organized in different ways. While vertical and horizontal containers will organize the components vertically and horizontally, respectively, containers will give you more freedom to place the components wherever you want.

Building custom portals for Dynamics 365 Customer Engagement

If we have a requirement to give access to Dynamics 365 Customer Engagement processes and data to users who are not part of the organization and who do not act on behalf of it, the option we will have is to use Power Pages (formerly Power Apps portals). Power Pages is one of the products that we will find in Power Platform that allows us to design, build, and deploy web portals without the need for any development. Power Pages requires a Dataverse-enabled environment since the web configuration is based on records from a product-specific data model.

With Dynamics 365 Customer Engagement, being an application based on customer management, there are multiple scenarios in which we may need people outside our organization to access the data and processes implemented.

Power Platform portals are highly flexible both in their graphic design and in the functionalities and components that can be published. It presents a great ease of integration, not only with Dataverse data and processes but also with the rest of the Power Platform components.

Next, we will analyze some of the most common scenarios in terms of Dynamics 365 Sales, Dynamics 365 Marketing, Dynamics 365 Customer Service, and Dynamics 365 Field Service applications.

Partner portal

Some organizations have partner-based business models. It is very common to see this business model in software companies that sell from representatives or partners in different countries. Managing partners correctly, as well as having a unified view of the business being developed, helps not only to maintain and grow the partner channel but also to have a more accurate business analysis and forecast.

We can deploy a Power Pages/Power Apps portal based on a template or start from a blank portal, and from there, extend and customize it. The following are some of the functionalities we can expect in a partner portal:

- Partner contact management
- Tracking of partner leads
- Allocation of business opportunities to the partner
- Tracking of objectives set for the partner

- Managing the joint agenda

- Scheduling meetings with the partner

- Making sales documents available

- Providing FAQs

- Receiving notifications

- Viewing the forecast

- Managing joint documents (contracts, NDAs, and so on)

Being a partner portal, we can also extend the administration of partner members so that they're self-managed. In this way, a partner administrator could define the access and privileges for each member of their organization.

Customer self-service portal

The self-service portal is the most common use case for implementing a Power Platform portal. Self-management portals allow us to enable various functionalities so that customers can manage requests and consult knowledge base articles among the most common portals.

There is a wide range of self-service portals. Depending on the processes that an organization has implemented in Dynamics 365 Customer Engagement, you can publish more or fewer processes in the portal.

Among the most common functionalities in a self-management portal, we can find the following:

- Incident/case management, being able to create them, close them, and interact with a customer service agent through publications

- Chat and integrated chatbot

- Management of knowledge base articles, allowing you to search and give feedback on them

- Invoice and purchase history viewing

- Managing customer assets

- Call scheduling with the support team

- Managing notifications or mailboxes

- Managing contracts and entitlements

- Consultation of physical stores

- Visitor registration

- Contact form

As mentioned previously, these are just a few examples. Depending on each organization, the functions and processes may vary:

- If the organization runs projects and performs management with Dynamics 365 Project Operations, you may want to enable not only the ability to create a support ticket associated with the project but also the following:

  - View project status and historical status reports

  - View the project schedule and task forecast

  - View project financials

- If the organization provides in-territory services, such as repairs, installations, or other types of services at the customer's home or location, among other functions, you might want to include the following:

  - Real-time tracking of the location of the resource that will be going to perform on-site work

  - View of fieldwork history

  - Ability to manage a visit or work order

  - Asset management and ability to trigger IoT commands

In short, the self-service portals will be adjusted to the processes that the organization has defined and wants to enable for the customer.

How to start with a new portal

To create a new portal, you need to do the following:

1. Go to https://make.powerpages.microsoft.com/.
2. Select your environment.
3. Click on + **Create a site**:

Figure 4.36 – The Create a site option

4. Choose the template you want to use:

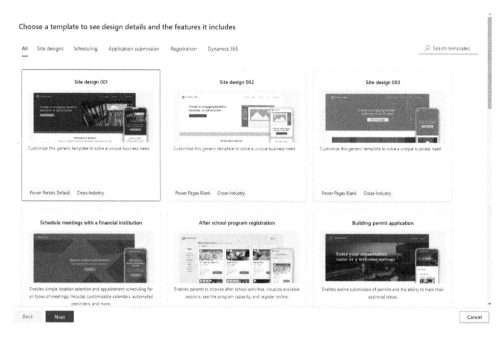

Figure 4.37 – Available templates

5.   Enter the name you want to give to your portal, the web address, and the language:

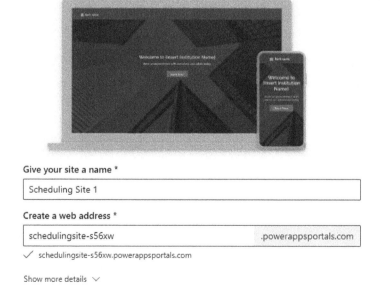

Figure 4.38 – Power Pages configuration

When the platform finishes the new portal deployment, you'll be redirected to the **Power Pages** home screen.

Summary

In this chapter, we looked at how we can extend Dynamics 365 Customer Engagement applications by creating standalone custom apps or portals. It is worth mentioning that the examples provided in this chapter are only a set of examples of actual deployments that have been implemented in projects; they are not intended to be a complete listing of the applications and portals that can be implemented. We began this chapter by understanding how to identify when a custom application or portal might be needed, and what technical and licensing considerations to take into account.

Then, we did a deep dive into identifying when a model-driven app or Canvas app applies to extend Dynamics 365 Customer Engagement and analyzed real-life scenarios for the different types of applications.

Finally, we looked at scenarios for building custom portals on top of Dynamics 365 Customer Engagement processes for Sales, Customer Service, Project Operations, and Field Service applications.

In the next chapter, we will look at scenarios where we can extend Dynamics 365 Customer Engagement with Canvas apps and Custom Pages components embedded in the application.

Questions and answers

1. Is it necessary to implement a custom application in every Dynamics 365 project?

    Answer: No. Native applications as they come out of the box are commonly used by organizations without the need to build a custom application.

2. What are the most common reasons to consider a custom application?

    Answer: Some of the most common reasons for building a custom application are the need to:

    *   Include external users as part of the processes

    *   Offer a much simpler UI and improve the UX

    *   Limit the use cases of the application

    *   Create a custom experience for specific users

3. Does every user have the right to access a custom application?

    Answer: Not necessarily. As with any other functionality, a user will have the right to access custom applications depending on the licenses the user has.

5
Dynamics 365 Customer Engagement with Custom Embedded Applications

With **Power Platform**, we can extend Dynamics 365 Customer Engagement applications by creating canvas app components to be embedded in the applications. This is thanks to the **convergence** strategy that Microsoft has put forward, in which little by little, canvas apps and model-driven apps have started to share components between them.

In this chapter, we will focus on the different ways we have to enable a canvas app experience from within a Dynamics 365 Customer Engagement application. You will learn how to create these applications from scratch and when they apply, and how to identify when an **embedded canvas app** is best and when a **custom page** is best. Finally, we will discuss some scenarios of real implementations in which these types of components were chosen to solve real-life requirements.

By the end of this chapter, you will have learned how to identify in which cases a canvas app component is a good option for deployment within a Dynamics 365 Customer Engagement application, and how to build one.

In this chapter, we will cover the following:

- How to identify whether an embedded canvas app or custom page is a good option as a solution in a Dynamics 365 Customer Engagement deployment
- How to build custom pages and some real deployment scenarios
- How to build embedded canvas apps and some real deployment scenarios

Technical requirements

To work with Dynamics 365 Customer Engagement, it is necessary to have an environment with one of the supported licenses. However, the topics covered in this chapter do not require any Dynamics 365 application.

The following are required for this chapter:

- Any Dynamics 365 Customer Engagement license (of the available ones) with administrator permissions in an environment
- A supported browser

Canvas apps within a model-driven app

Before we dive into how to create a canvas app within a Dynamics 365 Customer Engagement application (or any model-driven app), it is important to understand what options we have first.

When we want to improve the **user interface** (**UI**), we have many options to do so without the need for custom development, as we have already mentioned in *Chapter 2*. Among the options we have is to build canvas apps that will be accessed from the Dynamics 365 Customer Engagement application, with an embedded application experience. For this, we can choose between building a **custom page** and an **embedded canvas app**.

Unlike custom pages, embedded canvas apps include a native component that retrieves data from the record in which it is embedded. This is one of the most important differences between the two types of applications. In custom pages, we can enable the context of the registry in which it is launched as a dialog, but for this, we will need to make use of a few lines of code.

Embedded canvas apps were the first native option offered by Microsoft to have a canvas app as part of a model-driven app, and it has also been one of the first firm steps on the road to Power App convergence.

The following table tries to summarize the most relevant aspects for you to consider when you evaluate a custom page versus an embedded canvas app.

Feature	Custom Page	Embedded Canvas App
Components	A limited number of components available	All the components available in a regular canvas app
Pass parameters from a model-driven app	It's possible to pass parameters by using Power FX	It's possible by using the native **ModelDrivenFormIntegration** control in the Power Apps studio

Apps per form	There is no limit of custom pages per form	Up to three
User experience (UX)	The custom page takes the full page, or it's open as a dialog	The embedded app is part of the model-driven app form, embedded in a section

Table 5.1 – Custom page versus embedded canvas app

Regardless of the differences presented in the previous table, Microsoft's current recommendation is to opt for a custom page over an embedded canvas app when possible.

Now that we understand the options we have when embedding a canvas app into a Dynamics 365 Customer Engagement application, let's go deeper into what custom pages are, what particularities we will find with them, and some real examples of custom page implementation.

Custom pages

Power Platform allows us to create pages in a model-driven app with the power of a canvas app. These custom pages are another step towards the convergence announced by Microsoft between the different types of Power Apps. They allow us to incorporate components with great design flexibility, such as dialogs, full pages, or side panes.

Custom pages are a low-code option to incorporate components to improve the UI and UX. This enables us to incorporate additional functionality, and actions that interact with the Dynamics 365 Customer Engagement application. However, it's not limited to Dataverse data, as we can use the Power Platform connectors to integrate data from other applications.

To deploy a side pane or a dialog, we'll require some development skills since it's not a no-code/low-code approach.

In this section, we will look in detail at some of the most important considerations to keep in mind when we start working with custom pages as components of our solution.

> **Note**
> It's important to remember that custom pages are a new component in the Power Platform, and therefore they have some limitations and known issues. I suggest consulting the Microsoft documentation for the most updated information on limitations and known issues.

Multi-screen custom pages

By default, custom pages allow only one screen. However, for dialog scenarios, it is common to need more than one screen. For this, as we can see in the following screenshot, we must enable the multi-screen experience from the custom page display configuration.

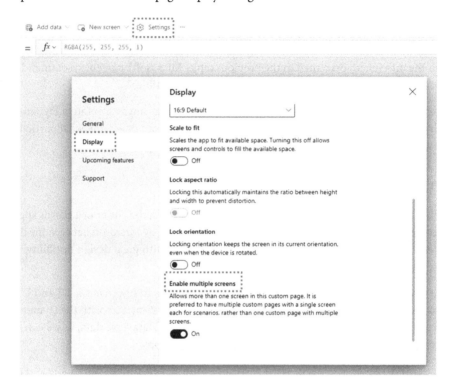

Figure 5.1 – Multiple screen configuration

By doing so, the possibility of adding new screens to the custom page will be enabled, as we can see in the following screenshots:

Before enabling multi-screen configuration

After enabling multi-screen configuration

Figure 5.2 – Command bar before and after enabling the multi-screen capability

By using the newly available **New screen** button, we are able to select the screen type we want to add to the custom page. The available screen types are limited to empty screens or screens with containers.

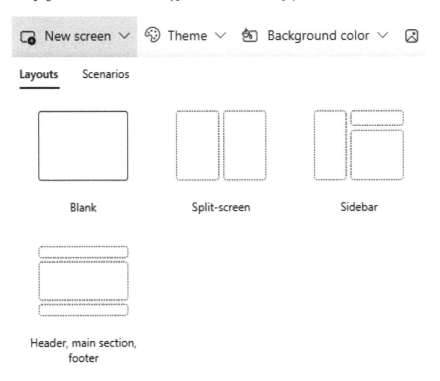

Figure 5.3 – Available screen layouts for a custom page

As we can see in the screenshot, there are only four possible screen formats that we can add. We can leverage the predefined layouts that include containers, such as **Split-screen**, **Sidebar**, and **Header, main section, footer** layouts.

Using Power FX in our custom pages

When building a custom page, we can make use of the Power FX functions as we do in standalone canvas apps. However, since a custom page is in the context of a model-driven app (Dynamics 365 Customer Engagement or Power App), some formulas have different behaviors than what we are used to in a canvas app.

Among the outstanding functions to be used in a custom page is the **Navigate** function. Using it, we can navigate between different screens of the same application or navigate within the model-driven app. In the latter case, we can navigate views or table forms, determine which one in particular, and even pass parameters that allow us to speed up management.

Navigating between screens of the same custom page

If we want to navigate to another screen within the custom page, we use the Navigate() function as we would in any canvas app:

Figure 5.4 – Navigating between screens of the same custom page

As we can see in the figure, after indicating the target screen, we can set the transition mode as in any canvas app.

If we want to return to the previous screen of the custom page, we can use the Back() function. This function is very practical when we are building a **dialog** in the Dynamics 365 Customer Engagement application. However, it's important to remember that the Back() function doesn't send any parameter back to the model-driven app. Currently, if we need to do so, it'll require a different approach, such as using JavaScript.

> **Note**
> The classic dialog functionality was decommissioned some time ago, so it was pending to have native functionality that would allow us to create dialogs quickly and easily.

Navigating to a Dynamics 365 Customer Engagement table

If we want to navigate to a Dataverse table, the first thing we have to do is to add the table as a data source:

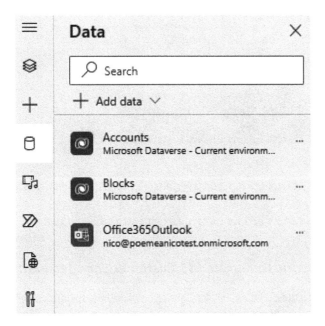

Figure 5.5 – Data sources included in the custom page

In this example, we have the **Accounts** and **Contacts** tables added, in addition to the Office 365 Outlook connector, so we can navigate to a form or a view of these tables only.

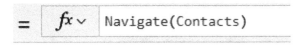

Figure 5.6 – Navigating to the default table view

If we want to navigate to the default view of a table in the model-driven app, the syntax of the function is very simple, being that we only have to add the name of the table to which we want to navigate. An interesting fact is that this table doesn't need to be added to the model-driven app or the site map.

Figure 5.7 – An error in a function when a screen transition condition is applied

As we can see in the example, when we want to navigate to a table in the model-driven app, we get an error if we try to define a transition between screens, since we are not navigating between screens.

Navigating to a specific Dynamics 365 Customer Engagement table view

If instead of navigating to the default view, we want to navigate to a specific table view, we must use a syntax similar to that we would use in a gallery that uses a Dataverse view to filter the rows.

Figure 5.8 – Navigating to a specific table view

In this way, we can conditionally set which destination view we want to navigate to and customize the UX.

Navigating to a Dynamics 365 Customer Engagement record

If instead of a view, we want to navigate to a particular record, we only have to indicate which record we want. For example, if we have a gallery on the custom page, we can navigate to the record in question in the **OnSelect** value of the record in the gallery.

Figure 5.9 – Navigating to a record

If you want to navigate to a table row when selecting it from a gallery, it is not necessary to indicate which is the destination table since this is defined in the gallery itself. If no particular form is specified, it will navigate to the default form.

Navigating to a Dynamics 365 Customer Engagement record in a specific destination

However, if we wanted to, we could indicate which form we want to go to to view the record.

Figure 5.10 – Navigating to a record in a specific form

The destination page identified in the `Navigate()` function can either be a specific form of a table or another custom page.

Figure 5.11 – Navigating to a record in a specific custom page

In this second scenario, in the **Item** property of the target custom page form, we have to use the `Param` function to pick which record to open.

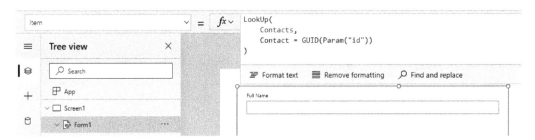

Figure 5.12 – Destination form's item property configuration

In this example, for the form of the destination custom page, we are searching in the `Contacts` table for the record that we selected in the previous custom page.

Navigating to a table form in create mode

It is also possible to open a new form in the Dynamics 365 Customer Engagement application. In doing so, we can also include parameters to set default values.

As we can see in the screenshot, by setting the target as `Defaults(Entity Name)`, we are indicating that the default form of the table should be opened.

```
fx ∨    Navigate(
            Patch(
                Defaults(Contacts),
                {
                    'First Name': "Nicolás",
                    'Last Name': "Fernández"
                }
            )
        )
```

≣ Format text   ≣ Remove formatting   𝒪 Find and replace

Create new contact with parameters

Figure 5.13 – Navigating to a new form including parameters

As mentioned before, if we want to set default values, we can do so by including the parameters in the `Navigate` function.

Components in a custom page

Custom pages support both reusable canvas app components, with a low-code approach, and **Power Apps component framework** (**PCF**) controls, with a pro-code approach. This allows us to think, design, and build custom pages in a scalable and time-optimized way by reusing standardized components.

Unlike the canvas apps that we can build and deploy as standalone, the components for the custom pages cannot be created directly on the custom page and must be used from the component library.

On the other hand, in order to make use of the PCF, we must enable it within the custom page we are building.

Power Apps component framework for canvas apps

Enables Power Apps component framework feature that allows the execution of code that may not be generated by Microsoft when a maker adds code components to an app. Make sure that the code component solution is from a trusted source. Learn more ⌁

Allow publishing of canvas apps with code components

 Off

Figure 5.14 – PCF for canvas apps feature

The preceding screenshot shows the option to allow canvas apps to be published with code components, which can be found in the features configuration in the Power Platform environment manager: `https://admin.powerplatform.microsoft.com`.

Text localization for a custom page

When implementing Dynamics 365 Customer Engagement, it is very common to deploy the solution in more than one language. Custom pages allow us to manage the localization of the application by importing RESX web resources, which allow us to reference the label of the controls and ensure consistency between the language in which Dynamics 365 Customer Engagement is deployed and the embedded custom page.

The process to include text localization in a custom page is a three-step process: enable the language in the environment, add the mentioned RESX web resource file, and manage the localized RESX and the references in the controls.

Enabling the language in the environment

As we already know, Dataverse/Dynamics 365 Customer Engagement environments can have more than one language configured. When configuring the environment, we have to define what the base language will be. Then, we can add additional languages to the environment from the Power Platform administration portal.

In order to configure the custom page to support more than one language, we first have to enable this language in the environment.

Adding the mentioned RESX web resource file

Once the language is enabled, we have to create a RESX file for each one. If we have more than one language, all the files must be named in the same way.

Then, for each language, we have to add the file to the solution as a web resource.

After adding all the web resources to the solution, we have to publish all the changes.

Finally, we have to go to the editor of the customized page and add the web resource. It is necessary to add all the web resources, as adding one is enough.

Managing the localized RESX and the references in the controls

Once we have added the web resources to the custom page, we have to edit the tags so that they take the value corresponding to the language in which the model-driven app is running.

Tips for designing a custom page

Designing a standalone canvas app is different from designing a custom page, as custom pages are meant to be used as a model-driven app component.

Some key design tips to consider are as follows.

Supported controls

Custom pages are a new and evolving product. Currently, they only support a particular set of components, among which we can find the following:

- **Display components**: Labels
- **Input components**: Text boxes, date pickers, buttons, combo boxes, checkboxes, toggles, radio groups, sliders, ratings, edit forms, display forms, and rich text editors
- **Layout components**: Vertical containers and horizontal containers
- **List components**: Gallery
- **Media components**: Icons and images
- **Custom components**: Code components and canvas components

Many of the display and input controls are based on the new modern controls introduced for canvas apps for Teams, and are based on Fluent UI.

Styling controls to align with model-driven app controls

When working with custom pages, we have to remember that these pages will be embedded into a model-driven app as a component of these applications. That is why it is important to try to align the design of the custom page with the layout of the model-driven app. This is set with the default values when creating a custom page in the modern app designer.

Some of the most important considerations when building custom pages are as follows:

- Controls need different font sizes. Since custom page text has an upscaling of 1.33, we need to keep this in mind when defining the font size. For the page title, if we used 12.75, we would get a font size of 17. For a normal label, we should use 10.52 to get a font size of 14. And finally, for a small label, we will set the font size to 9.02 to get a final font size of 12.

- The primary buttons should have these style settings:

```
Color=RGBA(255, 255, 255, 1)
Fill=RGBA(41,114,182,1)
Height=35
FontWeight=Normal
```

- Secondary buttons should have the following style settings:

```
Color=RGBA(41,114,182,1)
Fill=RGBA(255, 255, 255, 1)
BorderColor=RGBA(41,114,182,1)
Height=35
FontWeight=Normal
```

These considerations, while not critical, will help us to provide a better UX.

Creator Kit components

Finally, it is important to remember that Microsoft has developed the Creator Kit. This is a set of components for different types of applications, which can be used to improve the UX. These components are compatible with custom pages.

The Creator Kit also includes a custom page template to quickly start working with custom pages.

How to start with custom pages

We can create a custom page from a solution, or the app designer. You can also start by using the custom page template included in the Creator Kit.

To create a custom page from a solution, you need to do the following:

1. Go to https://make.powerapps.com.
2. Go to **Solutions**, and enter a solution:

Figure 5.15 – Selecting a solution

3. Click on **+ New**, and then **Page** under the **App** section:

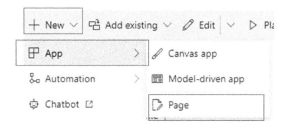

Figure 5.16 – Creating a new custom page

4. This will open the page designer:

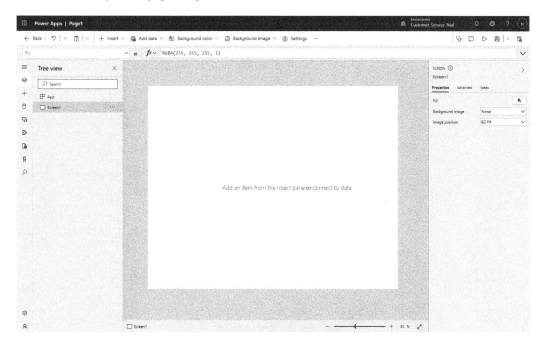

Figure 5.17 – Custom page designer

Now, to create a custom page in the app designer, you need to do the following:

1. Go to https://make.powerapps.com.
2. Go to **Solutions** and enter a solution.
3. Select any model-driven app and click on **Edit**:

Figure 5.18 – Editing a model-driven app

4.   Click on + **Add Page** in the ribbon or the menu:

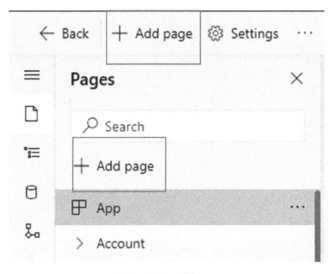

Figure 5.19 – Add page

5. Select **Custom**:

Figure 5.20 – New page wizard

6. Enter a page name in the **Name** field and select **Create a new custom page**:

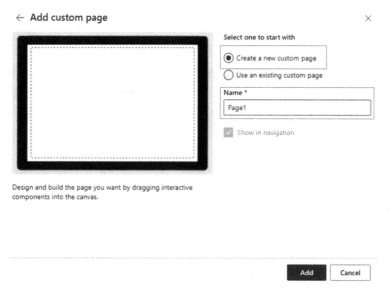

Figure 5.21 – New page wizard

7. This will open the page designer:

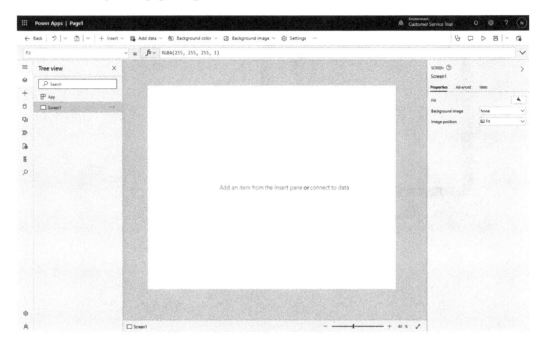

Figure 5.22 – Custom page designer

Once you have the new blank page, you'll build your custom page like any other canvas app.

Custom page examples

As was mentioned at the beginning of this chapter, custom pages can be deployed as dialogs, as a side pane in the productivity pane, or as a full page. The following are some examples of custom pages used in projects.

Dialogs

As mentioned before, one of the possibilities for displaying a custom page is as a dialog.

Having a new native functionality to implement dialogs has been a breakthrough for Dynamics 365 Customer Engagement. Previously, we had the classic dialog functionality, but since it was deprecated by Microsoft, we were waiting for a native option that would replace it.

It is common to see the implementation of wizard-style dialogs that assist the user when creating a new record as part of projects. This allows the organization to maintain consistency in the registration process while ensuring that the user is aware of all the steps required.

Productivity panel tools

The productivity panel allows us to enable different tools in the application so that users can access them quickly.

With custom pages, we can deploy tools for users without the need for custom development. Some of the uses of custom pages are as follows:

- **Swiss Army Knife**: A custom page to group different actions to automate mundane repetitive tasks

- **Real-time inventory and ordering**: By integrating the custom page with the ERP where operations are managed, agents using it can quickly search for orders or store inventory availability without the need for costly or complex integrations

- **KPIs**: We can configure a custom page that consolidates the most relevant KPIs, taking data from both Dynamics 365 Customer Engagement and other systems

Full pages

The third format available for custom pages is a full page. It is very common to find very specific requirements about the initial screen that users see when entering the application. Sometimes, a native panel or a Power BI panel are the most common options. However, when custom pages are added to the scenario, it opens up the possibility of having a fully customizable page. Having a custom page as a home screen will allow us to do the following:

- Have multiple listings of the most relevant records, either from the same table or different tables

- Have KPIs on screen, in a flexible layout without the need for Power BI licenses

- Display information from other systems or data sources other than Dataverse, without complex integrations

- Have an automation orchestrator that can be executed on demand

Now that we have covered custom pages, let's discuss how to use embedded canvas apps.

Embedded canvas apps

Embedded canvas apps are practical when we need to work with an application as part of the registration form, and where we need data from the registration or associated records.

Embedded canvas apps have the **ModelDrivenFormIntegration** control, which allows us to take the context of the record in which the embedded canvas app is running, and work with its data and the related record data.

The embedded canvas app can interact with the form of the model-driven app in which it is located. In this section, we will see how we can work with embedded canvas apps and some case studies.

Using the ModelDrivenFormIntegration control's properties

When we create a canvas app embedded into a model-driven app, we will see that a special control will appear in the Power Apps Studio. This control, **ModelDrivenFormIntegration**, is the one that allows us to obtain context data from the registry where we are.

There are several properties and actions of the embedded canvas apps, such as the following:

- **DataSource**: This property is automatically configured when the canvas app is embedded and determines which table it will be acting on

- **OnDataRefresh**: This is used to refresh the data source to which it is connected and set or update variables

- **RefreshForm** and **SaveForm**: These are actions that allow us to update the form in which the application is embedded or save the record

- **NavigateToMainForm**, **NavigateToView**, and **OpenQuickCreateForm**: These are actions that allow us to interact with the model-driven app, enable navigation steps, or quickly open a creation form

Embedding a canvas app into a model-driven app

To embed a canvas app into a model-driven app, you need to do the following:

1. Go to `https://make.powerapps.com`.
2. Go to **Solutions** and enter the solution you want to work with.
3. Select the table where you want to embed the canvas app.
4. Navigate to the forms, and enter the main form where you want to embed the canvas app.
5. Select a section in the form in which you want to embed the canvas app.
6. In the **Components** area, click on **Canvas app** in the **Display** section:

Figure 5.23 – The Canvas app option in the Components area

7. Complete the required values.

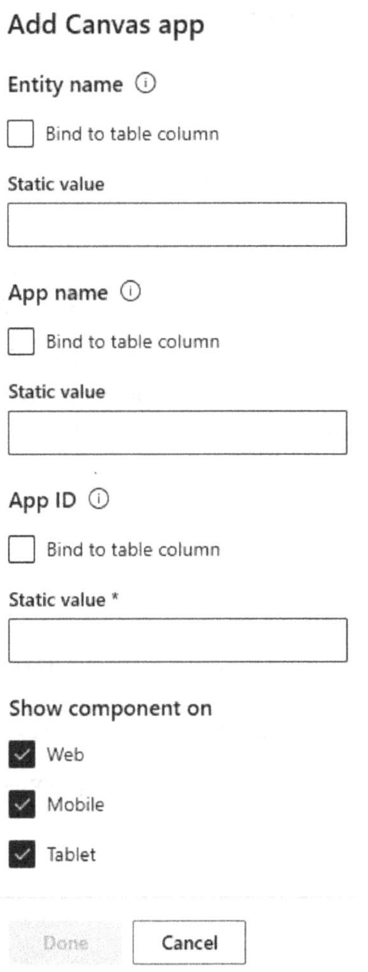

Add Canvas app

Entity name ⓘ

☐ Bind to table column

Static value

[   ]

App name ⓘ

☐ Bind to table column

Static value

[   ]

App ID ⓘ

☐ Bind to table column

Static value *

[   ]

Show component on

☑ Web

☑ Mobile

☑ Tablet

[Done] [Cancel]

Figure 5.24 – Adding the Canvas app form

Notes

Entity name: Allows you to specify the name of the table that will provide the data to the embedded app.

App name: Allows you to specify the name of the canvas app to be embedded.

App ID: You need to enter the ID of the app that will be embedded.

You can bind any of these values to a column.

8. Save and publish it.

It's important to remember that the canvas app will not be published when you publish the form or the model-driven app.

Common embedded canvas app scenarios

Some real scenarios for the implementation of an embedded canvas app are as follows:

- *Document management*: Enabling an improved experience for document management when it is integrated with SharePoint. By embedding the canvas app, we can modify the UI of the SharePoint document sub-grid, and from this, we can offer a friendlier UX.

- *Enabling Artificial Intelligence (AI) models*: As we will see in *Chapter 6*, it is possible to embed AI models into our applications. These applications with AI components can be embedded in a Dynamics 365 Customer Engagement form, in order to facilitate integration. In this way, we could have a predictive model within our Dynamics 365 Customer Engagement record, powered by AI Builder within the canvas app.

- *Asset visualization*: We can improve the way to visualize our customers' assets by enabling an embedded application with an interface that includes multimedia content (images, floor plans, or others) within the application.

- *Improving the product catalog*: With an embedded canvas app, we can enhance the product catalog experience by incorporating shortcuts to access the sales literature associated with the products, as well as digital assets that may be related, such as videos or brochures.

As with most things we can design in Dynamics 365 Customer Engagement, there is no definitive answer as to the best approach. In each scenario, we must weigh up the dependencies and limitations of our design decisions.

Summary

In this chapter, we have analyzed the different options we have for utilizing canvas apps as part of a Dynamics 365 Customer Engagement application. We identified the options we have and the most common use cases that each of these solves. We reviewed the particularities of custom pages when interacting with model-driven apps in detail. On the other hand, we also analyzed the **ModelDrivenFromIntegration** control that allows us to take the data from the registry in which the embedded canvas app is located, as well as the actions that we can execute from the canvas app on the model-driven app.

In the next chapter, we will go into the Dynamics 365 Customer Engagement extension capabilities that Power Automate offers us when empowering the user. We will analyze some of the most common use cases in which we can benefit from Power Automate in the context of Dynamics 365 Customer Engagement applications.

Questions and answers

1.   How can we deploy a custom page in a Dynamics 365 Customer Engagement app?

     Answer: We can deploy a custom page as a dialog, side pane, or full page.

2.   Can we leverage the Power Platform connectors when we use a custom page?

     Answer: Yes, since custom pages are still canvas apps, it is possible to use connectors to work with data from other applications.

6

Extending Your Apps with AI and Mixed Reality

In recent years, we have witnessed how business applications, in particular Dynamics 365 Customer Engagement, have evolved, incorporating new technology version by version. If you have worked with previous versions of Dynamics CRM (1.2, 3.0, 4.0, 2011, 2013, 2015, or 2016), when working with Dynamics 365 Customer Engagement applications, you will have quickly seen how it has changed in two areas: the technology or functionality incorporated and the predominant no-code/low-code approach to customizing and extending the applications.

In this chapter, we will learn how to incorporate into our Dynamics 365 Customer Engagement applications two of the technology trends of the moment: **artificial intelligence** (**AI**) and **mixed reality**. We will understand some of the most common scenarios in which we can implement solutions that have these capabilities. We will identify the different types of AI models that **AI Builder** offers and how to start using them. Finally, we will learn how we can incorporate mixed reality components into our **Canvas Apps**.

By the end of this chapter, you will have learned how to incorporate AI and mixed reality components into Dynamics 365 Customer Engagement processes.

In this chapter, we will cover the following topics:

- Working with AI Builder
- Mixed reality

Technical requirements

To work with Dynamics 365 Customer Engagement, it is necessary to have an environment with one of the supported licenses. However, the topics covered in this chapter do not require any Dynamics 365 application.

The following are required for this chapter:

- Any Dynamics 365 Customer Engagement license (any of the available ones) with administrator permissions in an environment

- AI Builder subscription supported browser

Working with AI Builder

AI Builder is a solution within **Power Platform** that allows us to incorporate AI models without the need to develop or create complex algorithms. It offers different AI models that can be used by anyone. AI Builder uses Azure services, simplifying its implementation so that any user can make use of it.

Within AI Builder, we find two categories of models:

- **Pre-built models** are those that we only need to connect to our applications or Power Automate flows and make use of them. They do not require any configuration or parameterization.

- **Custom models** are those that need input from our business to be trained, although they do not require any data scientist knowledge either.

AI Builder models are available for use in Power Automate Cloud flows and, in some cases, in Power Apps applications.

To include the AI Builder control in a Canvas app, we can use the **AI Builder** button in the command bar:

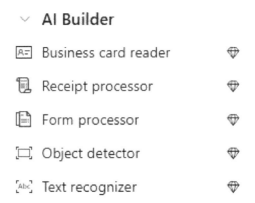

Figure 6.1 – AI Builder models available in Power Apps

As we can see, natively, we can only include some AI Builder models in a **Canvas App**. However, there is a new functionality in Preview that allows you to use the different models through **Power Fx functions**.

> **Note**
>
> Although it is not specific to this component, when we want to work with AI Builder, we must validate the availability of the different models according to the region: `https://docs.microsoft.com/en-us/ai-builder/availability-region`.

Pre-built models

As we have already mentioned, pre-built models are those that we can use without any prior configuration. These models are easily adapted to different business processes and are a quick way to start introducing AI to applications.

Let's quickly review what pre-built models are available in AI Builder.

Business card reader

The *Business card reader model* allows us to extract the main data from a business card. Once the data has been extracted, we can process it, create a lead or a contact, search for it in a database, and much more.

This model is used in Dynamics 365 Sales Enterprise, allowing each user to make use of it. Natively, we can find it in the Quick Create forms, as shown in the following screenshot:

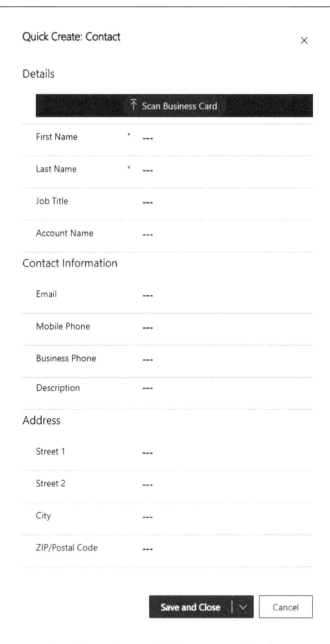

Figure 6.2 – Quick Create form with the business card reader component

This template can process images in JPG, BMP, and PNG formats, but currently only in English.

Let's learn how to add the business card reader AI Builder component to a canvas app:

1. First, you need to enter the app where you want to add the component.

2. Then, from the ribbon/command bar, click on + **Insert**, and then on **Business card reader** in the **AI Builder** section:

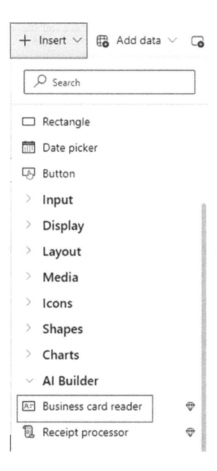

Figure 6.3 – Business card reader component in Canvas App

3. Then, you need to add the form or fields where you'll capture the data the business card reader will read from the business cards. To reference the data in the AI Builder component, we will have to define the default property of the fields using the component definition, as shown in the following screenshot:

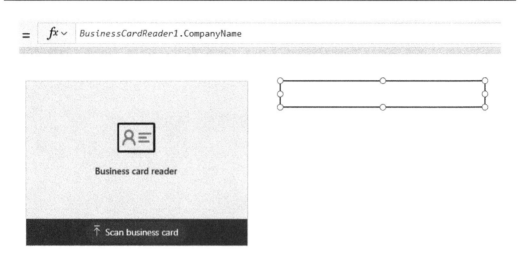

Figure 6.4 – Referencing business card reader data to define the default properties on fields

Now, you can work with the data to save it in Dynamics 365 Customer Engagement or perform validations with the contacts that exist in the environment.

Category classification

The *category classification model* allows us to process texts and classify them automatically into categories predefined by Microsoft related to customer feedback: Issues, Compliments, Customer Service, Documentation, Price & Billing, and Staff.

If we need to extend the categories, we can make use of the homonymous custom model.

Entity extraction

The *entity extraction model* allows us to process text and extract data identified by predefined entities. We can group this into three categories: general data, location data, and personal/organizational data.

General data:

- Events names
- Speed references
- Language
- Color
- Temperatures

- URLs

- Weights

- Date and time (mention the weekday or month, either by direct, indirect, or relative mention)

- Percentages (whether mentioned as a number or in words)

- The positive or negative sentiment (Boolean)

Location data:

- City

- US states

- Continent

- Country or region

- Zip codes

Personal/organizational data:

- Age

- Organization name

- People's names

- Email

- Phone numbers

If we need to extend these entities, we can make use of the homonymous custom model, as explained later in this chapter.

ID reader

The *ID reader model* allows us to extract US passport and driver's license data from images. The supported formats are JPG, PNG, and PDF.

Invoice processing

The *invoice processing model* allows us to process this type of document from a JPG or PNG image, or a PDF document. The model will extract the most relevant data from an invoice, including the following:

- Amounts

- Postal addresses

- Customer ID

- Dates
- Invoice lines, including product quantities, descriptions, unit price, total price, and taxes

For each piece of data that's extracted, the model will also provide a confidence percentage. This confidence level allows us to set confidence thresholds and do automatic processing or determine manual steps.

If we need to extend the model, we can make use of the customized document processing model. We'll describe this model in the *Custom models* section.

Key phrases extraction

This *key phrases extraction model* allows you to process text and extract the most important talking points from it.

Language detection

The *language detection model* allows us to process texts and identify which language they are in. The result is a list of detected languages, with the numeric value (between *0* and *1*) for the confidence level for each language.

Receipt processing

The *receipt processing model* uses **optical character recognition** (**OCR**) to detect the most relevant information on receipts, whether printed or handwritten.

At the time of writing, the model supports receipts from Australia, Canada, the United States, Great Britain, and India, but only in English.

Sentiment analysis

The *sentiment analysis model* allows us to process texts and identify them as positive or negative. Each sentence of the text is analyzed and weighted with a sentiment score. The total score of the text will be the sum of the sentiments of each sentence.

The sentiment analysis may give a positive, negative, neutral, or mixed sentiment, and will give a confidence level between 0 and 1 for both sentences and the total text.

Text recognition

The *text recognition model* allows you to identify and extract words from documents and images using OCR, whether they are printed or handwritten texts.

Text translation

Finally, the *text translation model* allows you to process text and translate it into no more than 10,000 characters per process. In addition to the translated text, the model will report the source language identified.

In addition to the pre-built models, we can leverage the AI Builder engine to train our custom models. In the next section, we'll take a deep dive into the different available custom models.

Custom models

Custom models are those that we must train to be able to use in our business processes and applications, such as the prediction model, category classification, entity extraction, object detection, document processing, and image classification.

These models are already programmed and only need to be trained with our business data. This means that we do not need to be data scientists to be able to do it, but we do need to know our business to provide the best possible data sample for model training.

Prediction model

The *prediction model* allows us to analyze patterns in historical data. From this, we can associate these patterns with possible outcomes. This model can predict the answer to a question where the former is a binary answer (between two options), multiple choice, or a number.

Category classification

The *category classification model* allows us to process texts and classify them automatically while considering the categories defined by us. The model will process the text and identify these categories in the context of the analyzed text.

Entity extraction

The *entity extraction model* allows us to train the model for custom entities. When we use the entity extraction model, we process texts and extract the data that matches the entities that we defined. This model is very useful when the pre-built model does not offer us all the entities we need.

Object detection

The *object detection model* allows us to process images and identify the different objects and their quantity. This model requires training on each of the objects we want to identify, in each of the possible formats, shapes, or presentations.

Document processing

This *document processing model* allows us to process entire documents and extract the most relevant information from them.

This model supports both structured or semi-structured documents and unstructured or free-format documents. Once we have defined the type of document we want to process, we must train the model to identify the data that is relevant to our business. This could be a single type of data, such as table format or the state of checkboxes.

At the time of writing, the model supports not only one-page documents but multi-page documents, where tables may be split over more than one page.

Image classification

The *image classification model* allows us to integrate the image classification models created in Lobe to be used by AI Builder.

> **Note**
> Lobe is a Microsoft desktop application that allows you to manage custom image detection models.

Working with AI Builder

Regardless of whether we work with a custom model or a pre-built one, the way we have to work with AI Builder is very similar. Of course, it will be a little easier if we do it with pre-built models since we will not have the tasks of training and retraining the model. We can identify up to five steps to start working with AI Builder:

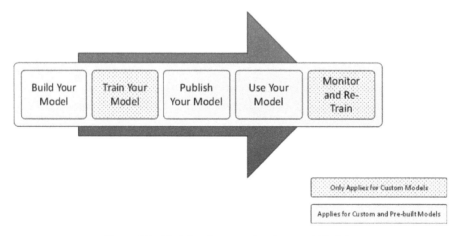

Figure 6.5 – High-level steps to implement AI Builder

The preceding diagram represents the five steps we must follow to get a good custom AI Builder model:

1. The first step is to create our model. For that, we have to understand what outcome we want to achieve, what data we have to process, and what impact it will have on our business process.

2. The second step is to train. This step only applies to customized models. This step is one of the most important, because the level of training we give to the model, and the quality of the data sample with which we do the training, will be the quality of the results it offers us every time we use it. We must remember not to train the model with perfect data, but to train it with the most realistic data possible. This applies not only to the data that we can find in Dynamics 365 Customer Engagement or other business applications but also to images or documents of all types and conditions when we do document processing or object detection.

3. We should publish the model without seeking to have the perfect test result first, as this will allow us to expose the model to real data and be able to improve it based on these results.

4. Monitoring and re-training are important, not only because achieving a perfect model requires several interactions, but also because our business may change, which forces us to incorporate new variables or conditions into our model.

5. As the model is used, we must evaluate it, and understand if it requires any adjustment or retraining.

Once we have followed these steps, we will have an AI model implemented without development or the need for data scientists, thanks to AI Builder.

Common use cases

There are several business scenarios in which the implementation of AI Builder applies. This list does not seek to reflect all of them, but the most common ones I have encountered in recent years:

Use Case	AI Builder Model
Simplify on-site business card capture at events	Business card reader
Automate how invoices received by email are processed	Invoice processing/document processing
Automate how contracts received by email are processed	Document processing
Customer purchase prediction	Prediction
Automate shelf display control in department stores	Object detection
Automate email sorting	Category classification
Identify fraudulent behavior	Prediction
Automate negative sentence alerts	Key phrases extraction
Automate expense reporting	Receipt processor

Table 6.1 – Common uses cases to implement AI Builder

AI Builder's versatility allows us to create applications for business processes of the different Dynamics 365 Customer Engagement applications, either by custom or pre-built models.

As we have learned, AI Builder is the perfect no-code approach to start integrating AI models into your Dynamics 365 Customer Engagement applications. By understanding the pre-built models, we can quickly identify which one fits our requirements or if we need to train a custom model. In addition to the AI models that we can implement, we can also extend our applications by including another trending technology, with mixed reality features. In the next section, we'll learn how to work with the mixed reality components in Power Apps.

Mixed reality

Mixed reality is the combination of physical reality and virtual reality. For some years now, Microsoft has incorporated applications with mixed reality within its portfolio of Dynamics 365 applications. Among them, we can find the following:

- **Product Visualize**: This was an application that allowed us to visualize 3D models of the products related to an opportunity, and take notes on them. This application is currently deprecated.

- **Remote Assist**: This is an application that allows us to make a call between two or more people and share the video with mixed reality components such as arrows and drawings, and even visualize documents.

- **Guides**: This is an application that allows us to define guides for operators to carry out training or follow the step-by-step process of the tasks to be performed. Thanks to the anchors and 3D instructions, the operator will know what to do at all times.

- **Layout**: This is an application that allows us to position multiple 3D models in space to design a space.

Additionally, Power Platform incorporated mixed reality capabilities as components and functionalities that we can enable in Canvas Apps. At the time of writing, we can visualize and manipulate 3D models and work with measurements and markers, as shown in the following screenshot:

Figure 6.6 – The Mixed Reality menu in Power Apps Studio

> **Note**
>
> To make use of these capabilities, the device has to support mixed reality.

Let's take a look at each of these features.

Working with 3D models

We can join the first two options, **View in MR** and **View Shape in MR**, since in both cases, they refer to being able to view 3D models in mixed reality. The main difference between both is that in the first case, a model that we have saved in some specific source is displayed in mixed reality, while in the second case, we can see a 3D model of a cube generated by the same component in mixed reality.

View shape in MR

By adding a view shape component to MR, we enable the application to generate a 3D model of a cube. Here, we will be able to work with different properties:

- Cube dimensions – height, width, and depth

- Unit of measure

- Enable shadows

- Enable markers

- Button properties:

Figure 6.7 – Place a cube

This is an example of a button showing an icon and text.

By clicking **Place a cube**, we can rotate it and place it in a space:

Figure 6.8 – Native 3D model of a cube

The preceding screenshot shows an example of a cube generated by Canvas Apps.

View in MR

By adding a view to the MR component, we can enable the application to generate 3D models based on a data source that we determine. For example, we could have a SharePoint list in which we store the 3D models. Then, from the gallery in the Canvas App, we can select it.

Once the object has been added, we can do the following:

- Change its position
- Rotate it
- Take a picture

Since Product Visualize was deprecated, if we need a mixed reality experience to show our customers the products in their opportunities, we can build a solution with a Canvas App. Our custom solution could include Dynamics 365 Sales, SharePoint, and a Canvas App as part of its architecture, as shown in the following figure:

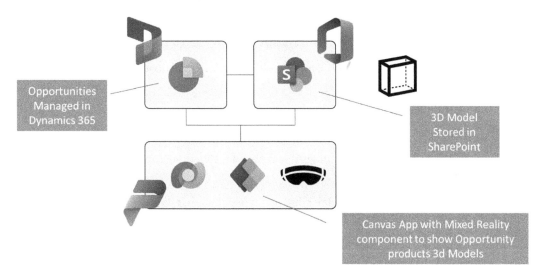

Figure 6.9 – High-level architecture diagram

As shown in the preceding diagram, we can build a Canvas App on top of Dynamics 365 Sales and SharePoint. Let's analyze each component:

- **Dynamics 365 Customer Engagement**: We can manage opportunities in Dynamics 365 Sales. Each opportunity will have opportunity products.

- **SharePoint**: We can link each product from the product catalog with a file saved in a SharePoint list. The SharePoint list will be used to manage the 3D models.

- **Canvas App**: We will use the Canvas App to navigate through the opportunities. When we select an opportunity product, we'll be able to view it in mixed reality.

Working with measurements

Another use case in which we can incorporate mixed reality into our applications is for taking measurements. Using a camera, we can determine the points, or anchors, to draw the lines we want to measure. As a result, we will obtain the captures taken, as well as the measurements in distance, volume, and area, and information about the segments of the measured object.

Work with markups and markers

Finally, the last of the use cases currently available incorporates markups and markers.

Markups are similar to those found in remote assist. They allow us to incorporate different mixed reality elements anchored in space. In this way, we can have arrows or drawings made in ink, to point out or highlight what we are seeing.

On the other hand, markers are similar to that found in Dynamics 365 Guides. We can create virtual markers to improve the precision and persistence of media that are placed using mixed reality controls.

Once the marker has been detected by the mixed reality control, it will load the media that's been aligned and placed on top of the marker.

Summary

In this chapter, we looked at the art of adding AI and mixed reality extensions to our Dynamics 365 Customer Engagement applications.

First, we reviewed what AI Builder is and the different types of models. In doing so, we were able to identify the differences between custom and pre-built models, and for which scenarios each applies.

Then, we learned about the possibilities that Power Platform offers us to incorporate mixed reality into our applications. We reviewed the different types of actions we can perform and commented on some practical examples.

At this point, you have the knowledge base to start extending your applications with AI and mixed reality.

In the next chapter, we will start talking about how we can extend Dynamics 365 Customer Engagement by adding automations with Power Automate.

Questions and answers

1. What is the name of the AI solution in Power Platform?

    Answer: AI Builder

2. What are the differences between the pre-built and the custom models?

    Answer: Pre-built models are ready to use and don't require any configuration or training. Custom models require training to learn the particularities of our business.

Part 3:
Building Custom Processes for Dynamics 365 Customer Engagement Applications

We can take advantage of Power Automate's capabilities to create new business processes or modify existing ones, as well as incorporate new processes or automation.

In this part, we will cover what we can do with Power Automate to facilitate the work of users while optimizing our processes in Dynamics 365 Customer Engagement.

This part has the following chapters:

- *Chapter 7, Automations in Dynamics 365 Customer Engagement Apps*
- *Chapter 8, Working with Data*
- *Chapter 9, Integrating Artificial Intelligence into Processes*

7

Automations in Dynamics 365 Customer Engagement Apps

Power Automate is one of the core solutions of Power Platform and is used to build automation and business processes. We can identify three main components of Power Automate: **cloud flows**, **desktop flows**, and **business process flows** (**BPFs**).

When we think about using Power Automate in our solutions, the first thing we should do is identify the type of process we need to cover the business requirement that was presented to us, and then move on to design, build, and test it. Cloud flows are useful to create automations using more than 700 native **connectors** offered by Microsoft, connectors created by independent publishers, an organization's own connectors, or any application that has APIs available. Desktop flows are useful when we need to automate actions or integrate applications that do not have APIs available or even apply some custom logic that is not possible or too complex to do in cloud flow. Desktop flows are known as **robotic process automations** (**RPAs**). BPFs, on the other hand, are not automations but components that allow us to define processes in their phases and tasks. BPFs allow us to establish a standardized process and provide a visual guide to users. This allows them to understand at any given moment which phase a process is in and what the next expected action is.

In this chapter, we will focus mainly on understanding how we can empower users by creating automations such as cloud flows. We will look at some of the most common scenarios in the context of **Dynamics 365 Customer Engagement** applications, with examples so that you can start creating your own automations.

By the end, you will have learned how to correctly identify when a cloud flow is a viable solution, and how to create different automations in the context of Dynamics 365 Customer Engagement.

In this chapter, we will cover the following topics:

- Automating simple tasks for customer service agents
- Alerting users of the next best action
- Automating BPFs
- Sending automated communications
- Automating alerts and reports
- Creating approval processes

Technical requirements

To work with Dynamics 365 Customer Engagement, it is necessary to have an environment with one of the supported licenses. The topics covered in this chapter may require some of the applications of any particular Dynamics 365 application.

The following are required for this chapter:

- Any Dynamics 365 Customer Engagement license (any of the available ones) with administrator permissions in an environment
- A supported browser

> **Note**
> In this chapter, we will refer to Power Automate and its components. It is therefore important to quickly review the most basic concepts of cloud flows:

- **Trigger**: A trigger represents the event that states a cloud flow. There are three categories of triggers that define the cloud flow types: instant (manually triggered), automated (event-based), and scheduled.
- **Action**: An action represents each automation that could happen during a cloud flow execution. Actions could happen in another system, could be calculations or processing in the cloud flow, or could be some of the controls available, such as conditions or switches.

Automating simple tasks for customer service agents

One of the main reasons to automate a task is because it is a repetitive and mundane task that does not add any value to the user performing it manually. This applies to any business process where we encounter repetitive tasks, whether for sales, marketing, field service, project management, or customer service.

In particular, customer service agents are faced with multiple challenges to provide the best service, and any-time optimization is highly beneficial. Having to look up customer data that is in another system, needing to create a case or record an action, and having to open a record or close a case are some of the most common actions an agent has to do. In turn, to maintain the quality of service, a customer service area has multiple actions that it needs to automate to correctly articulate all the steps. Some of these are as follows:

- **Service-level agreements (SLAs)**: When an organization has defined SLAs, it is important to apply the correct SLA to each customer, every time. At the same time, being able to establish actions before expiration, compliance, or prior to expiration as an alert, is important to ensure the best **user experience (UX)**.

> **Note**
>
> SLAs enable organizations to enforce support policies and ensure that customers receive support within the expected timeframe. An SLA can have several **key performance indicators (KPIs)**, such as first response time or resolution time. An organization could define a default SLA for each customer, apply a much more granular policy that applies different SLAs to different categories of customers, or define the SLA as part of a customer service contract.

- **Automatic record creation**: Talking about automatic record creation is very generic and we can find multiple applications. However, in the context of customer service, there are some clear examples. Dynamics 365 Customer Service allows us to configure rules for creating and updating records and for activities (emails, social activities, tasks, phone calls, appointments, service activities, and personalized activities). These rules will allow us, among other things, to automatically create a case when we receive an email to a specific mailbox.

Natively, Dynamics 365 Customer Engagement applications offer these and other features, thanks to which we can easily configure automations. In many cases, the automations executed are Power Automate cloud flows, which are configured from Dynamics 365 Customer Engagement.

Next, we will see how we can configure some of these automations to automate simple and repetitive tasks for customer service agents.

Macros

As part of Dynamics 365 Customer Service, we have the ability to configure **agent scripts** to help agents when they are having a conversation with a customer. At the same time, we can standardize the way agents manage conversations. This is a widely used tool in contact centers as they allow staff to maintain a high level of quality in conversations and save time in management.

In Dynamics 365 Customer Service, when configuring an agent script, we will be able to establish three different types of steps: text instructions, a link to another script, or a **macro**. Let's look at these in more detail:

- Text instructions will consist of a title and a message for the agent. The agent will be able to use it to give the correct message to the customer or ask the right question. Once it is done, you can mark it as completed.

- A link to another script allows agents to navigate to another script that will have new steps. This allows us to have scripts defined for specific use cases, and avoid huge scripts.

Macros are automations that we can create in a simplified Power Automate editor, and that we will execute on demand. These will be executed in the context of the conversation in which we are located and can take variables to give context to the actions performed.

What can we do with macros?

Macros are intended to perform simple actions, such as filling out a form, opening a record, speeding up the closing of a case, and other repetitive and mundane actions. In this way, we can automate these repetitive tasks, reduce unintentional errors, ensure that the actions are executed correctly, improve the agent experience and the UX, and even reduce the time it takes to manage conversations.

When creating a macro, there will be four types of connectors that we can use: **Productivity Automation**, **Session Connector**, **Omnichannel Connector**, and **Flow Connector**. You can see a representation of these in *Figure 7.1*:

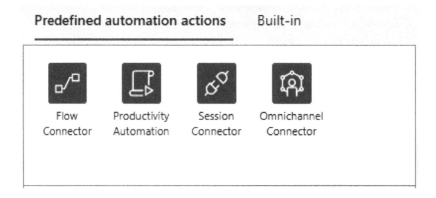

Figure 7.1 – Predefined automation actions in the macro's designer

In the previous screenshot, we can identify the four available predefined automation actions in the macro's designer.

> **Note**
>
> A session is an individual work area for a conversation, contact, or case, in the Omnichannel Engagement Hub application and Workspace application. Sessions are defined by a session template, and these are linked to the workstreams. Sessions will have multiple tabs, and on each tab, an agent can access records, dashboards, or even third-party applications. Agents can work with multiple sessions at the same time, allowing them to keep a group of tabs with contextualized information to work with in each session.

Let's analyze which actions are available on each connector:

- The **Productivity Automation** connector provides actions to be performed with model-driven app operations, such as opening a form, a record, or a view. The available actions are shown here:

Figure 7.2 – Productivity Automation connector's actions

Let's understand each action presented in the previous screenshot:

- **Open a new form to create a record**:

  - This action allows us to open a table in the form that we define. Likewise, we can set certain columns to be filled automatically, being able to be defined dynamically or predefined.

  - This action is useful when we want to speed up the processes of creating records, such as cases, tasks, or others. For example, if an agent has to create a case for the customer they are talking to, they can speed up the process thanks to this macro, since the case creation form can be partially completed.

- **Open an existing record:**

  - This action allows us to open any existing record in the environment. For this, we will have to define which table we want to target, the ID of the record we want to open, and the form we want to use.

  - This action is useful when we want to open specific records related to the client or the conversation—for example, customer assets, contracts, or the customer 360-degree view.

- **Open a record grid:**

  - This action allows us to open a view of a table. For that, we must define which table, the view ID, and the type of view we want to open.

  - This action is practical when we need to open a list of system records.

- **Search the knowledge base for the populated phrase:**

  - This action allows us to automate a search in the knowledge base based on a phrase.

- **Do a search based on the phrase:**

  - This action allows us to automate a relevance search on a phrase.

  - This action is useful when we want to do a search over multiple tables.

- **Update an existing record:**

  - This action allows us to update an existing record from data we are working with or predefined data.

  - This action is useful when we want to update, for example, the customer's typification.

- **Open an email form with predefined template:**

  - This action allows us to open the email form with a template that we predefine.

  - This action is useful to save time and ensure that the right template is selected, at various points in the case life cycle.

- **Action to resolve case:**

  - This action allows us to automate the resolution of the case.

- **Autofill form fields:**

  - This action allows us to complete fields of an open form.

- **Clone current record:**

- This action allows us to create a copy of a record in which the session is open. It is worth mentioning that the action does not save the record but rather opens a new record form and copies the fields.

- **Open knowledge base article**:

  - This action allows us to open a predefined knowledge base article.

  - This action is very handy when we have a recurrently consulted article and we need to make it available to agents quickly.

- **Save the record**:

  - This action allows us to save the record we are positioned on. This action will fail if all the required data is not completed.

- **Clone input record**:

  - This action allows us to clone a record by passing it the parameter of the ID of the record to clone. As in the previous case, the action does not save the record but copies the fields into a new record form.

> **Note**
>
> A macro is not limited to a single action of this connector when executed.

- **Session Connector** offers actions that execute operations related to the session in which the agent is located, such as opening or refreshing a tab. The available actions are as follows:

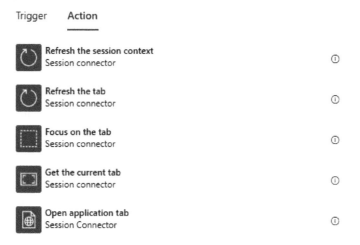

Figure 7.3 – Session Connector's actions

Let's understand each action presented in the previous screenshot:

- **Get the current tab**:

  - This action allows us to get details of the tab in which we are positioned.

  - This action is very practical when we want to get the ID to then perform the **Refresh the tab** or **Focus on the tab** actions.

- **Open application tab**:

  - This action allows us to open a new tab based on a tab template.

  - This action is very practical when we want to open in a new tab a web resource or a third-party application in an embedded way in our application, and thus be able to facilitate the management of the agent. In this way, instead of having to change the browser or application, the agent will be able to consult other applications in the same Customer Service session in which they are working.

- **Refresh the session context**:

  - This action allows us to refresh the session context that was defined at the beginning of this session.

  - This action is very practical when some change was made in the session and we need to update the context for some next action.

> **Note**
> The session context is the conversation, case, or contact for which the session was open.

- **Refresh the tab**:

  - This action allows us to refresh a tab.

- **Focus on the tab**:

  - This action allows us to position a tab that we define as the active tab in the session.

> **Note**
> A macro is not limited to a single action of this connector when executed.

- **Omnichannel Connector** offers us actions that execute operations related to the Omnichannel for Customer Service application. The available actions are as follows:

Figure 7.4 – Omnichannel connector's actions

Let's understand each action presented in the previous screenshot:

- **Send KB article in chat**:

  - This action allows us to send to the chat conversation a knowledge base article obtained in the **Search the knowledge base for the populated phrase** action.

- **Link record to the conversation**:

  - This action allows us to link a specific record with the active conversation.

- **Unlink record from the conversation**:

  - This action allows us to unlink a specific record with the active conversation.

- **Flow Connector** will be able to execute cloud flows as part of the macro. This opens up the possibility not only for automated actions to be performed in the Omnichannel for Customer Service application but also for actions to be performed on other systems, whether they are validations or integrations.

Finally, the macros have a **Condition** control to perform conditional validations during their execution.

Now that we know the actions available in the macros, let's review how to start working with them.

How to create a macro?

We can create a macro from different places: from the **Customer Service admin center** application, from the **Omnichannel admin center** application, or from the **App profile manager**.

Customer Service admin center

As we can see in the following screenshot, from the **Customer Service admin center** application, we must select **Productivity** in the site map under **Agent experience**. Then, we need to select **Manage** for the **Macros** option:

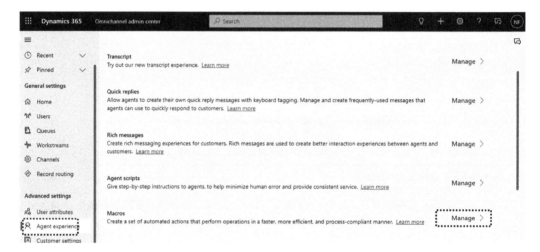

Figure 7.5 – Customer Service admin center

The most likely scenario for you to configure macros from the **Customer Service admin center** is that you have a customer service implementation without the Omnichannel Engagement Hub application.

Omnichannel admin center

As we can see in the next screenshot, from the **Omnichannel admin center** application, we must select **Agent experience** in the site map under **Advanced settings**. Then, we need to select **Manage** for the **Macros** option:

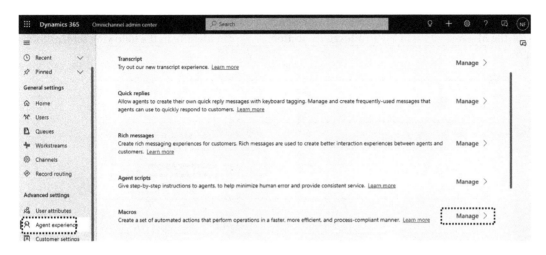

Figure 7.6 – Omnichannel admin center

The most likely scenario for you to configure macros from **Omnichannel admin center** is that you have a customer service implementation with the Omnichannel Engagement Hub application included.

App profile manager

To access **App profile manager**, we need to follow the next steps:

1. As we can see in the next screenshot, from make.powerapps.com, we have to open **App profile manager** from any of the applications available:

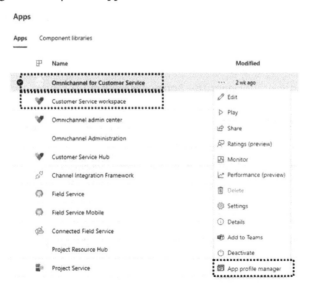

Figure 7.7 – Selecting App profile manager

2. Then, under both **Customer Service workspace** and **Omnichannel Admin Center**, we will find the **Macros** option in the **Productivity** section, as we can identify in the following screenshot:

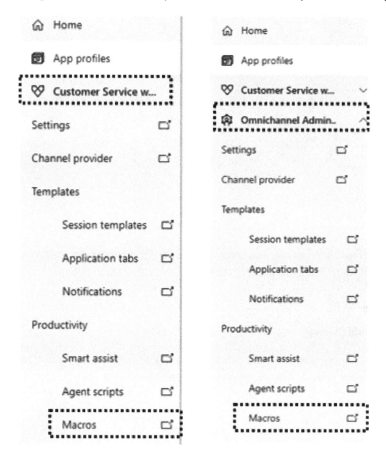

Figure 7.8 – App profile manager

The most likely scenario for you to configure macros from **App profile manager** is that you are making adjustments to app profiles.

However, all three ways are correct and will have the same outcome.

Why use a macro?

Repetitive and non-value-adding actions often carry a high risk of errors as users tend to underestimate them. By setting up macros, we ensure that actions are performed flawlessly while offering the agent a better experience when managing a conversation.

Now that we already know how to leverage macros, we can now learn how to alert users of the next best action for an account, opportunity, or other scenarios.

Alerting users of the next best action

Being able to identify the next best action to take with a customer is almost like finding a unicorn for many businesses. To achieve this, there are several approaches in Power Platform, from the implementation of Intelligent Recommendations to more low-code options such as making use of the assistant (formerly known as Relationship Assistant).

The assistant offers interactive cards with the most relevant information for the salesperson, from appointment reminders to customer information. The assistant can be accessed from the following:

- **The navigation bar**: At any time, we will be able to access the assistant from the Dynamics 365 navigation bar.
- **Dashboards**: It is possible to embed the assistant component in dashboards.
- **Forms**: It is possible to embed the assistant component in a table form. When doing so, the cards we will see in it will be only those related to the record.
- **Mobile application**: The assistant will also be available from the mobile application.

The assistant is part of Dynamics 365 Sales Insights, and we can get it if we have Dynamics 365 Sales Premium, Dynamics 365 Sales Enterprise, or Dynamics 365 Sales Insights licenses. In the case of having only Dynamics 365 Sales Enterprise licenses, we will not have access to the Assistant Studio, so we will not have the possibility to extend it.

In order to create custom cards, we need to have Dynamics 365 Sales Premium or Dynamics 365 Sales Insights licenses, as this will give us access to the premium assistant.

The premium assistant will allow us to create customized cards, as well as customize the UX by optimizing the ranking of cards, prioritizing individual cards, or assigning cards to specific user roles.

When working with the Assistant Studio, basically what we are going to do is set up cloud flows that will use the Dynamics 365 Sales Insights connector to create an action card.

In order to create a personalized card, in addition to having the necessary license, the configuration of the Dynamics 365 Sales Insights application is required. To do this, you need to do the following:

1. On the Sales Hub application, go to **Sales Insights settings**:

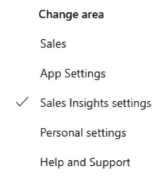

Figure 7.9 – Sales Insights settings in the Sales Hub sitemap

2. Go to the **Insights cards** option, under the **Assistant Studio** group:

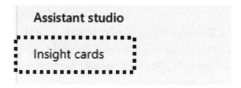

Figure 7.10 – Insights cards option

3. Click on the + **New card** option:

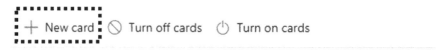

Figure 7.11 – + New card option

4.   Accept the Sales Insights settings and wait for it to be installed:

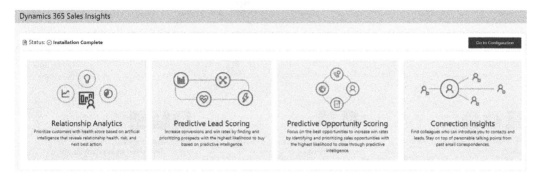

Figure 7.12 – Dynamics 365 Sales Insights installing screen

Once the process is finished, we can create new cards from the Power Automate cloud flows editor. To access it, we need to go to the new **Home** sub-area under the **Assistant studio** group, in the **Sales Insights settings** area:

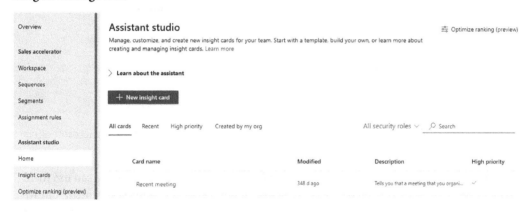

Figure 7.13 – New Assistant studio group options in the sitemap

As we can see in the preceding screenshot, after we install the Dynamics 365 Sales Insights application, two new sub-areas will be available for the Assistant Studio: **Home** and **Optimize ranking (preview)**.

Where to start

To start working with custom cards, we must go to the Assistant Studio. There, we should choose to create a new card.

As we can see in *Figure 7.11*, in addition to creating new cards, we will also be able to manage existing cards.

By selecting + **New insight card**, we will enter the Power Automate cloud flows editor. There, we can choose to start from scratch or use one of the existing templates:

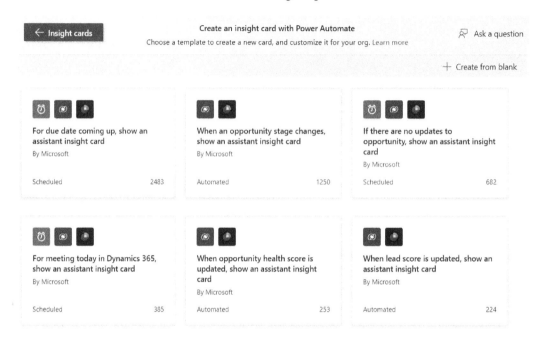

Figure 7.14 – Power Automate designer accessed from Assistant Studio

We can quickly identify many business scenarios already solved in the templates that Microsoft offers us, as we can see in the screenshot.

Something we must always remember is that being Power Automate cloud flows, we can use them not only as a trigger to an event within Dataverse/Dynamics 365 Customer Engagement, but we can also make use of manual triggers, scheduled or from events that happen in external systems or applications. At the same time, if we want to do some kind of evaluation, validation, or calculation prior to the creation of a card, we can make use of the more than 700 Power Platform connectors available, or a custom connector.

This allows us to include, as part of the action cards, information from other systems, or even Power BI indicators. For example, we could create an action card for the following scenarios:

- For the account manager to contact a customer when they are close to consuming credits from a subscription, which is managed in a system external to Dynamics 365 Customer Engagement

- For the account manager to propose a specific playbook based on the customer's accounting status

> **Note**
>
> A playbook is a Dynamics 365 Sales native feature. It allows organizations to configure action plan templates, to be instantiated in different types of sales-related records, such as opportunities, accounts, or offers. Playbook templates will include a set of activities that will be created when they are activated in an opportunity or other record.

When we talk about proposing a next best action, we have to understand that this can mean different things for different organizations. In short, it refers to proposing an action based on the context—but what is an action?

With Power Automate, we will be able to create customized cards for the assistant that include a title, a description, and two actions, one primary and one secondary. These actions can be the following:

- **Open record**: Allows us to define the table and record we want to open, as well as the form we want to use

- **Open URL**: Allows us to define a URL that we want to open

- **Launch playbook**: Allows us to define the playbook template we want to launch and the context in which it should be launched

- **REST API**: Allows us to define the endpoint, the method, and the URL to invoke the API

- **Custom action (CRM process) (this being a CRM process)**: Allows us to invoke a custom action, defined as global or for a Dynamics 365 table

You can see a screenshot example of some of the aforementioned actions here:

Figure 7.15 – Comparison of two cards with different actions

The previous screenshot presents a comparison between two different cards with different actions. We can quickly identify that the attributes required for the primary and secondary actions are different since the actions are different.

As we can see from the following screenshot, the Dynamics 365 Sales Insights connector has two available actions:

- **Choose custom action (CRM process) for insight card**: Allows us to define which custom action will be invoked on the card
- **Create card for assistant V3**: Allows us to define the attributes of the card

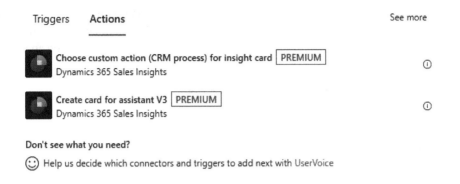

Figure 7.16 – Dynamics 365 Sales Insights actions

The possibilities for validations or actions are as wide as what we want to do with Power Automate. This gives us enormous flexibility in challenging us on what we need to create to offer the best action to sellers.

Let's now review how to work with BPFs, and how and why we could automate them.

Automating BPFs

BPFs are an excellent option when we want to provide users with a visual tool to guide them on how to manage a process. When we define a BPF, we will work with the following concepts:

- **BPFs**: These flows correspond to the process we are defining. They will be composed of several consecutive stages, and may also present branches to the process.

- **Stages**: The stages of the BPFs will represent a phase of the business process. Each phase will be associated with a single table, being able to change the table between consecutive stages. Each stage will be composed of steps. To move from one stage to the next, click on the **Next stage** button.

- **Steps**: These steps refer to the things that the user must do:

  - Data to be completed

  - Flows to execute

  - Actions to execute

Additionally, for each of the stages, we can add workflows that are automatically executed when entering the stage or exiting the stage.

The transition between stages, as I mentioned before, is a manual action on the BPFs. However, it is common to encounter the requirement that the transition is automated from the evolution of the record. Certainly, depending on the nature of the requirement, we can opt for different solution approaches. Here, we will focus exclusively on some scenarios in which Power Automate is a viable option.

Since these are just examples, and the construction of a cloud flow does not escape any other cloud flow, we will not go into detail on how to build them.

We must consider that every time we create a BPF, a table is created to manage its records. This table will be related to the Process Stages table, from which we will be able to create flows for its automated transition. This is the key part to automate the transition.

Updating the record

We may want to advance the BPF when some data in the registry is updated. To ensure that the phase change is always performed, we must think of a process that is executed at the server level and not only at the client level.

In this case, the trigger will be the record update, limited to the attribute(s) that we want to validate and contemplate to evaluate the phase change.

This scenario is very common to advance the following:

- **Sales processes** (in Dynamics 365 Sales) when BPF steps or opportunity attributes are completed
- **The case management process** (in Dynamics 365 Customer Service) when incorporating investigation or possible response information
- **Case management** (in Dynamics 365 Customer Service), or **work order management processes** (in Dynamics 365 Field Service), for scenarios that include IoT and automated processes
- **The event management process** (in Dynamics 365 Marketing) when advancing event planning

Updating related records

Sometimes, we want the BPF stage change to occur when a parent or child record is updated.

Some scenarios are as follows:

- **When the parent case is updated**, we want both the BPF of the record in question and the child cases to be updated
- **When updating the status of an offer**, we want the BPF of the opportunity to be updated
- **When a booking is updated**, we want the BPF of the work order to be updated

Updating a record in another system

Finally, it is possible that the trigger for the BPF step change may occur in another system. This is common for processes that take place in more than one system—for example, the following:

- If, in order to progress through a certain stage of the business process, an action must first be taken in the **enterprise resource planning (ERP)** on the account

- If a ticket to be escalated is managed in an external system, we may need input from that system to advance the business process

These are just some examples of where we may need to automate the transition of stages of a BPF. Let's now see how we can extend applications.

Sending automated communications

Dynamics 365 Customer Engagement applications have the customer at the center of their processes, so it is normal to expect to have multiple communications between the organization and the customer. Being able to automate part of these communications ends up being highly beneficial for users and organizations. It helps to save time in manual tasks, and this time can be applied to tasks that provide more value for the user, the business, and the customer.

However, communications generated from Dynamics 365 Customer Engagement applications need not be limited to communications with customers.

In this section, we will discuss how we can use Power Automate to automate the sending of communications, as well as real examples of required communications.

The first thing to understand is that we can automate communications from Dynamics 365 Customer Engagement applications to different types of recipients, among which we will find accounts, contacts, and system leads (they can be customers, suppliers, partners, or other types of relationship), but also system users and stakeholders of the processes but not necessarily Dynamics 365 users. When we talk about messages sent to system users or stakeholders, we will refer to these messages as alerts or notifications. Although this definition is subjective, I believe it is extremely practical when analyzing the processes in a project (or during pre-sales).

The second point to understand is that there are several ways to automate communications, but in this case, we will limit ourselves to the communications that we can automate with Power Automate cloud flows.

It should be noted that Dynamics 365 Marketing allows us to automate the sending of communications, and this would be the correct approach for marketing communications. These examples will be left out of the analysis done in this chapter.

We need to understand what will be the trigger and the message we want to send. For this, we have as many options as offered by the Power Platform connectors. That is, we can have communications sent by the following kinds of triggers:

- **Manual**: When executing the automatism, the communication will be sent.

- **Scheduled**: The communication will be sent to the recipient on a recurring basis according to the scheduled trigger.

- **Event-based**: The communication can be sent when an event is performed (creation, modification, deletion, and so on) of a record in Dynamics 365 Customer Engagement or in another system. If the trigger is in another system, it is also possible that we want the communication to be made from Dynamics 365 Customer Engagement to centralize communications with customers.

Next, we need to understand which types of communications we can send. Here is a list of the most commonly used types of communications, and the scenarios in which they are used:

- **Email**:

    - Email is one of the most widely used channels, although it is increasingly being overtaken by other channels such as SMS, Teams, and even push notifications

    - When we send to customers (another type of account, contact, or lead) from Dynamics 365 Customer Engagement, we can take advantage of email engagement capabilities to track emails

    - There is a myriad of scenarios for sending emails, but here, I try to summarize the most relevant ones:

        - When a case changes status, you can automate sending a notification to the customer

        - When a resource reservation is created for a work order or service activity, you can automate the sending of a notification to the customer

        - When a case is resolved, you can automate the sending of a Dynamics 365 Customer Voice satisfaction survey

        - When a work order is closed, you can automate the sending of a Dynamics 365 Customer Voice satisfaction survey

        - When a quotation is activated, you can automate the sending of the quotation summary based on a template

- **SMS**:

    - SMS is the preferred channel when we want to send a communication to the customer and want to ensure the immediacy of receipt

    - Here are some of the most common examples of using SMS as a communication channel:

- When updating a resource reservation, you can automate the sending of an SMS with detailed information to give the best predictability of when the technician will be arriving

- When updating the information of an appointment or a scheduled call

- When a case classified as critical is resolved

- **Push notifications**:

  - Push notifications have been gaining importance in recent years, although not all organizations have mobile apps for their customers

  - Because of the nature of the channel, the scenarios that apply to an SMS also apply to a push notification

- **IoT messages**:

  - IoT messages can be sent to customer assets

- **Message by instant messaging (IM) app**:

  - IM notifications, such as WhatsApp, have also been gaining importance in recent years because of their immediacy

  - Because of the nature of the channel, again the scenarios that apply to an SMS also apply to a message by an IM application

- **Post on a self-service portal**:

  - When an organization has a self-service portal in place where the customer can create and manage incidents or cases, communication as a post in an incident begins to take on relevance

  - It is normal to want to automate messages at each change of phase or status of the case resolution process, as well as the sending of a satisfaction survey when it is closed

  - This type of post applies to other self-management processes that may be enabled in the portal, such as appointment or visit management

Now that we've learned some real-life examples of customer communications, let's analyze some examples of automated alerts and reports.

Adaptive Cards

Adaptive Cards is an easy way to format a message to include an enhanced UX, action buttons, and advanced components such as maps:

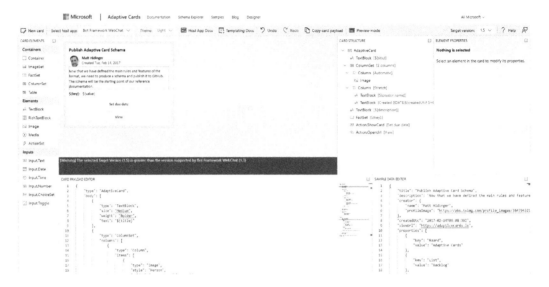

Figure 7.17 – Adaptive Cards designer

In the previous screenshot, you can see what the card designer (`https://adaptivecards.io/designer/`) looks like. You can quickly design your adaptive card with drag and drop functionality, and then define the properties of each element by selecting it:

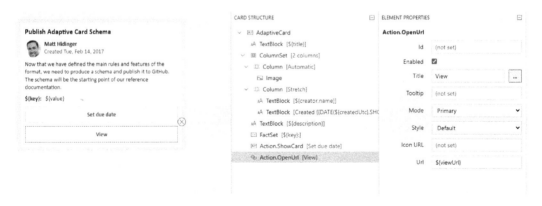

Figure 7.18 – Adaptive Cards designer

In the previous screenshot, we can see how the URL property of the button can be defined from the **ELEMENT PROPERTIES** section. For simple scenarios, we can create these cards without any development knowledge. However, for more advanced scenarios, we will have to work with JSON code, which will require pro-code skills.

Automating alerts and reports

As I mentioned earlier, we refer to alerts as notifications that we can automate for system users or stakeholders. Just as for communications, with Power Automate cloud flows, we can create different types of alerts or notifications with reports on Dynamics 365 Customer Engagement processes. These alerts will depend on the business requirements of each organization, but they will all have more or less the same basic structure:

- **Trigger**:

  - May be from an event that happens in Dynamics 365 Customer Engagement, by a scheduled or on-demand flow.

- **Validations**:

  - It is not mandatory to have validations as part of the flow, although we often encounter these. Validations will allow us to ensure that we send the correct notification/alert.

- **Message shaping**:

  - We will be able to build the message in different ways. Among the things we will be able to do are the following:

    - Obtain dynamical content from Dynamics 365 Customer Engagement records.

    - Select a Dynamics 365 template that we want to use.

    - Create HTML tables with dynamic content.

- **Send an alert**:

  - Finally, we will send the message through the corresponding channel.

When implementing the different Dynamics 365 Customer Engagement applications, we will encounter multiple scenarios in which we will apply to extend the solution with alerts or automated reports. We will try to summarize some of the most important considerations when working with these requirements.

Recipient

When collecting alerts and reporting requirements, it is important to understand who will be the recipient of each alert. The considerations we should have when designing the automation may change in the following scenarios:

- The user is a Dynamics 365 Customer Engagement user in the tenant:

  - In this scenario, as the recipient is a Dynamics 365 Customer Engagement user, we have a lot of flexibility when designing the alert. We can think about messages inside the application as well as outside the application. That is, the alert the user receives could be an in-app notification, keeping everything within the context of Dynamics 365 Customer Engagement. However, we could also send them an alert through some external channel (email, Teams message, and so on) with a link to the record(s) for which the alert is sent. That way, the user could receive the message, but if they needed more details, they could access the corresponding Dynamics 365 application. It is very common to need to send notifications to Dynamics 365 Customer Engagement users. These are just a few examples of alerts:

    - When some user creates an opportunity related to an owned account

    - When a customer often completes a web form integrated with Dynamics 365

    - When an opportunity is about to expire

    - A daily summary of pending tasks

    - When a task is assigned to a user

- The recipient is an Office 365 user in the tenant but does not have licenses that give them reading privileges over Dynamics 365 Customer Engagement:

  - In case it is an Office 365 user in the tenant, but does not have any license that gives them reading privileges over Dynamics 365 Customer Engagement, we will be limited by not being able to generate an alert within Dynamics 365 Customer Engagement. Nor will it make sense for us to add a link to Dynamics 365 Customer Engagement as part of the message. However, we could add some action button that ends up performing an action within Dynamics 365 if the cloud flow is properly licensed.

- The person who will receive the notifications is not a user in the tenant:

  - It is very common to need to send notifications to users in the organization who do not have access to Dynamics 365 Customer Engagement. These are just a few examples of alerts:

    - When a high-priority opportunity is missed

    - When a case is created for an issue for a VIP customer

    - Opportunity status

- Case status

- When a satisfaction survey is negative

- When a process is not compliant

Finally, sometimes we need to notify users from other organizations about an action that happens in Dynamics 365 Customer Engagement. In these cases, in addition to the limitation of not having access to Dynamics 365 Customer Engagement applications, there are also limitations in terms of the channels available to contact you.

Channels

When analyzing the possible channels for sending alerts, we have to consider what is the optimal experience for the user who will receive the alert. Among other considerations, we have to contemplate the following:

- **Frequency of notifications**: We must consider the most effective channel for alerts that have a high cadence to avoid users getting fed up and dismissing the alerts.

- **Urgency of notifications**: If the alerts have a high urgency, we must think of a channel that guarantees that they will be seen quickly. A message in Teams or an SMS are usually the most immediate channels.

- **Format of notifications**: Will the alert be plain text? Will it include a link? Do we need an action button? Could we use an Adaptive Card? These are some of the questions we should ask ourselves to identify the best channel for sending the alert. It is not the same to send information from multiple records by SMS as it is to send it in a table as part of an email.

Once the recipient and the channel have been identified, we still have to define the rest of the flow that will constitute the alert. This could include data validations, and the message itself, that we will include as part of the flow.

Creating approval processes

Finally, one of the most frequent automation we have in Dynamics 365 Customer Engagement projects has to do with extending native processes to support approval processes. This can apply to different business processes, although it is very common to have this type of requirement for approvals of discounts or commercial conditions.

Power Automate offers approval flows as a native capability to integrate into our processes. To create an approval flow, we must add the **Approvals** connector to our cloud flow, as an action.

When working with the connector, we will have two options: use the **Start and wait for an approval** action or use the **Start an approval** action, and then close the flow with the **Wait for an approval** action. Let's look at these in a bit more detail:

- For the first action, **Start and wait for an approval**, the cloud flow will trigger the approval and wait for the result of the approval before continuing the flow

- The second one, where only the approval is started, allows us to define actions to be executed between starting the flow and waiting for its result

When we start an approval flow, the first thing we have to define is the type of approval we want to execute. The options are **Approve/Reject - Everyone must approve**, **Approve/Reject - First to respond**, **Custom Responses – Wait for all responses**, and **Custom Responses – Wait for one response**:

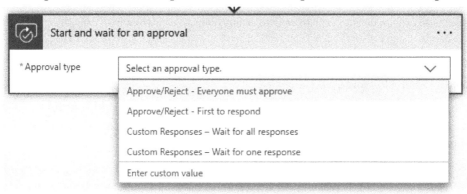

Figure 7.19 – Approval types

In the previous screenshot, we can see the types of approvals available. We can better understand how the approval types work with the following table:

	Approve/Reject	Custom Responses
Everyone must approve/Wait for all responses	The approval flow will have two possible outcomes: approve or reject. The approval action will wait for responses from all recipients of the approval flow before defining the outcome.	When configuring the action, we must define the options that the approvers will have when receiving the approval messages. The approval action will wait for responses from all recipients of the approval flow before defining the result.
First to respond/ Wait for one response	The approval flow will have two possible outcomes: approve or reject. The approval action will define the outcome of the first response received.	When configuring the action, we must define the options that the approvers will have when receiving the approval messages. The approval action will define the result of the first response received.

Table 7.1 – Approval types definition

> **Note**
>
> In January 2023, it is expected that Power Automate will support sequential approvals. This feature will help makers to create multilevel/stage approval flows. The approval flow will advance to the next stage/level, only if all the approvers in the previous stage approved it.

In *Table 7.1*, we can see the different possible combinations of response types and the number of expected responses.

As part of the approval definition, we can add a link to Dynamics 365 Customer Engagement to access all the information needed to make a decision.

Now that we have gone through these six most common scenarios of automations, we will be able to build to empower users. We must always keep in mind that these automations seek to simplify the use of the application, keep all stakeholders informed, and ensure compliance with processes.

Summary

In this chapter, we have learned about how to respond to the six most common scenarios that we can encounter in Dynamics 365 Customer Engagement projects. We started by detailing how we can automate mundane and repetitive customer service agent tasks with macros. We saw which types of actions we can do and why they are important when wanting to provide tools that empower agents and improve the UX. We then went on to understand how we can create suggestions for users with interactive cards with the assistant and the Assistant Studio. Leveraging the customer data we have in Dynamics 365 or other systems, we can analyze what is the next best action and propose it to our sales force.

We then covered how we can work with BPFs, and in what ways we can automate the transition of stages.

We also understood the types of automated communications we can have, both for customers, users, and stakeholders. We reviewed the most relevant considerations and constraints to keep in mind when designing a solution.

Finally, we analyzed the types of approval processes that Power Automate offers natively.

For each of these extensions that we can build with Power Automate, we reviewed real business scenarios to which it applies.

In the next chapter, we will continue to discuss extensions that we can build with Power Automate, but in this case, we will focus on how to work with Dynamics 365 data, both for data validation and integration between systems.

Questions and answers

1. Why should we use macros?

   Answer: Macros allow organizations to increase agent experience and customer satisfaction and reduce the handling time for cases and conversations.

2. Which license do I need to access the Assistant Studio?

   Answer: The Assistant Studio is part of the Dynamics 365 Sales Insights application. Organizations have the right to use this application if they have Dynamics 365 Sales Premium or Dynamics 365 Sales Insights licenses.

8

Working with Data

As we saw in the previous chapter, Power Automate offers multiple capabilities to automate repetitive tasks, thus empowering users. However, the use cases for which Power Automate offers a solution are many more. One of the most important aspects whenever we implement any Dynamics 365 Customer Engagement application is working with data. However, Power Automate is not the only tool that Power Platform offers us to work with data when we need to perform data validations, build integrations between systems, or perform data synchronization.

In this chapter, we will delve into real scenarios of Dynamics 365 Customer Engagement implementations where it was required to work with data, and we will analyze the possible solutions with Power Platform. For each of these cases, we will see which Power Platform solution is a valid option, and the considerations to take into account. As always, it's important to remember that regardless of having multiple no-code/low-code options, when designing a solution we must consider the specific conditions of each case to determine if it is the best design approach. Sometimes, we will need to consider a pro-code approach, as it could be the best solution. But this is even more important when faced with the need to solve integrations or large-volume data processing.

By the end of the chapter, you will have learned how to identify which are the viable options when designing a solution that requires working with Dynamics 365 Customer Engagement data.

In this chapter, we will cover the following topics:

- Validating data
- Integrating systems
- Synchronizing data

Technical requirements

To work with Dynamics 365 Customer Engagement, it is necessary to have an environment with one of the supported licenses. However, the topics covered in this chapter do not require any Dynamics 365 application.

The following are required for this chapter:

- Any Dynamics 365 Customer Engagement license (any of the available ones) with administrator permissions in an environment

- A supported browser

Validating data

When users work with Dynamics 365 Customer Engagement applications, often they are working with customers' data related to the different processes covered in Dynamics 365 (such as opportunity management, case management, and others), or even with products or assets data. On many occasions, it is necessary to validate data that is manually entered by a user. In some cases, this validation has to happen in real time in order to continue with a process, while in other cases data validation can happen in the background, as an asynchronous process.

When designing a data validation solution, the first thing to identify—in addition to the data to be validated—is the *why*; that is, what is the purpose of the validation. This will allow us to define how we are going to do the validation.

In this section, we will review some of the most common examples that we can find in our implementation of Dynamics 365 Customer Engagement and how we can solve them, thanks to the capabilities that Power Platform offers.

Considerations in designing data validations

When a user is working with a Dynamics 365 Customer Engagement application, they may need to perform data validation as part of the process they are developing. As presented in the following diagram, the most common scenarios in which validation is required are in the context of the record they are working on, on related records, or on an external system:

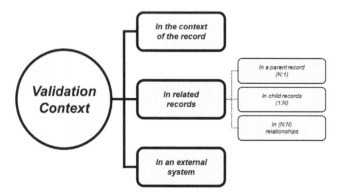

Figure 8.1 – Validation contexts

As we can see in the preceding screenshot, when the context of validations is on related records, we refer to either of the following:

- **Parent records (N:1 relationships)**: For example, if the automation is in the context of an opportunity, the validation could be at the customer level

- **Child records (1:N relationships)**: For example, if the automation is in the context of an opportunity, the validation could be at the opportunity product level

- **Multiple related records (N:N relationships)**: For example, if the automation is in the context of an opportunity, the validation could be at the competitor level

It is possible that when a user is working in a Dynamics 365 application, we may need the validation to be triggered automatically in some cases, while in others, it could be executed manually. This will depend on the business process we are implementing.

However, data validations will not be limited to only being triggered when a user is working in Dynamics 365 Customer Engagement. In many cases, we will need to run background processes in which we will need to perform data validations. These validations can be executed after an event performed by an integration, or from a scheduled process. Thus, we will have three triggers to launch a data validation: manual, event-based, or scheduled.

We must take into account that when we talk about a validation based on an event, we can find an event that happens at the server level as well as at the client level. That is to say, an event can be the change in an attribute of a record having saved the record, or simply having modified it in a form.

An example of a validation performed at the client level would be this: when the agent completes the first level of typing of the case, the application validates if the second level has data and puts it as required by the system. On the other hand, an example of validation at the server level would be this: when we complete a reservation, the system validates if there is another reservation open for the work order, and if not, it closes it. This second example is an example of logic that brings us Dynamics 365 Field Service out of the box.

Finally, we must consider the way in which data validation is performed. This may be synchronous or asynchronous. Asynchronous validations are triggered and executed in the background, while synchronous validations are executed in real time. We will use the synchronous ones when we need the result of the validation to continue with the process we are executing. For example, a user wants to close a Dynamics 365 Customer Service case, but to do so, certain registration data must be completed. This validation must be performed in real time since the result depends on whether or not the main action is allowed to be performed.

Once the data validation has been defined, we must establish the subsequent action. Depending on the validation execution mode, we will be able to choose one or another post-validation action. For example, if we take the previous example, if what we want is to receive an error message on the screen and prevent the process from continuing, this can only be achieved with synchronous validation.

In summary, we can consider that there are going to be context, trigger, execution mode, and post-validation actions considerations, and based on those we will be able to define the best solution, as shown in the following screenshot:

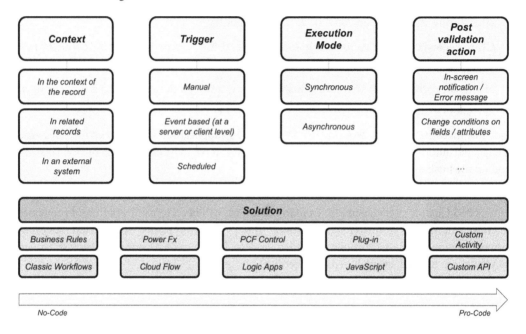

Figure 8.2 – Validations considerations

With these considerations, we can now think about the types of solutions we can consider. As presented in the previous screenshot, when we think about the ways in which we can perform data validation in Dynamics 365 Customer Engagement, we will have no-code/low-code solutions, as well as options that require development, or pro-code.

Among the former, we can find business rules, classic workflows, Power FX, and cloud flows. Let's now analyze each of these solutions.

> **Note**
>
> It is important to have a global vision of the solution since it is possible that we use different types of mechanisms to perform validations, and among these, there may be dependencies or considerations. A frequent example is when we work with client-side logic, and include business rules and JavaScript that are executed in the same form. If you are not careful, you can get a solution that is complex to manage and prone to failure.

Business rules

As we have already seen in *Chapter 3*, business rules can be used to apply business logic on a record. This type of validation will be only in the context of the record in which we are not able to validate related data or data from external systems. We can consider that they are triggered by an event, or rather in the pre-saved action of an event, whether it is applied on forms or at the table level. The execution mode of a business rule will be synchronous.

The actions that we will be able to establish post-validation for business rules are presented here:

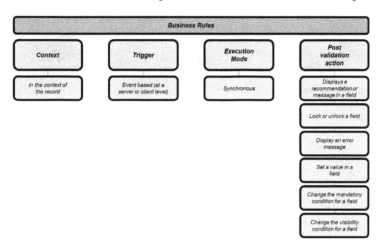

Figure 8.3 – Business rules considerations

The preceding diagram summarizes the considerations to be taken into account when evaluating a business rule as a possible solution for data validation.

Classic workflows and cloud flows

Classic workflows allow us to define validations and actions declaratively without the need for any development. This functionality is the predecessor of the current cloud flows, but we can find four main differences between them:

	Classic workflows	Cloud flows
Execution mode	Synchronous and Asynchronous	Asynchronous
In the context of…	Record and parent record in Dynamics 365 Customer Engagement/Dataverse	Any of the +700 Power Platform connectors

Table 8.1 – Classic workflows and cloud flows comparison

> **Note**
>
> Currently, the use of cloud flows is recommended as long as this approach meets the requirements. Classic workflows have not been the focus of Microsoft's investment in recent releases, and there is a risk that they will be deprecated in the near future. It should be noted that there is no confirmation from the manufacturer on the actual continuation or deprecation of this functionality and that for the time being, it remains a viable option.

As mentioned in the previous table, when we work with classic workflows, we can use data from the record on which the automation is being executed, or related data.

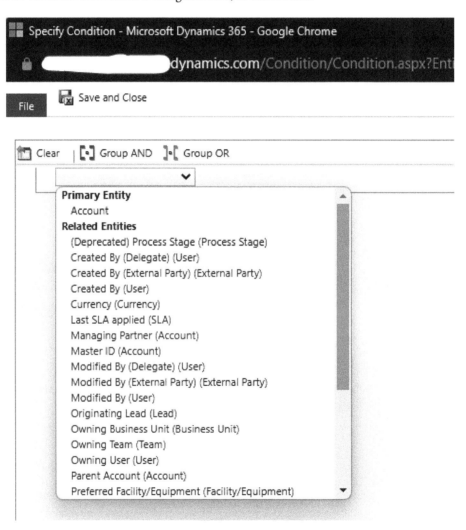

Figure 8.4 – Example of Account's relationships available in a condition step

In the previous screenshot, we can see that the context of the conditions that we can create to make a validation is limited to the main table/entity and related tables, but only with an N:1 relationship. Validations may be done considering multiple conditions and applying logical operators on these conditions (AND and OR).

There are a variety of actions that we can execute after a validation are multiple. Natively, we will find the following:

- Create a record

- Update a record

- Assign a record

- Send an email

- Execute a child workflow

- Perform an action

- Change a status

- End the workflow

Also, we may have workflow activities available that have been developed within the organization. Dynamics 365 Customer Engagement solutions, as with **independent software vendors' (ISVs')** solutions, could also deploy workflow activities when installed in a Dynamics 365 Customer Engagement environment. For example, if we have Dynamics 365 Marketing, or if we deploy a native portal, we will find workflow activities specific to those solutions.

When a workflow is executed synchronously, we have to consider that until the workflow is finished executing, we will not be able to continue working on the application. For this reason, it must be evaluated if there is a real need to have the workflow running synchronously. Finally, if the workflow will be executed synchronously, we can define when it will be executed:

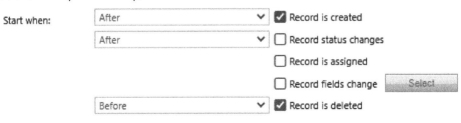

Figure 8.5 – Synchronous workflows: automated trigger rules

As we can see in the preceding screenshot, a classic workflow can be executed:

- After the record is created
- Before or after:
    - a change of status
    - a change in another attribute
    - being assigned
- Before being deleted

Additionally, we can configure a workflow to be executed manually so that it will not be limited only to being executed from an event:

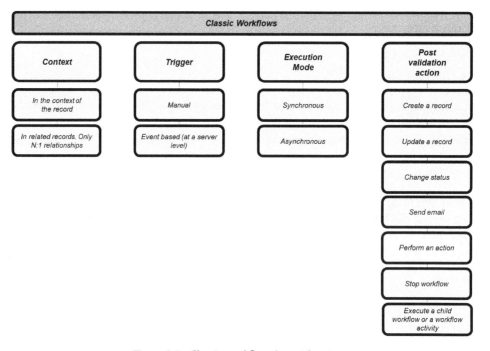

Figure 8.6 – Classic workflows' considerations

The previous diagram summarizes the considerations to be taken into account when evaluating a classic workflow as a possible solution for data validation.

On the other hand, Power Automate cloud flows are a great tool to validate data, especially when we need to make complex queries within Dynamics 365 Customer Engagement, or when we need to consult external systems. As we already know, when running a cloud flow, we can make use of the +700 native connectors that Power Platform offers us, as well as the custom connectors that we have developed. Unlike the classic workflows in which we could choose whether we wanted them to be executed as synchronous or asynchronous processes, cloud flows will be executed as asynchronous processes. This will be the major conditioning factor since sometimes we will want the result of the validation to allow or block a process. For those cases, we will have to resort to another solution approach that does allow us to create synchronous validations:

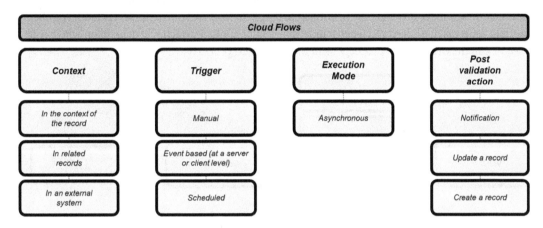

Figure 8.7 – Power Automate cloud flows' considerations

Since it is a cloud flow, we can configure it to be executed on demand, with a manual trigger, scheduling it to be executed on a recurring basis, or on the basis of an event (creation, modification, or deletion of the record). In the preceding diagram, we can see a summary of the considerations that we must take into account when designing a data validation with a cloud flow.

One of the most important elements that we will have at our disposal to use when working with cloud flows is AI Builder. In the next chapter, *Chapter 9*, we will see how we can get the most out of this type of use case.

However, it is worth mentioning that we will not be limited only to the three post-validation actions listed in the diagram (notifications, updating records, and creating records), but these are an example. As I mentioned earlier, by being able to make use of Power Platform connectors, the options for post-validation actions are extensive.

Power Fx

As the conversion between canvas apps and model-driven apps progresses, we find more no-code/low-code capabilities. This path of unifying the different types of Power Apps is closely tied to the capabilities that Dynamics 365 Customer Engagement applications will have. This is because, as we have established before, Dynamics 365 Customer Engagement applications are model-driven apps built by Microsoft. In *Chapter 3*, we introduced the concept of the command bar and talked about the possibility we have to customize actions in it without development. We saw that as part of this customization, we can incorporate Power Fx formulas as part of the logic to be executed, or the display conditions of the commands.

Both at the time of executing an action and defining whether the command is visible or not, we will be able to perform validations. The first aspect to consider is that when introducing validations as part of commands, these will be linked to the application in which we have these commands. This means that these validations will only be present at the client level and not at the server level. Another important aspect is to understand when validations will be applied, which will depend on whether it is executed in the OnSelect property or in the Visible property:

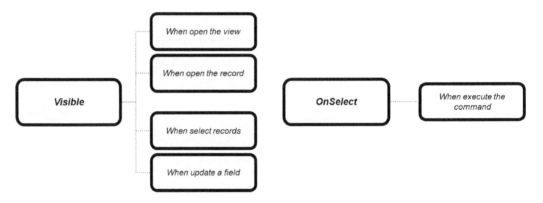

Figure 8.8 – Data validation applied on command bar's commands

The validations that we can add in the Visible property will define when the command will be visible to the user. This validation will help to maintain consistency and will reinforce when it is appropriate to execute a specific action. In the case of view command bar commands, the validation will be applied both when the view is opened and when the view records are selected. This is because among the validations that we could be doing are validations on the number of records selected or the data of the selected record.

For example, if in a view we want a command to be displayed only if there is one record selected, we must add this function to the Visible property of the command:

```
If(CountRows(Self.Selected.AllItems)=1,true,false)
```

In the same way, if we want the number of records to be at least one, the function we should add would be the following:

```
If(CountRows(Self.Selected.AllItems)>0,true,false)
```

In these examples, we can see that the validation we are doing is on the set of records in the view, simply considering the total number of records as a condition to make the command visible or not.

On the other hand, validations that we add in the `OnSelect` property will only be executed if we execute the command manually.

Sometimes, we will need to execute different formulas depending on a condition. Based on what we have already seen, we could have two commands whose visibility depends on the condition we are evaluating. However, the evaluation of the condition can be added in the `OnSelect` property. This way, we would have to maintain a single custom command.

It is worth mentioning that it will depend on the business requirements whether we should opt for one or the other option.

Regarding the context in which validations can occur, we can use Power Fx functions not only to take data from the record or view in which we are located but to also take data from related tables. For example, if we wanted to condition an action from a parent record, we could do the validation as part of our function, as we can see here:

```
Notify(If(Self.Selected.
Item.'Primary Contact'.'First Name'="Nico","Hello","Goodbye"),
NotificationType.Information)
```

We can see that we are doing the validation within the action we want to perform, and that depending on the result of the validation, we will condition the main action.

In this example, the action we want to do is to send an onscreen notification, with the `Notify` function. We can see that the message is of type `Information`, and its value depends on the validation that we want to do, and depending on the result of the validation, the message will be one or another. The validation that we are doing in this example is simple. We are simply validating if the first name of the primary contact of the record in which we are positioned is equal to `"Nico"`. If the primary contact's name is Nico, the information message will be `"Hello"`, and if it is another value, the message will be `"Goodbye"`. This is a simple example of a notification that will depend on data from a parent record.

Currently, Power Fx functions in custom commands only support Dataverse as a data source, and only a set of functions, among which we will find: `Patch`, `CountRows`, `If`, `Notify`, `Navigate`, `Now`, `DateAdd`, `RecordInfo`, `DataSoruceInfo`, `Confirm`, and `Launch`. It is recommended to consult the official documentation on a recurring basis for updates on the supported functions, in `https://docs.microsoft.com/en-us/power-apps/maker/model-driven-apps/commanding-use-powerfx`:

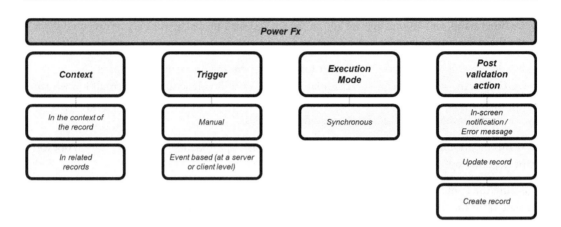

Figure 8.9 – Power Fx's considerations

The preceding diagram summarizes the considerations to be taken into account when evaluating whether to use Power Fx as a possible solution for data validation.

Validation examples

These are some real cases of validations, and how they can be solved with a no-code/low-code approach:

Scenario	Possible solution
Validate if a customer already exists in ERP	Cloud flow
Validate that opportunities are close to expiring	Cloud flow
Validate if there are selected records in a view	Power Fx
Validate that an attribute of the parent record is consistent with an attribute of the record in question	Classic workflow
Validate the value of an attribute	Business rule
Validate that a record exists before creating it	Cloud flow

Table 8.2 – Validation examples

Next, we will analyze how to integrate different systems with a no-code/low-code approach.

Integrating systems

It is very unusual to find Dynamics 365 Customer Engagement implementations that do not require integration with other systems. As for other requirements, Dynamics 365 Customer Engagement allows us to propose solutions with a no-code, low-code, or pro-code approach. In this section, we will analyze the most important considerations to take into account when evaluating possible solutions for a system integration requirement, and the most relevant characteristics of the most used no-code/low-code approaches to integrate systems.

Systems integration considerations

When presented with a requirement to integrate Dynamics 365 Customer Engagement with another system, we have to analyze in detail not only the purpose of the integration (whether to synchronize data, simply visualize it, or execute actions in another system), but also aspects of how, when, and what to integrate:

Figure 8.10 – System integration key considerations

As we can see in the preceding diagram, we can summarize the four most important aspects to take into account: *why*, *what*, *when*, and *how*. Let us briefly analyze each of these aspects:

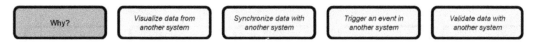

Figure 8.11 – System integration "why" consideration

In the preceding diagram, we can see some of the most important reasons why we will have to perform an integration between systems:

- **Visualize data from another system**

  - When the need to display data only arises, it means that the data does not have to be synchronized. That is, the data does not have to be replicated in Dynamics 365 Customer Engagement. This is very common in scenarios where a process happens in another system (SAP, ServiceNow, and so on), and we need to make part of the process available in Dynamics 365 Customer Engagement. Two key points to keep in mind are that if you can only visualize the data, what we can do with that data in the context of Dynamics 365 Customer Engagement will be limited (for example, incorporate this data into reports, dashboards, or view filter conditions), and secondly, this type of integration will not affect the storage capacity of Dataverse.

- **Synchronize data with another system**

  - In this case, we must consider that this will affect the storage capacity of Dataverse, so we have to be very clear about which data we really need to synchronize, in addition to other considerations such as data governance and data structure. We will discuss data synchronization between systems in detail in the next section of this chapter.

- **Trigger an event in another system**

  - If we need to execute an event in another system, we must have identified the unambiguous form of identification of the action and the record on which to execute the event in the target system.

- **Validate data with another system**

  - In the previous section, we already talked about some of the most important considerations for data validation scenarios.

Once we understand the *why* of an integration, we have to understand in detail what we have to integrate. To understand the *what*, it is not enough just to know what is the data to be integrated—we have to consider other aspects:

Figure 8.12 – System integration "what" consideration

As we can see in the previous diagram, to know the *what*, we must understand not only the structure of the data but also the volume of data to be integrated and if it requires some kind of transformation. Finally, we need to understand the data mapping between the source and target system.

The next point to solve is the *when*. This factor is not minor, and should not be taken as isolated data but rather in the context of the rest of the considerations:

Figure 8.13 – System integration "when" consideration

As we see in the preceding diagram, we need to identify whether the integration should happen online or as an offline process. Secondly, we have to understand how often the integration should be executed.

Last but not least, we need to understand how we can/should integrate with the other system. This covers both security and governance aspects, as well as how we are going to be able to connect:

Figure 8.14 – System integration "how" consideration

In the previous diagram, we can see that there are many aspects to consider in order to define how we are going to integrate. The first point corresponds to the definition of whether the integration will be in near-real time or as a batch process. A near-real-time integration is very common in scenarios where we must synchronize data for its prompt management.

Another relevant point regarding how we will integrate has to do with the integration capabilities of the other system. The first point is to understand if the other system has documented APIs, or if integration via APIs is not possible. If it does have APIs, we then need to know whether there is a native Power Platform connector available to perform the actions we need, or a custom connector in the organization. A related aspect to consider is where the system is hosted, as the integration capabilities will also depend on this. The scenarios, and the complexity, will vary depending on whether we have to connect to a system that is in the cloud, a system that is in an on-premises architecture, or a system that runs on the user's terminal. Finally, in terms of integration capabilities, we need to understand whether there are limitations or constraints to be taken into account by the organization's integration strategies. It is not uncommon to encounter restrictive strategies for the use of connectors, especially when we need to integrate with solutions such as SAP.

Security is another aspect of great importance when analyzing how we can integrate between systems. This includes considerations such as impersonating a user or managing service users.

The last two most important aspects to consider are integration governance and data governance. The latter will gain a lot of importance if we are in a bi-directional data synchronization scenario.

Once we have done the analysis taking into account these considerations, we will have to define what will be the solution to build an integration. As I mentioned at the beginning, integrations are not limited to no-code/low-code solutions. On the contrary, in many cases, the solution will require the use of code, so it can be considered pro-code. However, there are several no-code/low-code options available for the resolution of integrations, such as cloud flows, embedded applications, dataflows, desktop flows, and virtual tables:

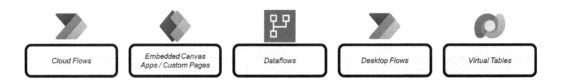

Figure 8.15 – Possible no-code/low-code approaches for system integrations

Next, we will analyze each of these approaches presented in the preceding diagram, to learn more about the scenarios in which they could be applied.

Cloud flows

Power Automate cloud flows are a very good tool to make integrations between systems when we have to integrate with other systems that are in the cloud, and where the processing work is not very high.

> **Note**
> We have to keep in mind that cloud flows are meant for simple, low-critical, light integrations. This is because they can present limitations when processing integrations, and in those cases, we should discard this option and consider another approach, such as a logic app.

The advantages of using cloud flows to solve integrations are obvious:

- It is a no-code/low-code approach, which does not generate dependencies with custom developments
- They can make use of the +700 native connectors, as well as the custom connectors that we develop
- Can be triggered by events within Dynamics 365 Customer Engagement, events in another system, scheduled work, or manually
- We will have governance tools to monitor executions and detect possible improvements

An interesting aspect to consider is the possibility of having Per Flow licenses, allowing us to assign a high-performance profile for our flows. However, as I mentioned, cloud flows have several limitations to keep in mind when evaluating them as an integration option. I recommend consulting the complete list as Microsoft updates them frequently, in Microsoft's *Learn* portal.

However, despite having limitations that make it not the best approach for complex integrations, for simple integrations of low level of complexity, it is a viable option, but it has to be the architect's decision whether it is defined as a cloud flow or another approach.

Embedded canvas apps and custom pages

As I mentioned earlier in this chapter, embedded canvas apps and custom pages allow us to natively introduce a canvas app in the context of Dynamics 365 Customer Engagement. By being able to make use of the +700 Power Platform connectors, we will be able to embed data from other applications in the Dynamics 365 Customer Engagement screen to work with them. We can also choose to create or update Dynamics 365 Customer Engagement records with the data available in the embedded application.

This approach is preferred when we are working with systems with which we can integrate the available Power Platform connectors and when we do not need to synchronize data, but only make it available. On the contrary, if we need to persist this data in Dynamics 365 Customer Engagement, this would not be the best approach to consider.

Dataflows

Dataflows allow us to create data **extraction, transformation, and loading** (ETL) processes, defining the data source and target tables. Once a dataflow is created, the data update frequency can be configured. Dataverse is one of the possible destinations in which to store the data, so dataflows become a great tool for the configuration of data integration and synchronization processes.

Dataflows support both on-premise and cloud-based application connections, including Excel, Azure SQL Database, SharePoint, Salesforce, Oracle, TXT, JSON, and more.

Data transformation is performed with Power Query, with a no-code/low-code approach, although it also allows the incorporation of a pro-code approach by including M language.

Desktop flows

When we find ourselves in a scenario where integration through APIs is not possible, either because the organization's policies do not allow it or because the application does not support APIs, we have the possibility of building **robotic process automations** (RPAs) with Power Automate desktop flows.

Desktop flows allow us to automate processes that happen on the user's desktop. However, if the system we want to integrate with has an API, the use of this should be our preferred approach.

Virtual tables

The last of the approaches to be discussed is the use of virtual tables. Virtual tables are a component that has been available in Dataverse for some time, by which we can create tables whose data is not persisted in Dataverse, but in another data source. We can understand that virtual tables *compete* with embedded canvas apps or custom pages since in both cases, we can expose external data in the context of a Dynamics 365 Customer Engagement process. However, the first difference we will find is that the **user experience** (UX) is completely different with either approach.

With canvas apps, we need to build the user interface, and this will hardly resemble the interface of a model-driven app. Opposite to that, virtual tables natively use the graphical interface of model-driven apps. We can understand that the experience of a virtual table differs from a normal table only in the actions that can be performed on them, but there is no difference when accessing a record. For example, in virtual tables, it is not possible to enable auditing or create consolidated fields, since the data does not persist in Dataverse.

Originally, the use of virtual tables was a 100% pro-code approach, as it involved the development of virtual table providers. However, in 2022, Microsoft incorporated virtual connector providers by which we can connect our virtual tables without the need for code. The virtual connector providers automate part of the creation process to have virtual tables in Dataverse. This way, we can create virtual tables to connect to Excel, SQL, or SharePoint, without the need for any development.

To create a virtual table without the need for development, making use of the new functionality (which at the time of writing this book is in preview), let's see an example of how to create a virtual table whose data is in Excel:

1. The first thing we have to do is to install the **Virtual connectors in Dataverse** solution in the environment:

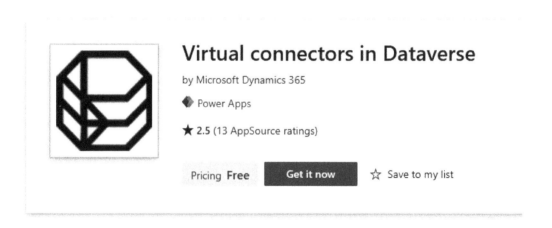

Figure 8.16 – Virtual connectors in Dataverse solution, in AppSource

2. Then, go to `https://make.powerapps.com` and create a connector. To do this, we will go to the left menu and select **Dataverse** and **Connections**:

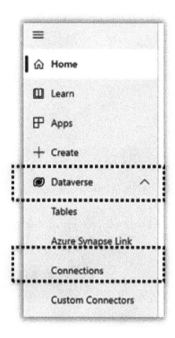

Figure 8.17 – Left-side menu in the Maker portal

3. We will create a new connector by selecting + **New connection**:

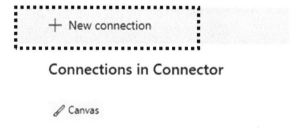

Figure 8.18 – + New connection

4. Then, we will look for the **Excel Online (Business)** connector:

Connections > **New connection**

Name	Type
Excel Online (OneDrive) Microsoft	Standard
Excel Online (Business) Microsoft	Standard

Figure 8.19 – Excel Online available connectors

5. The system will ask you to connect with the credentials that you want to use to access OneDrive, where the Excel file is saved:

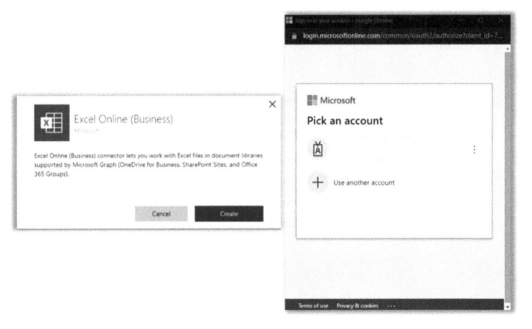

Figure 8.20 – Confirming the connector creation

6. Then, we have to go to **Solutions** and select an existing one or create a new one:

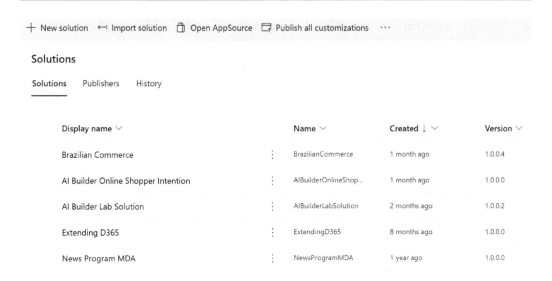

Figure 8.21 – Solutions page

7. Within the solution, we have to create a new connection reference:

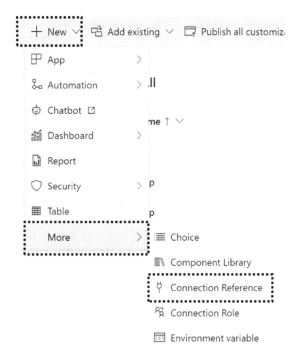

Figure 8.22 – Connection reference option in solution menu

8. In the connection reference form, select the **Excel Online (Business)** connector and a connection:

Figure 8.23 – Connection reference form

9. Now, we have to go to **Advanced settings**, accessing it from the gear icon in the upper-right part of the screen:

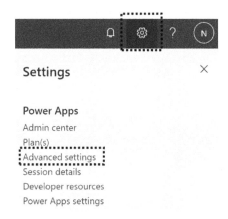

Figure 8.24 – Advanced settings

10. In the navigation menu, go to **Administration** and then to **Virtual Entity Data Sources**:

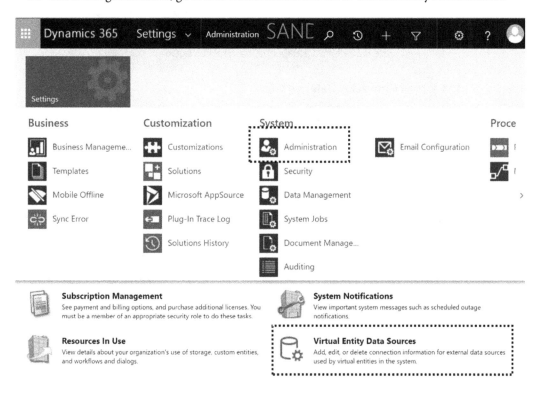

Figure 8.25 – Virtual Entity Data Sources sub-area

11. Click on + **NEW**:

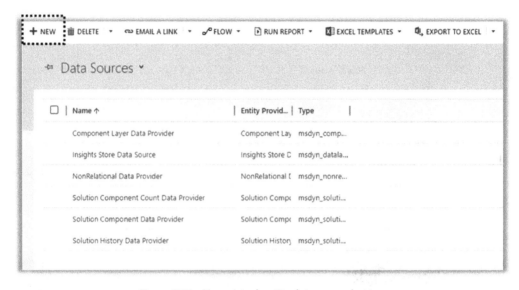

Figure 8.26 – New virtual entity data source button

12. Then, select **Virtual Connector Data Provider**:

Figure 8.27 – Data provider options

13. Name it, select a connection reference, and add the name of the Excel file:

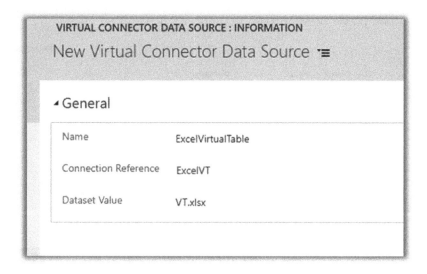

Figure 8.28 – New virtual connector data source form

14. When returning to the tables, we will be able to see that there is a new table called **Entity Catalog**, and then the name of the virtual table created:

Figure 8.29 – Entity Catalog table

15. We must access the table and edit the data:

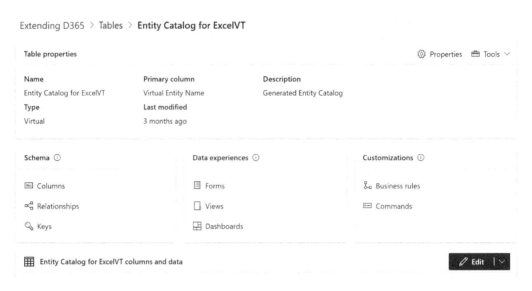

Figure 8.30 – Entity Catalog table

16. We select **Yes** on the **Create or Refresh Entity** field, and select values for the **Primary key of the Virtual Entity** and **Primary field of the Virtual Entity** fields:

Figure 8.31 – Entity Catalog form

17. After a few minutes, a new table will have been created with the name **Custom Entity**, followed by the name of the virtual table:

Tables

Recommended   Custom   All

Table ↑ ⌄	Name ⌄	Type ⌄
Custom Entity Tabla1	cr959_05fdaa5c238a4643b...	Virtual

Figure 8.32 – Custom entity table for virtual table

There are many options we have to integrate with systems to extend Dynamics 365 Customer Engagement. Next, we will discuss some of the most important considerations when working with data synchronization requirements.

Synchronizing data

As I discussed earlier, data synchronization is a type of data integration. However, not all data integration implies data synchronization. When working on Dynamics 365 Customer Engagement projects, it is normal to encounter data synchronization requirements. This is because organizations have processes in other systems that are relevant to processes developed in Dynamics 365 Customer Engagement applications. As examples, we can take the following scenarios:

Application	External processes
Sales	Customer creation in ERP Product catalog management in ERP Invoicing management in ERP Marketing application outside Dynamics 365
Marketing	Sales application outside Dynamics 365 Loyalty program managed in an external application Preferences or purchase data managed in an external database
Customer Service	Incident management escalated to a specific team that is managed in another ticketing system Knowledge base managed in another solution
Field Service	Invoicing management in ERP Asset management in ERP

Table 8.3 – Data synchronization scenarios

When evaluating data synchronization requirements, the most important aspects to consider are these:

Aspect	Consideration
Mode	Synchronization of data can occur in near real time or by batch processes.
Volume	The volume of data to be synchronized in each run may condition the solution approach to be proposed.
Tables and data structure	What are the tables and data structure to be synchronized; understanding if the same considerations of frequency, mode, and so on apply to all of them.
Direction	It is different to consider a unidirectional synchronization rather than a bi-directional one. It is important to identify the direction of synchronization as this can increase the complexity of the integration.
Data governance	When considering data synchronizations, it is important to know which system governs which data, down to the attribute level. For example, if the creation of a contact in an ERP must be synchronized with the CRM, what if the contact already exists in the CRM? - If the contact already exists in the CRM, is the data overwritten? - If the integration is bidirectional, which data is more important in the case of differences?

Table 8.4 – Key considerations for data synchronization

To solve the data synchronizations, we will have to come up with some method that allows us to move the data and not just display it. On many occasions, the solution we need will not exactly fall into the no-code/low-code category. This, far from being a problem, is a strength of the platform, in giving us more flexibility to choose different tools for different complexity levels.

Summary

In this chapter, we have delved into three common use cases when working with Dynamics 365 Customer Engagement data: data validation, system integration, and data synchronization. For each of these, we identified general considerations that allow us to think about what kind of solution we should propose. We were also able to see that even though the platform offers multiple no-code/low-code options, sometimes we must consider pro-code solutions to ensure the performance and scalability of the solution.

In the next chapter, we will delve into how we can make use of AI Builder to incorporate AI into our processes. We will work with three categories of models: text processing, forms and receipt processing, and predictive models. For each of these, we will go through step-by-step examples of how to start implementing AI models with Dynamics 365 Customer Engagement.

Questions and answers

1. Should we use a no-code/low-code approach for every data validation, system integration, or data synchronization?

    Answer: No. Power Platform is not only a no-code/low-code platform but also a pro-code one. Depending on the requirements and the considerations, a pro-code approach may be the best solution.

2. From a data validation perspective, which are the main differences between a classic workflow and a cloud flow?

    Answer: A classic workflow can only use the record on which the workflow is being executed—and its related record—to do data validations, and it can be executed in asynchronous and synchronous modes. On the other hand, cloud flows can use the +700 Power Platform connectors to connect with different systems or records to perform validations, but they can only be executed as an asynchronous flow.

9

Integrating Artificial Intelligence into Processes

Artificial intelligence allows us to accelerate business processes by incorporating data processing or even making predictions about possible outcomes. As we have already seen in *Chapter 6*, Power Platform allows us to incorporate different artificial intelligence models into our processes and use their results as part of our automation.

In this chapter, we will see in detail how we can make use of the models that AI Builder offers us in our business processes for text processing scenarios, forms processing, and predictive models. The application scenarios we will see will be related to native Dynamics 365 Customer Engagement processes. However, AI Builder is not limited to this and can be applied to any custom process, built-in Power Apps, or external systems.

It is worth mentioning that the use of these models will be conditioned by the requirements and processes we have in our Dynamics 365 Customer Engagement implementation. Regardless of the fact that we will see real examples, the instructions shared in this chapter are exclusively for getting started with the components and not for how to solve specific use cases.

Upon completion of this chapter, you will have learned, in a step-by-step manner, how to start using AI Builder models, both custom and pre-built.

In this chapter, we will cover how to use AI Builder models for scenarios such as the following:

- How to start working with AI Builder in the context of a cloud flow
- Prediction
- Text processing
- Forms and receipt processing

Technical requirements

To work with Dynamics 365 Customer Engagement, it is necessary to have an environment that has one of the supported licenses. However, the topics covered in this chapter do not require any particular Dynamics 365 application.

The following are required for this chapter:

- Power Apps Developer or Dynamics 365 Customer Engagement license (any of the available ones) with administrator permissions in an environment
- An AI Builder license
- A compatible browser

Working with AI

As with other Power Platform components, we must be aware that when using an AI Builder model, we can work inside or outside of a solution. It is worth remembering that, as a good practice, it is recommended to work with solutions as they facilitate the management and tracking of components/ objects that we create or modify.

To create a new AI model, we can do it either from the Power Apps maker portal or from Power Automate. Once created, we recommend that you add it to the solution we are working with.

To create a model and start using it, we have to do the following:

1. Go to the Power Automate maker portal: `https://make.powerautomate.com`.
2. In the navigation bar, go to **AI Builder** to display the available options:

Figure 9.1 – Power Automate maker portal navigation bar

3. Select **Explore** to select the custom model you want to build:

Figure 9.2 – AI Builder options

4. Select the custom model that you want to create:

Figure 9.3 – Select the custom model

5. Select **Get started** to train the custom model:

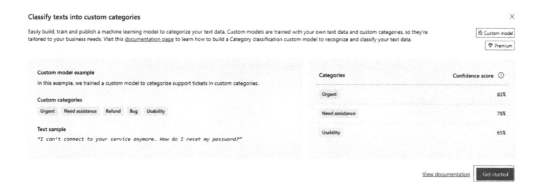

Figure 9.4 – AI Builder model wizard

After creating the custom model, we recommend that you add it to the solution we are working on.

> **Note**
>
> Adding AI Builder models to solutions only apply to custom models. Pre-built models cannot be added to solutions.

Once you have created your model, or in case you want to use a pre-built model, we can create a new flow from the solution by taking the following steps:

1. Go to the Power Automate maker portal: `https://make.powerautomate.com`.

2. In the navigation bar, go to **Solutions**:

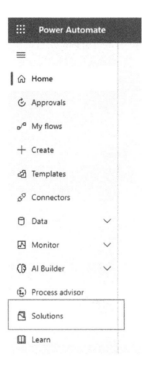

Figure 9.5 – Power Automate maker portal navigation bar

3. Edit the solution we want to work with:

Solutions

Solutions   Publishers   History

Display name ∨		Name ∨	Created ↓ ∨
✓ **Extending D365**	⋮	ExtendingD365	28 seconds a...
Case Suggestions AI Core	⋮	msdyn_CaseSuggest...	3 hours ago
CCA Case AI Solution	⋮	msdyn_CcaCaseAISo...	3 hours ago

Figure 9.6 – Edit solution

4. In the options bar, select **+ New**, then **Automation | Cloud flow**, and select the type of automation that we want to create:

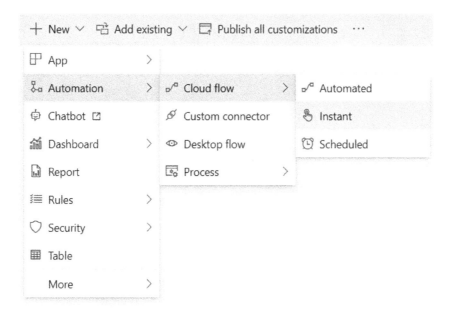

Figure 9.7 – Edit solution

5. In the wizard, we can select the trigger or skip this step. This is an optional step, as you may prefer to define the name after you have finished building your cloud flow, and you may want to evaluate different triggers in the editor:

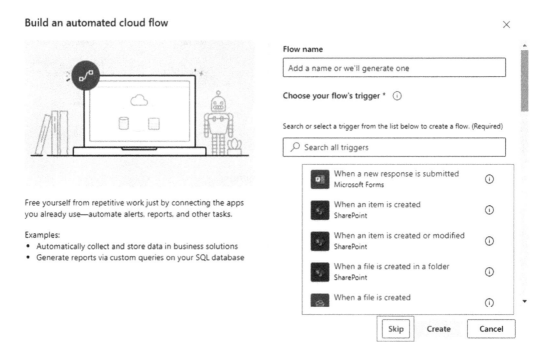

Figure 9.8 – New cloud flow wizard

6. Inside the flow editor, we can add an action using the AI Builder connector:

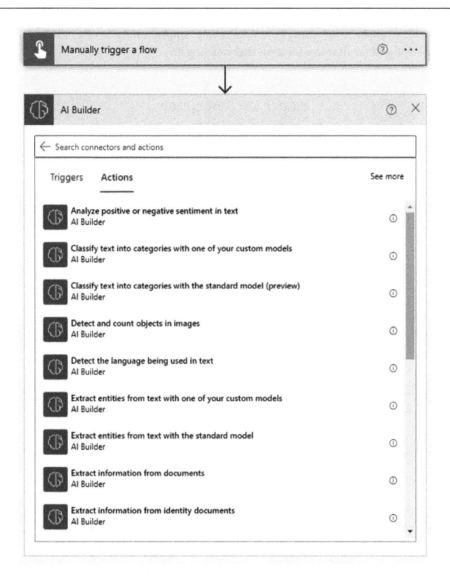

Figure 9.9 – Example of a cloud flow with the AI Builder connector

It is also possible to create a flow using Power Automate templates outside of a solution. If so, it is always advisable to add the flow to a solution after building it:

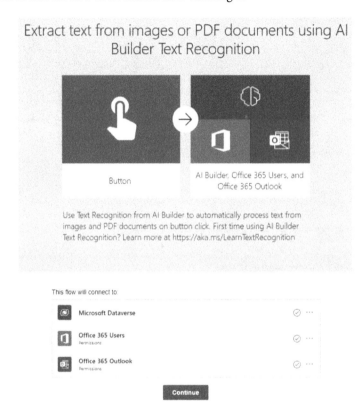

Figure 9.10 – Cloud flow template

Once we are working with the cloud flow editor, we can add one or more actions using the AI Builder connector. Each of the actions, corresponding to the different models, will be worked in different ways.

An important point to keep in mind about using AI Builder is its licensing. Some Power Apps and Power Automate licenses include credits for AI Builder (250, 500, or 5,000), and you can have up to 10,000 credits per month. Additionally, it is possible to purchase units of 1,000,000 credits to cover the AI Builder processing needs we will need.

To calculate how many AI Builder units we need, Microsoft offers us an online calculator where we can include the estimated usage of the different AI Builder models, and it will give us, as a result, how many units of AI Builder credits we will need.

Also, in the Power Platform licensing guide, we can find a table describing the number of credits required for the use of each model. For example, each page processed by the document processing model requires 500 credits, while each business card scanned by the business card reader model only requires 100 credits.

In the following sections, we will analyze some of the most important models, considering those that process text, forms, and receipts and predict results.

For each of the models, we will highlight the particularities of each action of the AI Builder connector to learn how to work with them.

Prediction models

The first of the models we will discuss will be the use of a predictive model as part of our process. AI Builder allows us to create a custom predictive model, which will learn from the patterns and outcomes of our business processes. We can use the predictive model for binary outcome analysis (only two possible outcomes), for multiple choice outcomes, or for a numerical prediction.

The binary prediction

The binary prediction will be used to predict simple patterns where the result is true/false, yes/no, and the like. The type of question that this model will be able to answer are as follows:

- Is the customer qualifiable?

- Is there a risk of customer abandonment?

- Is there a possibility of upselling?

- Is there a risk of diversion in the project?

If we need to consider more outcomes, then we need to think about multiple-outcome predictions.

Multiple-outcome predictions

As the name implies, multiple-outcome predictions allow us to predict more complex scenarios than binary ones. Some examples of this can be found in the following questions:

- What is the best product to offer the customer?

- What knowledge base article could I use?

- Will the field technician be on time, early, or late, or is it better to reschedule?

- What is the best resource for this project based on past performance?

However, if we need an indicator, or to quantify a prediction, then we can make use of the numerical prediction model.

The numerical prediction model

The numerical prediction model will give us a quantifiable result of the prediction. Some examples in the context of Dynamics 365 Customer Engagement are as follows:

- How many cases per day will each customer service agent have to handle?
- What is the minimum inventory I have to secure for each field technician?
- How many leads convert to opportunities per campaign?
- What is the risk of customer churn?

Now that we have reviewed the types of prediction models that we can configure let's review the steps required to configure a prediction model and how we can use it with Power Automate.

Training a prediction model

Since it is a customized model, the first thing to do is to train the model with the particularities of our business. Therefore, the only prior knowledge to configure the prediction model is to understand in detail the business process we want to predict:

1. The first thing to do is to go to https://make.powerapps.com or https://make.powerautomate.com and click on **Explore** in the **AI Builder** section:

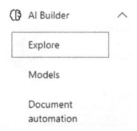

Figure 9.11 – Explore the area in the AI Builder section in the maker portal

2. Then, we have to choose the **Predict future outcomes from historical data** model:

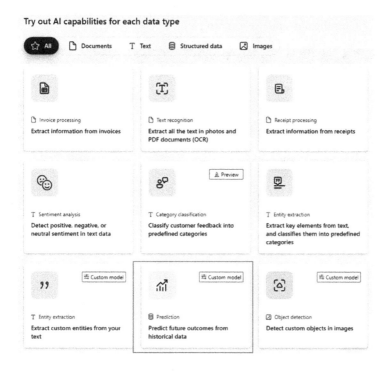

Figure 9.12 – The prediction model in AI Builder

3. In the wizard, we must select **Get started**:

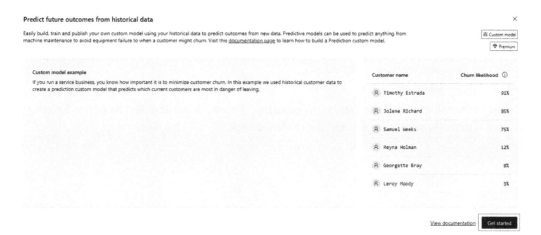

Figure 9.13 – The prediction model wizard

4. Once the configuration process has started, the first thing we have to do is to select the Dataverse **Table**, where the information we will use to train the model is located, and the **Column** of the table that contains the outcome we want to predict:

Figure 9.14 – Select historical outcome step

> **Note**
>
> Depending on the column we select, the model will interpret whether it will be a binary, multi-outcome, or numerical model.
>
> The AI Builder model supports yes/no, choices, whole numbers, decimal numbers, floating point numbers, and currency columns.

5. Select the columns we need to train the model. By default, all columns will be selected, but we can remove those that are not relevant to the analysis:

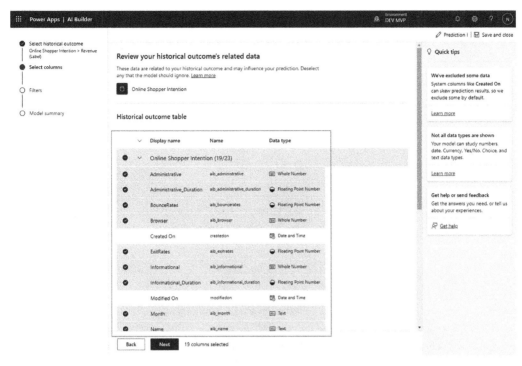

Figure 9.15 – Select columns step

6. We have the option to add filters to the historical data, which can be based on data from the table itself or from related tables. It is worth mentioning that we are not obliged to define filters; it is completely optional:

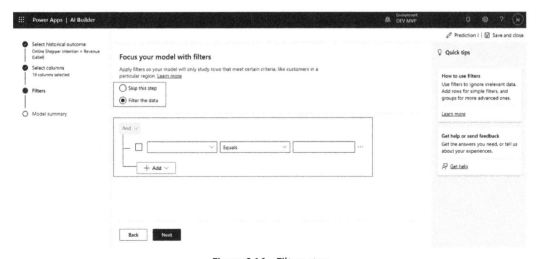

Figure 9.16 – Filters step

7. Finally, we have to train the model:

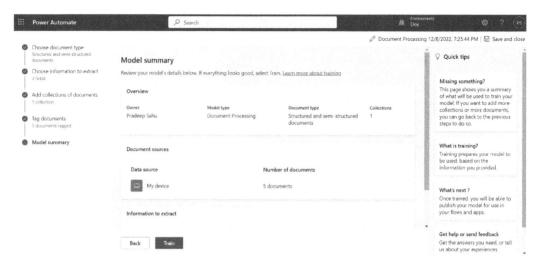

Figure 9.17 – Prediction Model summary

8. Once the training is finished, AI Builder will show us a summary of the trained model, where we can see the performance and the data that most influence the result:

Figure 9.18 – Trained model summary

9. To access more details of the model, you can click on **See details**:

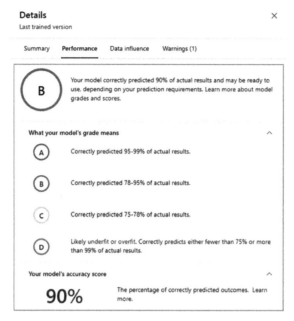

Figure 9.19 – Trained model details

As we can see in the preceding screenshot, in the details of the result, we have the accuracy score of the model, more details of the data that influence the model, and potential warnings to correct.

To start using the model as part of a cloud flow, we have to do the following:

1. Add any of the prediction actions from the **AI Builder** connector: **Predict**, **Predict whether something will happen by record ID**, or **Predict whether something will happen by field**:

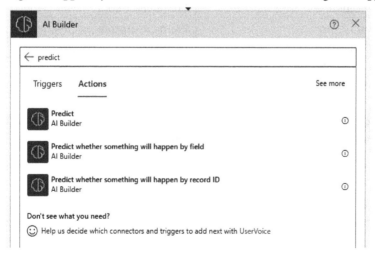

Figure 9.20 – Predict actions in AI Builder

2. Select the model and map the data (columns or record ID):

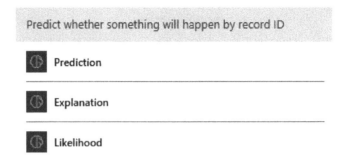

Figure 9.21 – Predict action outcomes

As a result of the action, AI Builder will return the prediction, explanation, and likelihood level.

Processing text

AI Builder models that perform text processing are diverse. Most of them are pre-built models, from which we can have more information about the texts we need to process. Among the models, we can find the following:

Model	Type
Text recognition	Pre-built
Language detection	Pre-built
Sentiment analysis	Pre-built
Category classification	Pre-built/Custom
Entity extraction	Pre-built/Custom
Key phrase extraction	Pre-built

Table 9.1 – AI Builder text processing models

Next, we will take a step-by-step look at how we can start using them and some practical examples of Dynamics 365 Customer Engagement application deployments.

Text recognition

The text recognition model allows us to process PDF documents and images and extract from them the text that the model identifies. We can leverage the text recognition model by including the recognize text in an image action as part of a cloud flow. In the context of a Dynamics 365 Customer Engagement implementation, this type of model allows us to automate the processing of documents to images that customers can share by different means. For example, if the customer sends the customer service center a picture of the screen of a device that is displaying an error, we might be able to process the image and provide an automatic response to the customer, depending on the error in question.

The **Recognize text in an image** action has, as its only input parameter, the image to be processed for text detection:

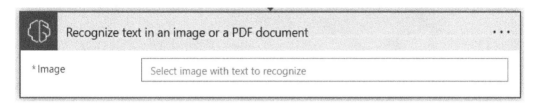

Figure 9.22 – Recognize text in an image input parameter

As we can see in the previous screenshot, the **Image** parameter is the only one we can define, and it is mandatory. However, this action will return multiple values, sorted by lines, among which we can identify the most important, as follows:

- The identified text
- The page number where the text was detected
- The coordinates of where the text is located

In order to use this data, we must apply the **Apply to each** control first to the results level and then to the lines level:

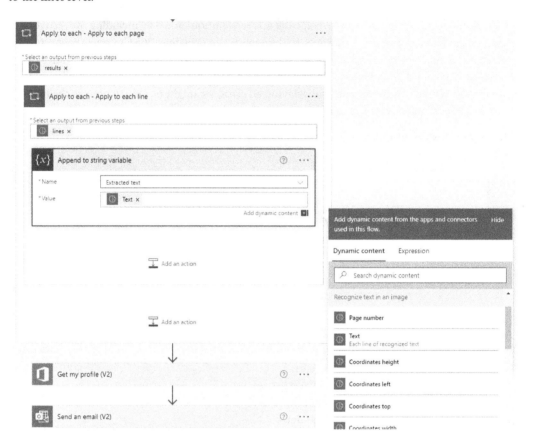

Figure 9.23 – Recognize text in an image action's output data in cloud flow

As we can see in the previous screenshot, once that is done, we will have the page number, text, and coordinates values.

Language detection

The language detection model will analyze the text we indicate and return information about the language identified and the confidence level of the result given. The unified routing capability of Dynamics 365 Customer Engagement uses this functionality to intelligently route conversations and cases.

When we work with this model as part of a cloud flow, we only have to pass text as a parameter, and we receive as an outcome of the action the list of identified languages and their respective confidence level:

Detect the predominant language of a text document   ✕

The language detection prebuilt model identifies the predominant language of a text document. The model analyzes the text and returns the detected language and a confidence score. Check out our learn module to get started with using a language detection model in a flow.

⅌ Prebuilt model
⊕ Premium

Type your own text

L'écran n'est pas assez grand.

30/5000

△ Analyze text   ↻ Random sample

Language code ⓘ   Confidence score ⓘ

fr   100%

By clicking **Use in a flow**, you are extending your expired trial for another 30 days free. Learn more   View documentation   Use in a flow

Figure 9.24 – Language detection wizard

In the preceding screenshot, we can see the structured response of some text analyzed in the AI Builder wizard. We can see that it identifies that the language is English with 97% confidence.

The language detection model uses Azure's language detection services, which currently support 115 languages. It should be noted that the AI Builder model has a processing limit of 5,120 characters, so if our text becomes longer, we must break it into blocks of less than 5,120 characters.

Sentiment analysis

The sentiment analysis model processes the indicated text, returning, as a result, the overall positive, negative, or neutral score, but also on each identified sentence.

Unlike the language detection model, the AI Builder's **Analyze positive or negative sentiment in text** action requires us to indicate the text to be analyzed but also the language of the text. For this reason, it is not uncommon to use the language detection model and the sentiment analysis model together:

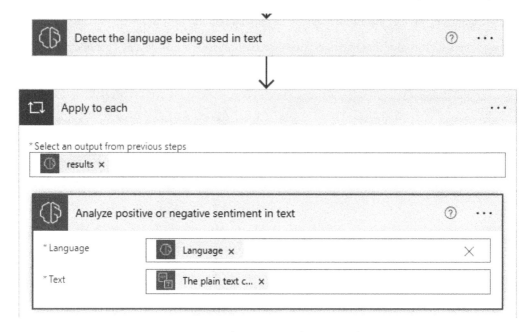

Figure 9.25 – Sentiment analysis example

The preceding screenshot represents an example of first using language detection and then using the result as the input parameter for the sentiment analysis. We could also add a condition between the two actions to ensure that only the sentiment analysis is performed for those confidence levels higher than 90%.

Just as we can use the output parameter of another AI Builder model as the input parameter of the sentiment analysis, we can also use the data returned by the sentiment analysis for another expression in the cloud flow:

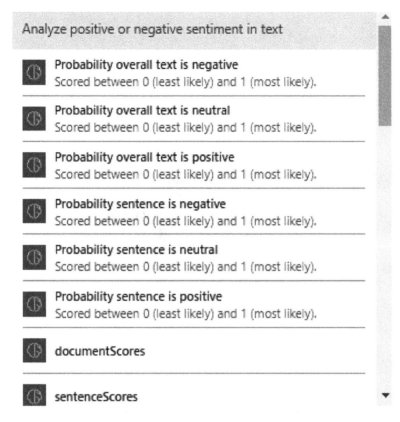

Figure 9.26 – Sentiment analysis action output data in cloud flow

As we can see in the previous screenshot, once the text has been analyzed, we can use it as dynamic data in the following actions; the probability of each sentence, of the complete text being positive, negative, or neutral, as well as the result of the analysis of the sentences and of the complete text.

Category classification

AI Builder offers us the possibility of processing a text to establish categories for it. This information we obtain is an insight that we can take to automate processes or to provide more information to the user so that they can make better-informed decisions. AI Builder offers the possibility of using a native, pre-built model for the category classification or creating your own model. Where we use the pre-built model, the categories that are identified are limited to those that are part of this model. However, if we want to train the model with categories specific to our business, we could use a custom model. Depending on which one we want to use, we will have to add one or the other action to our Power Automate flow.

Although in both cases, we will use a text as an input parameter, depending on whether we use the pre-built model or a custom model, we will need to add another input parameter:

Figure 9.27 – Custom category classification action versus pre-built category classification action

As we can see in the previous screenshot, for the pre-built model, in addition to the text to be processed, we must identify which language the model should consider for processing the text. In the case of custom models, we must identify which model we want to use for processing. In the case of custom models, language is automatically identified, as that is a property of the model itself, so it would be redundant to have to identify it again when we want to use it.

As in the case of the sentiment analysis model, when using category classification with Power Automate, we could take the language from a previous language detection action.

Entity extraction

The entity extraction model allows us to process text to extract specific data, such as cities, company names, or addresses. Like the category classification model, we will have two versions of the entity extraction model: the pre-built model and the custom model. The difference between the two is that in the pre-built model, we will only be able to extract those entities that are already pre-configured, while in the customized model, we will be able to define and train the model to identify new entities from our business model.

Once we have our custom model trained and published, or we might want to use the native model, we have to add the corresponding action in the cloud flow: **Extract entities from text with the standard model** for the pre-built model or **Extract entities from text with one of your custom models** for custom models:

Figure 9.28 – Custom entity extraction action versus pre-built entity extraction action

In the preceding screenshot, we can see the comparison between the action using the pre-built model and the action we must add to use a custom model. In both cases, we must identify the text we want to process, but depending on the model, we must add the language (for the pre-built model) or index the model (for the custom model).

Key phrase extraction

The key phrase extraction model will allow us to process text and identify the most relevant talking points in it. This pre-built model will process unstructured text documents and will result in a list of key phrases.

When using this model from a cloud flow, we simply need to identify the language of the text and the text to be processed. As we have seen before, if, for our business model, we can get texts in different languages, we can first process the text by the language detection model and then use the result for the extraction of key phrases:

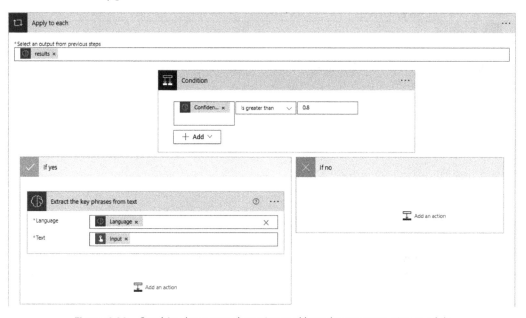

Figure 9.29 – Combine language detection and key phrases extraction models

In the previous screenshot, we can see how we can combine the language detection model with each of the results and execute the **Extract the key phrases from text** action. In this case, since we can obtain more than one language, as a result, we can first set a condition so that only the key phrases of those languages with more than 80% confidence are extracted.

Once the text is processed, we can use the extracted phrases to create records in Dynamics 365 and thus provide insights to users:

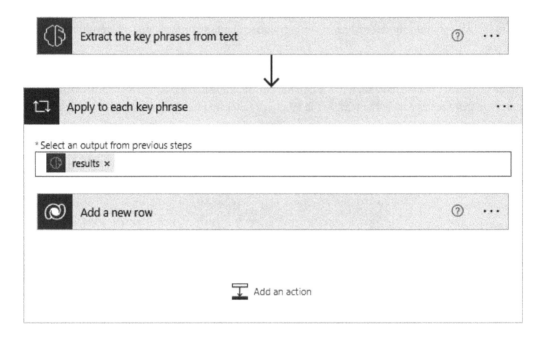

Figure 9.30 – Add a new row in Dataverse after extracting key phrases

As we can see in the previous screenshot, the result of the extraction of key phrases could be a list of results that we would want to use to create a record in Dataverse and **Apply to each** control automatically.

Now that we have reviewed the most important models for working with text, let's analyze the models for processing forms and receipts.

Processing documents and receipts

There are several pre-built and customized models that allow us to process specific types of documents, such as identity documents, business cards, expense receipts, or documents in general, such as invoices, delivery notes, or others. Unlike the models we analyzed in the previous section, these models have in common that they only extract the information from the documents and do not process the texts.

Business card reader

The business card reader model allows us to extract the person and the organization's data from business cards. With this data, we can create new contacts and accounts in our Dynamics 365 Customer Engagement implementation. As we saw in *Chapter 6*, this model is included in the Dynamics 365 Sales application, and we can make use of it both from the web and mobile application.

The business card reader model is commonly used in custom applications for booths at events to facilitate data capture. Another common use is to process cards that can be scanned by a third party or included as attachments. For the latter, using the model as part of a cloud flow is a valid option:

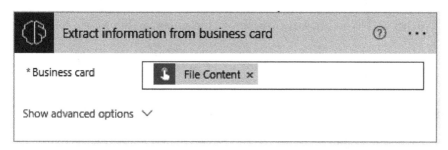

Figure 9.31 – Read business card information action in cloud flow

As we can see in the preceding screenshot, the AI Builder action of reading the business card only requires identifying the card we want to process. As it is a pre-constructed model, the result of this action cannot be customized to identify new attributes or data. Among the data that we will obtain when processing a card, we will find the image, personal data (first name, last name, full name, and position), contact data (phone, mobile, fax, email, full address, street, zip code, state, and country), and company data (name and website):

Figure 9.32 – Read business card information action output data in cloud flow

In the preceding screenshot, we can see some of the data that we will obtain when processing a business card as part of a cloud flow.

ID Reader

As we saw in *Chapter 6*, the ID reader model is a pre-built model that currently supports only US ID documents, such as driver's licenses and passports.

The ID reader model supports both JPG and PNG images, as well as PDF files, as long as they are no larger than 20 MB in size:

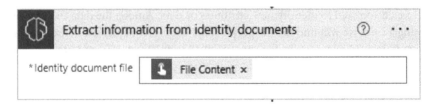

Figure 9.33 – Extract information from identity documents action in cloud flow

The previous screenshot shows us that to process an identification document with this module, we only need to identify the file we want to process in the cloud flow action.

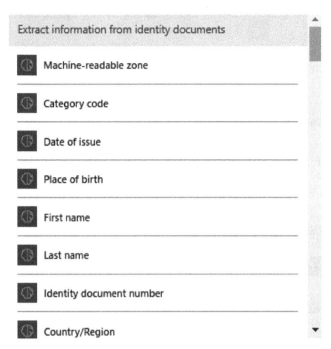

Figure 9.34 – Extract information from identity documents action output data in cloud flow

As we can see in the preceding screenshot, similar to the business card reading template, this template will result in the personal data of the owner of the document, along with the document's own data, such as the expiration date. This template can be used to streamline data capture, for example, for passport data entry when project resources require travel. We can take this as an example of applying the model in the context of a Dynamics 365 Customer Engagement application, such as Project Operations.

Receipt processing

Another pre-built model that AI Builder offers us to make use of quickly is the receipt processing model. This model takes the image of the receipt and extracts the most important data, such as purchase data and merchant data. This template is widely used to facilitate the recording of project expenses, sales representation expenses, or field technician expenses during the resolution of a work order:

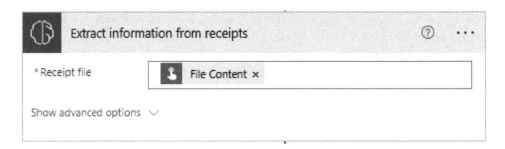

Figure 9.35 – Extract information from receipts action in cloud flow

As we can see in the previous screenshot, the template only requires us to indicate the file to be processed, which can be in JPG, PNG, or PDF format, and currently only supports receipts in English for Australia, Canada, India, the United States, and Great Britain:

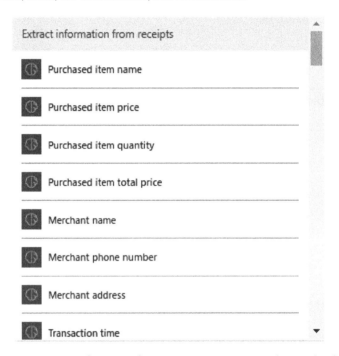

Figure 9.36 – Extract information from receipts action output data in cloud flow

In the preceding screenshot, we can see a reduced list of the data that will give us output data for the processing of a receipt. As we can see, among the data will be the information on each item of the receipt, including the name, quantity, and price, as well as the total amount, taxes, transaction date, and merchant data.

Document processing

Finally, among the models that can be grouped as document and receipt processing, we have the document processing model. Unlike the others, this model is customized, so we will have to train and publish it in order to use it.

The document processing model allows us to read and extract information from standardized documents, such as invoices, purchase orders, or delivery notes, allowing us to automate a process that, if done manually, does not provide value to the user.

When creating our document processing model, we have to do the following:

1. Select the type of document we will use; it can be structured or unstructured:

Figure 9.37 – Choose document type screen – document processing model

> **Note**
>
> **Structured documents** are those that have a defined layout with fields, checkboxes, tables, and other objects that we can identify and expect to have in all documents with this format. Invoices, delivery notes, or purchase orders are examples of structured documents.
>
> **Unstructured documents** are those that do not have a specific format that will be followed in each document. Examples of this type of document are contracts, letters, statements of work, or solution design documents.

2. Select the data to be extracted. For this, we will create each field or table that the model presents when analyzing a document. For tables, we must also define the columns that are part of the table:

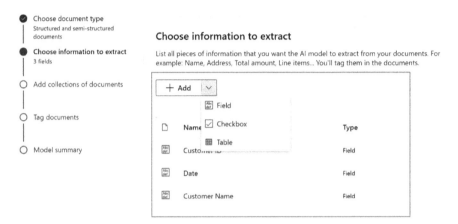

Figure 9.38 – Choose information to extract screen – document processing model

3. Add collections of documents to be used for training. Each document collection will correspond to a different layout or type of document that we want to add to this document processing model. This is practical when we have more than one different document format that we need to consider. When we process the document, the AI model will identify which layout it corresponds to and use the logic learned for that specific document type to extract the data. For example, if the model is for processing vendor invoices, and we have two vendors with different invoice formats, we can train a single AI Builder model to process both formats effectively:

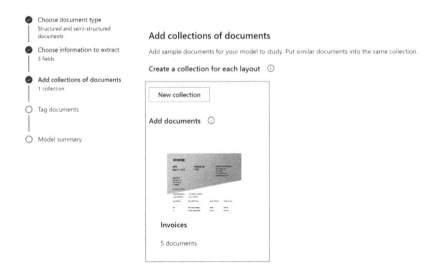

Figure 9.39 – Add collections of documents screen – document processing model

4. Define the labels on the documents. For each document we have uploaded, we must mark each of the data to be extracted. This step is essential to train the AI Builder model to identify these attributes correctly. When we mark a table, we must also define how many columns and rows it has, and we must correctly map the attributes of the table with the columns:

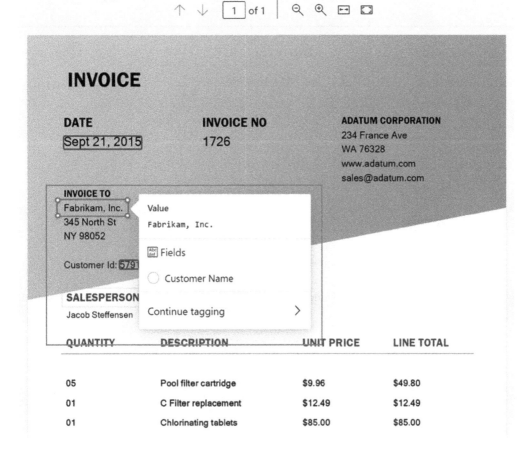

Figure 9.40 – Tag documents screen – document processing model

5. Finally, we must train the model:

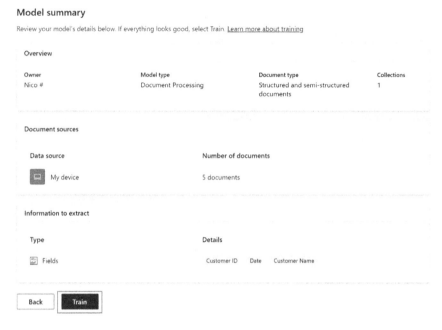

Figure 9.41 – Model summary screen – document processing model

When training is finished, AI Builder will indicate the accuracy score in general and for each extracted data point:

Figure 9.42 – Document processing accuracy score screen

As we can see in the previous screenshot, **Accuracy score** is **93%**, with **99** points for **Customer ID** and **Customer Name**, but only **80** for **Date**.

When we want to use this model in a cloud flow, we can do it by using the **Extract information from documents** action:

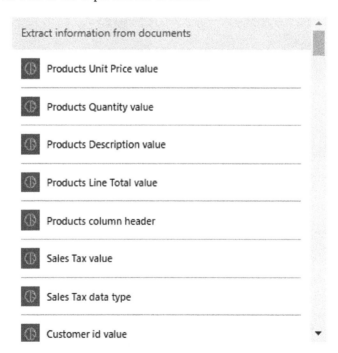

Figure 9.43 – Extract information from documents action in cloud flow

In the preceding screenshot, we can see that in addition to **Form**, we must indicate **Form type** and which **AI model** we want to use to process the document:

Figure 9.44 – Extract information from documents action output data in cloud flow

Finally, as a result, we have the different data that we have configured in the model. In the previous screenshot, we can see the example of an AI builder model built to extract data from invoices, including items from a table, such as the products of the invoice.

Summary

In this chapter, we looked at how we can begin to introduce AI models as part of our processes to speed up business processes and reduce the burden of manual tasks on users. First, we looked at the AI Builder prediction model. We saw some examples for which each type of prediction could apply, and we went through the steps necessary for setting up our first prediction model. Then, we reviewed the text recognition-based models. We looked at how we could use each one individually and how we could use them together.

Finally, we looked at the models based on processing different types of documents and receipts, delving into how we can train our own document processing model.

In the next chapter, we'll start working on how and for what purpose we can extend Dynamics 365 Customer Engagement applications with bots. We will start by understanding why bots are becoming increasingly important in a CRM strategy and then see, step by step, how we can go about deploying our first bot without development with Power Virtual Agents.

Questions and answers

1. Do I need a data science degree to work with AI Builder?

    Answer: Definitely not. AI Builder is intended to be used by business experts, not artificial intelligence experts. AI Builder allows you to quickly make use of pre-built models where no pre-configuration is needed and custom models where we need to have a deep understanding of the business model to help the model be trained correctly.

2. What is the purpose of introducing AI Builder to my processes?

    Answer: AI Builder will allow us to automate mundane and repetitive tasks from custom or pre-built models. From capturing data from a document or a business card to detecting objects in an image, each of these actions will mean significant time savings for users who will be able to focus on tasks that provide more value.

Part 4:
No-Code/Low-Code Bots
for Dynamics 365 Customer
Engagement

A bot can be a great self-service tool both for clients, to deflect the creation of cases, and for users, to be able to automate actions. In this part, you will get an overview of what Power Virtual Agents is and how to leverage it both for external and internal users.

This part has the following chapters:

10
Customer-Facing Bots

Today, self-service is one of the key factors for organizations when choosing a platform to develop their customer service strategy. This is due to the preference that their customers have when choosing how to communicate to solve a problem or seek information. Thinking about a digital contact center is synonymous with thinking about automated attention by intelligent bots that can make decisions in real time to provide the best service to customers.

A bot can be a great self-service tool for customers, also helping to divert the creation of cases, and automating actions – but what do you need to consider for its development and maintenance?

In this chapter, we will talk about Power Virtual Agents and how we can quickly deploy a chatbot to help our customer service strategy. We will see the step-by-step process we need to follow to not only set up a chat channel quickly but also integrate a bot into it. Then, we will identify the requirements to be able to deploy another bot in our voice channel, which will help us to obtain more information before the call reaches a teleoperator.

By the end, you will have learned about the basic concepts of Power Virtual Agents, and how to deploy a bot, both in a chat channel and in a voice channel.

In this chapter, we will cover the following points:

- Deploying a chatbot
- Enabling bots for the voice channel

Technical requirements

To work with Dynamics 365 Customer Engagement, it is necessary to have an environment that has one of the supported licenses. For this chapter, the following are required:

- Dynamics 365 Customer Service with Chat and Voice Add-in licenses with administrator permissions in an environment
- A Power Virtual Agents license
- A supported browser

Deploying a chatbot

Before getting into the technical aspects of deploying a chatbot, let's take a look at why we need one, and why Power Virtual Agents would be the ideal recommendation for a Dynamics 365 Customer Engagement project.

As I mentioned in the introduction to the chapter, customer preferences show a growing tendency to choose a channel that offers advanced and real self-management capabilities over agent-based channels. This is due, among other factors, to the fact that if the self-management channel is mature, it will allow the person to carry out the management quickly and effectively, avoiding delays in queues, or delays due to lack of skills or knowledge on the part of the agent attending them.

When we think about a new implementation of a digital contact center, it is crucial to think about having as simplified a system architecture as possible to achieve effective processes without the risks of complex integrations. Dynamics 365 Customer Service has evolved a lot in recent years, with the clear objective of offering a unified omnichannel service platform, powered by AI. With this in mind, in any Dynamics 365 Customer Service project, we have to evaluate which channels we are going to implement, and if chat is one of the intended channels, we have the possibility of using the native channel. By using native chat, we will have the clear benefit of simplifying our systems landscape, and we will take advantage of the native integration with Dynamics 365 Customer Service and Power Virtual Agents.

When choosing which bot to use, we have many options. We could choose a technology from another manufacturer, or opt for a bot based on Microsoft technology – but within the Microsoft brand, we can choose between Power Virtual Agents and Bot Framework.

As in each of the aspects of Power Platform that we have already discussed, when we talk about bots, we also have the dichotomy of no-code/low-code and pro-code. This is basically the distinction we have when we compare Power Virtual Agents and Bot Frameworks. However, Microsoft is investing a lot of resources into achieving convergence and synergies between both platforms, getting the best of both worlds, and allowing the extension of Power Virtual Agents with Bot Framework capabilities when we need it.

Now, let's see what steps we have to follow to create and deploy a Power Virtual Agents bot in the native Dynamics 365 Customer Engagement chat channel. Assuming that the implementation of Dynamics 365 Customer Engagement is done and that we have the chat channel deployed, what we will have to do first is to create a bot in Power Virtual Agents:

1. We will go to `https://make.powerapps.com`, make sure we are in the correct environment, and in the **Chatbots** section, we will click on **Create**.

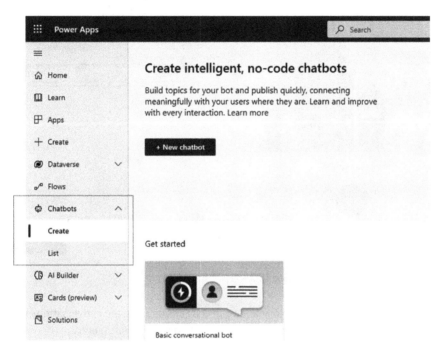

Figure 10.1 – Create area under Chatbots in the maker portal

2. Then, we have to click on + **New chatbot**.

Create intelligent, no-code chatbots

Build topics for your bot and publish quickly, connecting meaningfully with your users where they are. Learn and improve with every interaction. Learn more

+ New chatbot

Figure 10.2 – Adding a new chatbot in the maker portal

3.   Finally, we will have to define the name of the bot, the language in which the bot will have conversations, and the environment in which we want to create it.

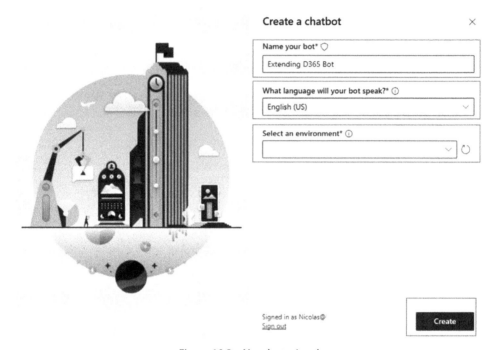

Figure 10.3 – New bot wizard

Now, we have our first bot created, and we will have to start configuring the conversations we want it to have. To do so, let's quickly review the basic concepts of Power Virtual Agents.

Figure 10.4 – The Power Virtual Agents navigation bar

As we can see in the previous figure, Power Virtual Agents has two main areas for configuring the bot's conversations: **Topics** and **Entities**. Topics are the structure that the bot will have to answer questions or expressions. Every topic will have a set of phrases that trigger it, and actions.

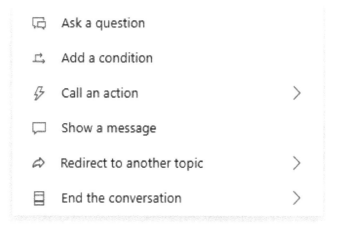

Figure 10.5 – List of possible actions to add to a topic

As we can see in the figure, the actions can be **Ask a question**, **Add a condition**, **Call an action** (for example, searching for a knowledge article in Dynamics 365, or executing a cloud flow), **Show a message**, **Redirect to another topic**, or **End the conversation** with a survey or transferal to an agent.

Additionally, we can have a fallback topic, which we will use when the bot cannot determine a specific topic to continue the conversation. It is common to want to manage these situations to try to get more details before escalating the conversation to a real agent.

Entities, on the other hand, are categories of information that the bot can obtain during the conversation. This is a fundamental aspect of natural language understanding, driven by artificial intelligence. Some native examples of this are age, city, color, continent, or duration. Some examples of personalized entities are the type of use (home, professional, or gaming), delivery preferences, or contact preferences.

Finally, as the bot progresses with the conversion, we may want to save some of the client's answers to use them later in another part of the conversation, at the moment of triggering automation, or when we escalate the conversation to an agent. For this, we will be able to use the variables.

To create our bot, we will need to create the topics and entities we need so that the conversations customers have with the virtual agent are productive and consistent. Let's see how we can create our own topics and entities.

Creating a topic

To create a new topic, see the following:

1. Go to **Topics** in the navigation bar inside Power Virtual Agents:

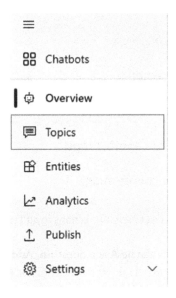

Figure 10.6 – The Topics section in Power Virtual Agents

2. Select + **New Topic** in the command bar:

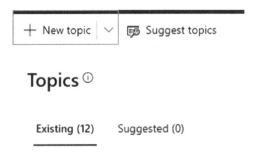

Figure 10.7 – New topic option in the command bar

3. Define the phrases that will trigger the topic:

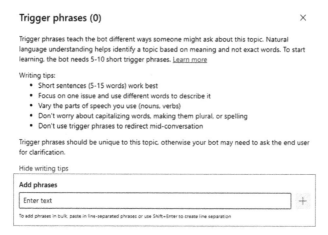

Figure 10.8 – Adding trigger phrases

4. Add actions to the topic:

Figure 10.9 – Adding an action to a topic

5. If we add an **Ask a question** action, we can see how a variable is automatically generated by the user's answer.

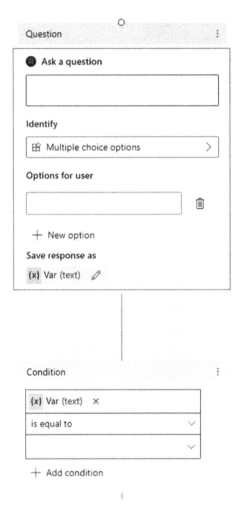

Figure 10.10 – Ask a question action

Now, let's see how to create a custom entity.

Creating an entity

To create an entity, see the following:

1. Go to **Entities** in the navigation bar inside Power Virtual Agents.

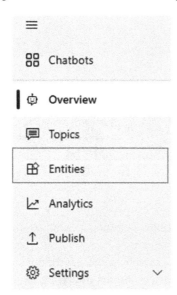

Figure 10.11 – The Entities section in Power Virtual Agents

2. Select **+ New entity** in the command bar:

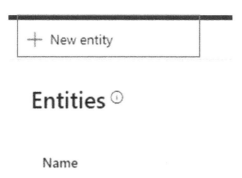

Figure 10.12 – The New entity option

3. Select the method you want to create:

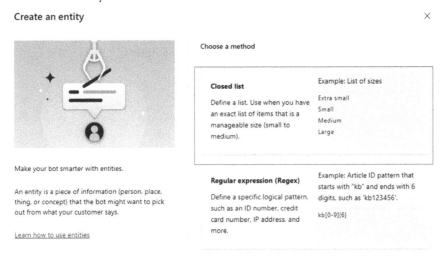

Figure 10.13 – Selecting the entity method

4. Complete the properties – for example, name, description, and options, including synonyms if applicable. We could also turn on **Smart matching** to enable the bot's understanding of natural language.

Figure 10.14 – Entity properties

Once we have configured our bot to have intelligent conversations with our customers, we can connect it to the Dynamics 365 Customer Service chat.

Connecting the bot with Omnichannel Engagement Hub

To connect Power Virtual Agents with Omnichannel Engagement Hub, we have to configure the handover to Dynamics 365 Customer Service, and then connect the bot to the omnichannel solution. For that, we will do the following:

1. From **AppSource**, we install the provided **Omnichannel Power Virtual Agents Extension**:

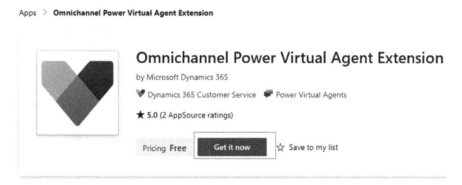

Figure 10.15 – Omnichannel Power Virtual Agent Extension in AppSource

2. Then, we have to go back to the Power Virtual Agents portal, go to **Manage**, and then to **Agent transfers**:

Figure 10.16 – The Agent transfers area for a bot

3. We will select the **Omnichannel** option.

Agent transfers

Connect to a customer engagement app to enable your bot to hand off a chat session to a live agent or other bot. Learn more

How would you like the bot to hand off chat sessions?

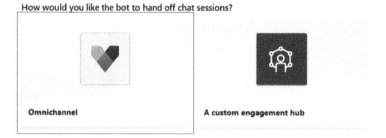

Omnichannel   A custom engagement hub

Figure 10.17 – Agent transfers options

4. We will click on the **Enable** option to escalate a conversation from Power Virtual Agents to a live agent.

Omnichannel   ✕

ⓘ Your bot doesn't have access to all the required variables and actions. Ask your admin about installing the Omnichannel package or follow this step-by-step walkthrough ⬀.

Turn on Dynamics 365 Omnichannel for Customer Service to seamlessly and contextually hand off escalated Power Virtual Agents conversations to live agents.

After you enable Omnichannel for your bot, you will manage individual channel deployment in Omnichannel. Learn more

By turning on Omnichannel, we'll enable Microsoft Teams for you. Power Virtual Agents uses Microsoft Teams to communicate with Omnichannel.

Figure 10.18 – Enabling omnichannel escalation in Power Virtual Agents

5. We have to select the environment this bot is connected to, and specify the **Application ID** information:

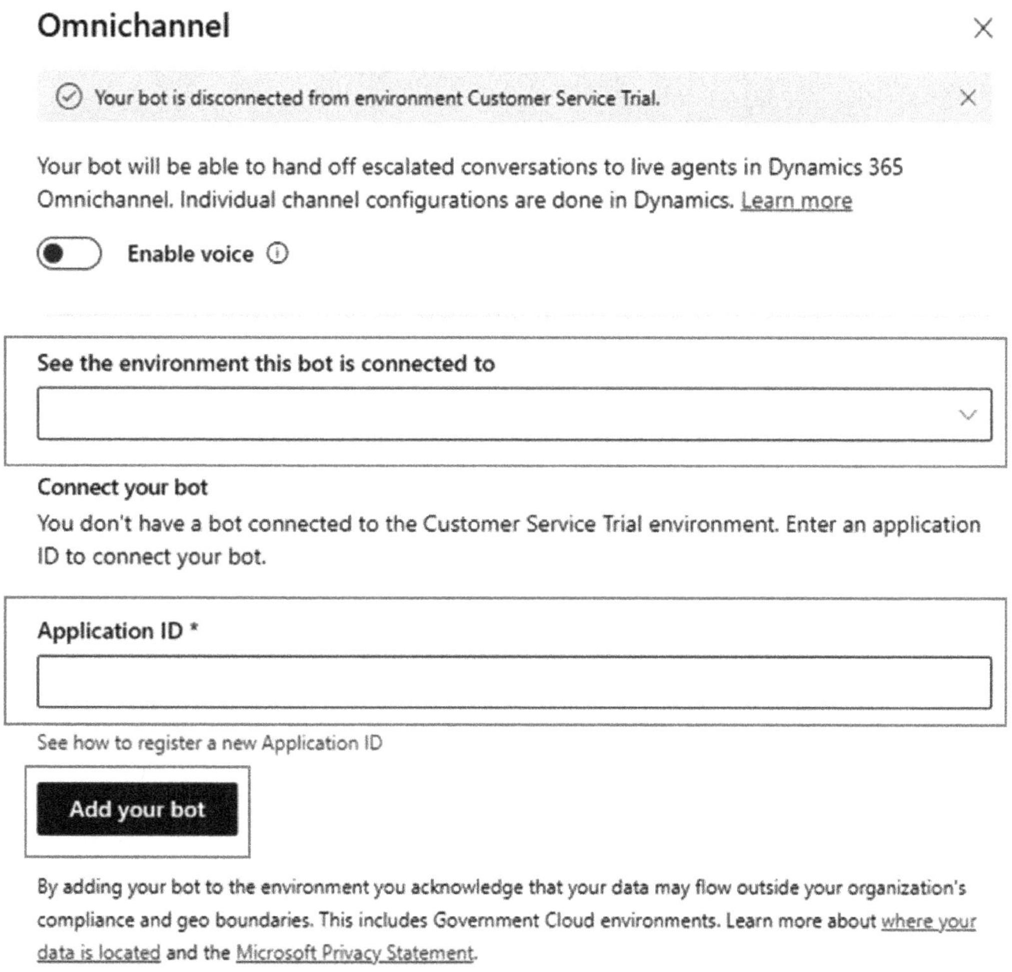

Omnichannel   ✕

⊘ Your bot is disconnected from environment Customer Service Trial.   ✕

Your bot will be able to hand off escalated conversations to live agents in Dynamics 365 Omnichannel. Individual channel configurations are done in Dynamics. Learn more

⬤ **Enable voice** ⓘ

See the environment this bot is connected to

[⌄]

Connect your bot
You don't have a bot connected to the Customer Service Trial environment. Enter an application ID to connect your bot.

Application ID *

[   ]

See how to register a new Application ID

[**Add your bot**]

By adding your bot to the environment you acknowledge that your data may flow outside your organization's compliance and geo boundaries. This includes Government Cloud environments. Learn more about where your data is located and the Microsoft Privacy Statement.

Figure 10.19 – Omnichannel transfer setup wizard

6.   Once we have clicked on **Add your bot**, we will see the confirmation and the option to **View details in Omnichannel**:

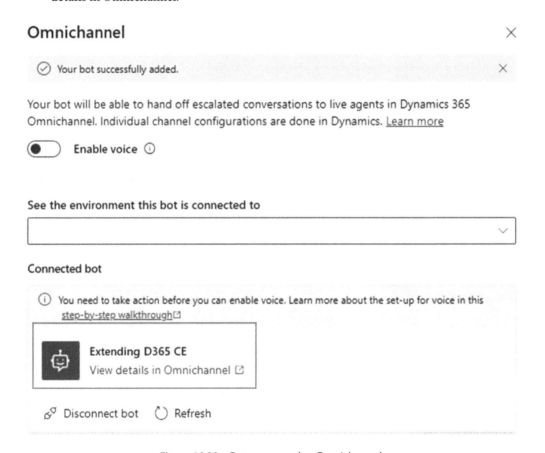

Figure 10.20 – Bot connected to Omnichannel

Finally, we have to go to the channel configuration in Dynamics 365 Customer Engagement. For this, we will do the following:

1.   Open the **Customer Service admin center** application.

2.   Go to **Channels**:

Figure 10.21 – The Channels subarea in the Customer Service admin center app

3. Select **Manage** in the **Chat** channel:

Channels

Add support channels to provide personalized service to customers on the channels of their choice.

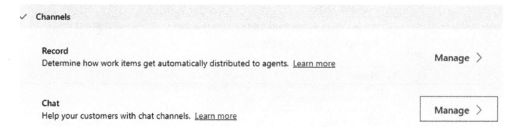

Figure 10.22 – Chat channel in the Customer Service admin center app

4. Select the workstream of the chat channel we want to link to Power Virtual Agents:

Figure 10.23 – Selecting the workspace to which to add the bot

5. In the **Bot** section, we click on + **Add bot**:

Bot Optional

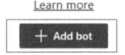

Add a bot

All incoming work will be routed to the bot first. If needed, your bot will transfer customers to the right queues to speak with human agents.

Learn more

+ Add bot

Figure 10.24 – The Bot section in the workstream

6. Search for the bot we want to link, and then click on **Save and Close**.

Figure 10.25 – The Add a bot form in the workstream

7. Once we have finished this, we will have configured our Power Virtual Agents in the chat channel.

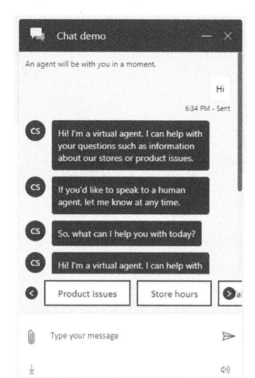

Figure 10.26 – Native chat channel with Power Virtual Agent integration

As we can see in the previous figure, the conversation was automatically attended by the virtual agent, who proposed different options to assist the customer.

Enabling bots for the voice channel

Power Virtual Agents also allows us to integrate with other channels, such as first-party voice – that is, we can configure a bot to answer calls, try to resolve them, or obtain important details for proper routing.

> **Note**
>
> This section covers some of the issues to consider when you want to enable bots for the voice channel. Only first-party voice is considered and not any existing third-party telephony systems that an organization may have.
>
> This section tries to present a simplified scenario, but it might not be the same as the one you will face in your organization or project.

If we want to connect our bot to the voice channel, we will have to install new extensions, configure the transfer, including the voice channel, and add the bot to the voice channel workstream in Dynamics 365 Customer Service to support the bot.

The extensions we need to install are two: **Omnichannel Voice Power Virtual Agent Extension** and **Power Virtual Agents telephony extension**.

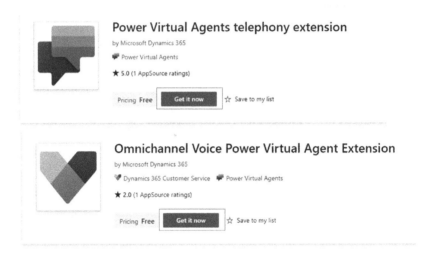

Figure 10.27 – Required extensions for the voice channel

As we can see in the previous figure, **Power Virtual Agents telephony extension** has no dependency on Dynamics 365 Customer Service since it works regardless of the engagement hub with which it is integrated.

After installing these extensions, we must do the following:

1.   Go back to the Power Virtual Agents portal, and go to **Agent transfers** in the **Manage** section.

2.   Select the **Omnichannel** option.

3.   Select **Enable voice**:

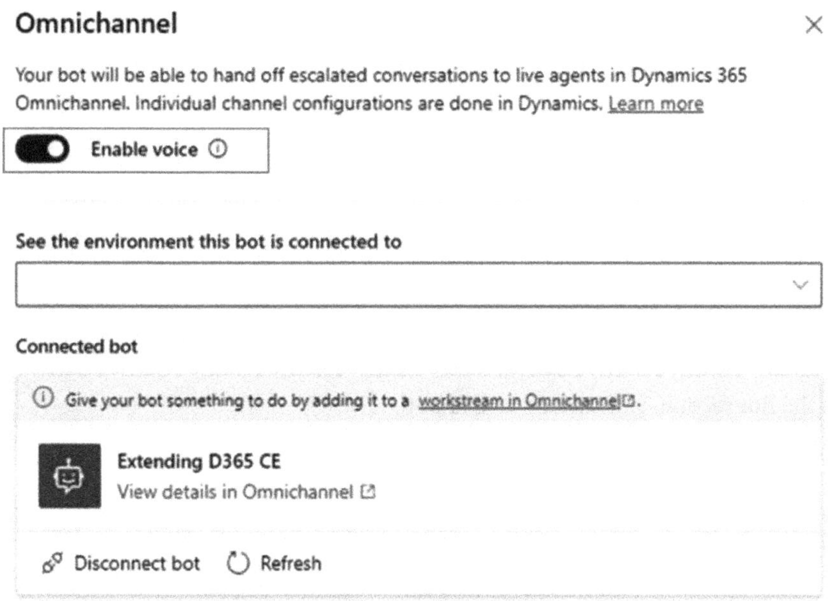

Figure 10.28 – Enable voice in Power Virtual Agents

To add the bot to the voice channel, we have to do the following:

1. Enter the **Customer Service admin center** application, and go to **Channels**.
2. Click on **Manage** in the **Voice** channel.

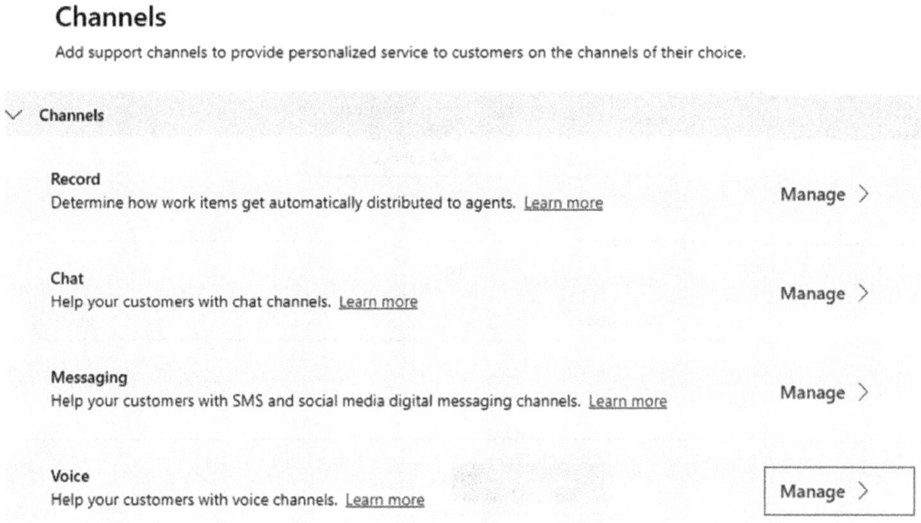

Figure 10.29 – Voice channels in the Customer Service admin center app

3. Enter in the voice channel workstream:

Figure 10.30 – Selecting the workspace to which to add a bot

4. Go to the **Bot** section, and click on + **Add bot**:

Figure 10.31 – The Bot section in the workstream

5. Select the bot and click on **Save and close**:

Figure 10.32 – The Add a bot form in the workstream

Once these steps are finished, we will have our bot deployed in the voice channel.

Summary

In this chapter, we reviewed the importance of bots in any organization's current digital contact center strategy. We saw how Power Virtual Agents is an ideal option to quickly deploy bots in digital and voice channels, without the need for any development.

We started by refreshing the basic concepts of Power Virtual Agents, and then we saw the step-by-step configuration of our bot in the native chat channel of Dynamics 365. Finally, we saw how easy it is to deploy a bot in a Microsoft voice channel by setting up an IVR that allows us to correctly route each call.

In the next chapter, we will discuss some use cases for deploying a Power Virtual Agents bot integrated with Dynamics 365 Customer Engagement for internal use by users in the organization.

Questions and answers

1. Do I need to know about machine learning to deploy a chatbot?

    Answer: No, you don't. Power Virtual Agents make it easier than ever. With just a bit of configuration, you can create and deploy your chatbot in a matter of hours.

2. Why bots are important in any customer service strategy?

    Answer: In recent years, there has been a growing trend in customer preference for self-service channels. This type of option allows customers to get a faster response, avoid waiting in queues, and manage their needs as and when they want.

    A customer service strategy that does not take these preferences into account faces a higher level of customer dissatisfaction.

    For this reason, a strategy that includes bots in the different channels where it is present, and where it makes sense to deploy a bot, is more likely to deliver a better customer experience.

11
Enabling Bots to Users

Deploying bots as part of our customer service strategy can be very beneficial, but we can't only utilize customer-facing bots. Members of our organization also have specific needs, for which having a powerful tool such as Power Virtual Agents developed for them can simplify day-to-day tasks.

Whether they are users of Dynamics 365 Customer Engagement or not, as with all members of the organization, we will find use cases in which automating tasks through a bot can be extremely beneficial.

In this chapter, we will focus on this facet of Power Virtual Agents, the bots for the users of an organization. We will discuss some of the most common use cases, and describe the most important considerations to keep in mind.

By the end of this chapter, you will have acquired a new approach to solutions built on Dynamics 365 Customer Engagement, with your users or affected members of the organization in mind.

In this chapter, we will cover the following points:

- Enabling Power Virtual Agents to easily search in the knowledge base
- Triggering automation from your virtual assistant

Technical requirements

To work with Dynamics 365 Customer Engagement, it is necessary to have an environment that has one of the supported licenses. For this chapter, the following are required:

- Dynamics 365 Customer Service (with a Chat Add-in license with administrator permissions in an environment)
- A Power Virtual Agents license
- A Microsoft Teams license
- A supported browser

Enabling Power Virtual Agents to easily search in the knowledge base

Possibly one of the most widely implemented use cases in Dynamics 365 Customer Engagement, and its previous versions of the Dynamics CRM system, must be the use of the knowledge base for internal users.

As we saw in the previous chapter, *Chapter 10*, it is very quick and easy to deploy a Power Virtual Agents bot in a Dynamics 365 Customer Service chat. This chat could be deployed in an internal portal built with Power Pages, but what if we didn't deploy any type of employee portal – how could we deliver a similar experience? Let's look at how we could deploy this capability in another channel.

Let's say we create a bot for users in the organization to query the Dynamics 365 Customer Engagement knowledge base.

For this, the first thing we will need to do is to create the bot itself.

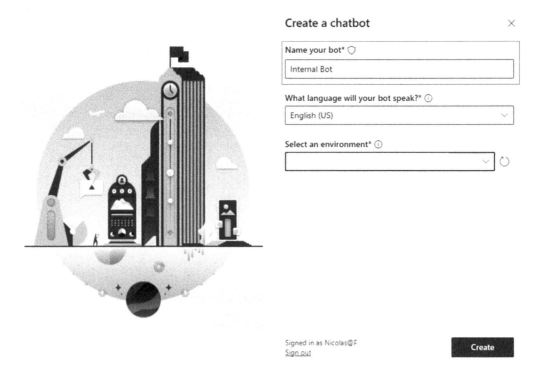

Figure 11.1 – Internal bot creation wizard

The figure here shows the wizard for creating the new **Internal Bot**. Once created, and before creating the topic to connect with Dynamics 365 Customer Engagement, the first thing to do is to create connection references in Dataverse.

Creating a connection

Power Virtual Agents offers us a native way to connect the bots with the Dynamics 365 knowledge base. To enable us to consult the knowledge base, it provides a Power Automate cloud flow with predefined actions. This cloud flow uses connections, such as Microsoft Dataverse and Content Conversion. To use the flow, first, we need to create these connections.

For this, we will do the following:

1. Go to `https://make.powerapps.com`.

2. Go to **Connections** within the **Dataverse** section.

3. Create a connection for **Dataverse** and **Content Conversion**, if they do not already exist in the environment:

    I.   For that, we will click on + **New connection**

    II.   Select the connector, and create the connection:

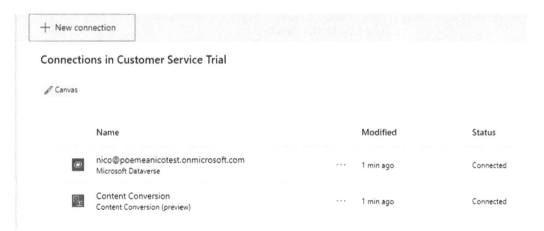

Figure 11.2 – Adding new connections

4. Then, we must go to solutions and select **Default Solution**, and we filter for **Connection references** objects.

Default Solution > **Connection references**

|≡   **Display name ↑ ∨**

🖤   Common Data Service (current environment)   ⋮

🖤   Content Conversion   ⋮

🖤   Dataverse   ⋮

🖤   Dataverse Connection for Swarming   ⋮

🖤   Microsoft Dataverse   ⋮

Figure 11.3 – Confirming the existence of the connection reference

5. We will confirm that the two connection references are there and that they have the connections we have created associated with them.

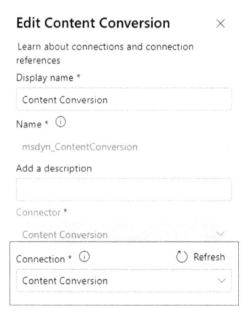

Figure 11.4 – Adding the connections to the connection references

6. Then, we must go to the cloud flows and click **Turn on** for the flow called **Search Dynamics 365 Knowledge article flow**.

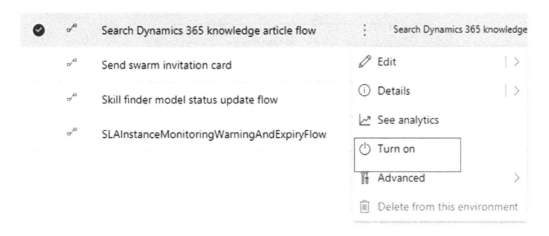

Figure 11.5 – Turning on the cloud flow

Adding the topics and entities

As we saw in *Chapter 10*, to personalize the conversations our bot will have, we need to create the topics and entities that are relevant to our business.

Adding the Search Dynamics 365 Knowledge article action

We now go to our bot to add the **Search Dynamics 365 Knowledge article** action as a topic node. For this, we will do the following:

1. Open the topic to which we want to add the action.

2. Add a **Question** action, and ask the user how we can help them.

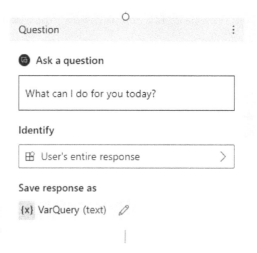

Figure 11.6 – Ask a question action

3. We add a second action, **Search Dynamics 365 Knowledge article**, and we put the result of the previous question as a search variable.

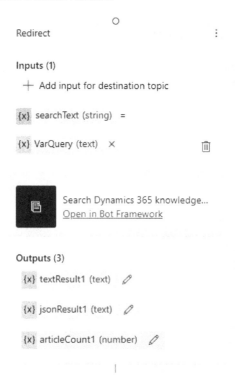

Figure 11.7 – The Search Dynamics 365 Knowledge article action

4. Finally, we add a **Send message** action, and in it, we put the result of the search of the knowledge base article.

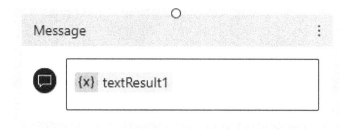

Figure 11.8 – The Send a message action

5. We can test the result in the test bot and check that it returns information from Dynamics 365 Customer Service.

Figure 11.9 – Test bot

Now that we have our bot configured, what we need to do is to deploy it in the channel of preference. When choosing the channel, the most natural channel for a user assistance bot is Microsoft Teams.

Deployment

To publish the bot in Microsoft Teams, see the following:

1. Publish the bot by clicking on **Publish**, and confirm by clicking **Publish** again.

Figure 11.10 – The Publish bot

2. Then, we go to **Manage**, and select **Channels**:

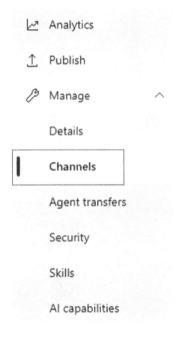

Figure 11.11 – The Channels section

3. Select **Microsoft Teams**:

Figure 11.12 – The Microsoft Teams channel

4. We click on **Turn on Teams**:

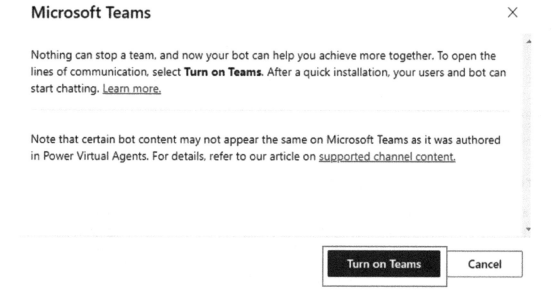

Figure 11.13 – Turn on Teams

5.   Once it's published, we will be able to test it in Teams.

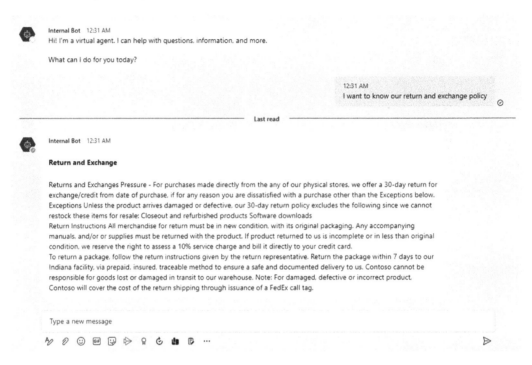

Figure 11.14 – Teams conversation with the bot

This is a simple way to empower the users of the organization, facilitating access to the information that is managed in Dynamics 365 Customer Engagement as knowledge base articles, without them having to navigate to access it.

Now, we will see other examples of actions that we can add to the bot conversation to help users.

Triggering automation from your virtual assistant

In addition to consulting knowledge base articles, Power Virtual Agents can be used to set up a series of actions that we want to execute from a bot in Microsoft Teams. Thanks to the integration between Power Virtual Agents and Power Automate, we can trigger a cloud flow from a bot conversation. This opens the possibility not only to interact with Dataverse or Dynamics 365 Customer Engagement but also to interact with any of the systems for which we have connectors available in Power Platform.

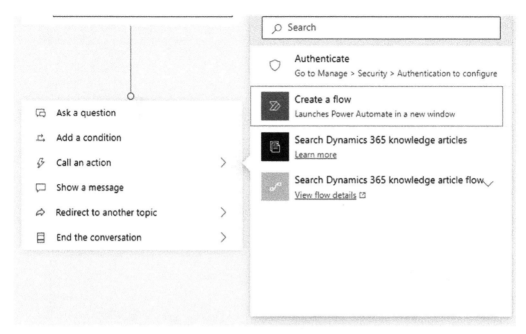

Figure 11.15 – The Create a flow action

The previous figure shows the **Create a flow** action, which allows us to invoke a flow and, with it, perform the actions we need.

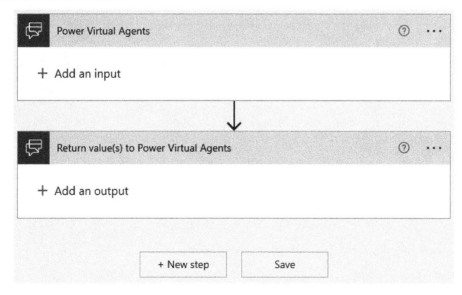

Figure 11.16 – Cloud flow template

In the previous figure, we can see that the Power Virtual Agents flow template is based on a Power Virtual Agents trigger to which we can add input parameters and outputs to return values to Power Virtual Agents.

Figure 11.17 – Output parameters in Power Virtual Agents

As we can see in the previous figure, the cloud flow action in the topic will return the output parameters defined in the cloud flow. These parameters can have a text format, yes/no format, or number format. For each output parameter, Power Virtual Agents will save the value in a specific variable.

Some examples of the actions that we could perform are as follows:

- Schedule a meeting
- Consult a record status
- Close an opportunity as win/close
- Create a new record in Dynamics 365 Customer Engagement
- Update a record in Dynamics 365 Customer Engagement
- Create a task
- Schedule a phone call

- Reschedule a work order
- Validate a field technician's ETA

These are just examples of some actions you can automate with a cloud flow triggered by a bot conversation.

Summary

In this chapter, we analyzed some use cases of the implementation of Power Virtual Agents in Dynamics 365 Customer Engagement, for internal users. We started by reviewing the employee self-service scenario, and how with Power Virtual Agents, we could quickly create and deploy a bot in Microsoft Teams to query knowledge base articles. Finally, we reviewed some examples of actions that we could automate by executing cloud flows from the bot conversation.

In the next chapter, we will begin to look at how we can extend data analysis capabilities by integrating with Power BI.

Questions and answers

1. Is Power Virtual Agents only for customer-facing bots?

   Answer: No. it's really common to deploy a bot in Teams to automate mundane tasks and to help users with day-to-day tasks.

2. Why do I need to configure a connection to use the Search Dynamics 365 knowledge article action?

   Answer: The Search Dynamics 365 Knowledge article action uses a Power Automate cloud flow that uses connections to Dataverse and Content Conversion connectors. To configure and turn on cloud flows, first, we need to configure the connections.

Part 5: Working with Advanced Dashboards and Reports with Dynamics 365 Customer Engagement

Power BI, as with all Power Platform tools, integrates natively with Dynamics 365 Customer Engagement, thus facilitating the construction of advanced reports and dashboards.

In this part, we will see how we can make use of Power BI connected to Dynamics 365, both as an isolated component and as an embedded component.

This part has the following chapters:

- *Chapter 12, Reporting Dashboards with Dynamics 365 Customer Engagement Data*
- *Chapter 13, Embedded Dashboards and Reports in Dynamics 365 Customer Engagement*

12

Reporting Dashboards with Dynamics 365 Customer Engagement Data

Power BI is the Power Platform solution that we will use for data exploitation via datasets, reports, and dashboards, which we will be able to create easily. Dynamics 365 Customer Engagement applications, being built on Dataverse, offer us the possibility to easily integrate with Power BI, and thus extend the native capabilities of reporting and analytics. To help us accelerate the creation of advanced reports, Microsoft offers several templates for data mining Dynamics 365 Customer Engagement applications.

In this chapter, we will learn how to connect Dynamics 365 Customer Engagement with Power BI, and the initial steps for creating reports and dashboards.

By the end of this chapter, you will have connected Dynamics 365 Customer Engagement with Power BI, and you will have created your first reports.

In this chapter, we will cover the following topics:

- Connecting Dynamics 365 Customer Engagement applications with Power BI
- Creating custom reports and dashboards based on Dynamics 365 Customer Engagement data

Technical requirements

To work with Dynamics 365 Customer Engagement, it is necessary to have an environment with one of the supported licenses. However, the topics covered in this chapter do not require a Dynamics 365 application.

The following are required for this chapter:

- Any Dynamics 365 Customer Engagement license (any of the available ones) with administrator permissions in an environment

- Any Power BI license

- Power BI Desktop

- A supported browser

Connecting Dynamics 365 Customer Engagement with Power BI

To connect Dynamics 365 Customer Engagement with Power BI, we have multiple options. The easiest way would be by using one of the Power BI apps for Dynamics 365 Customer Engagement. The most common way would be connecting directly to Power BI with Dataverse using the native connector. But we can also use an external data source, such as a data lake, where we export the data from Dynamics 365 Customer Engagement. An example of this would be using Azure Synapse Link for Dataverse.

Whether connecting via the native Dataverse connector or by exporting data using Azure Synapse Link, we will need Power BI Desktop to connect to the data source and build our reports.

Using the Dataverse connector

If we think of end users who want to build reports and dashboards and if they have a minimum knowledge of Power BI, they will most likely connect to Dataverse directly from Power BI Desktop. This option is valid, fast, and simple, and above all does not require advanced knowledge of data intelligence to make use of it.

To use the data in Power BI Desktop, we must create a connection to the Dynamics 365 Customer Engagement/Dataverse environment(s) with which we want to work. To do this, we must do the following:

1. Open Power BI Desktop and enter our credentials.

2. In the top bar, in the **Home** tab, in the **Data** section, click on **Dataverse**:

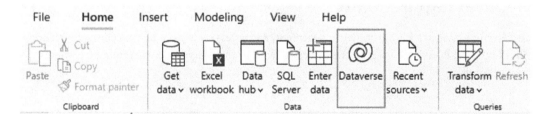

Figure 12.1 – Connecting to Dataverse in Power BI Desktop

3. If this is the first time we are connecting to **Dataverse**, it will ask us to sign in. To do this, click on **Sign in**, and enter your credentials:

Figure 12.2 – Signing in to Dataverse in Power BI Desktop

4. Once we have entered our credentials, click on **Connect**:

Figure 12.3 – Connecting to Dataverse after signing in to Power BI Desktop

5. When we do that, we will see the complete list of environments that we have available to the tenant:

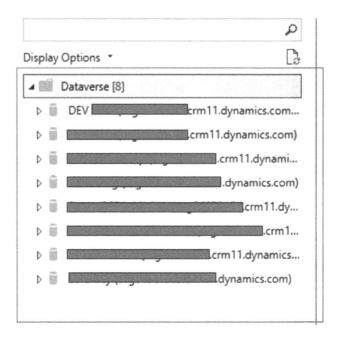

Figure 12.4 – Selecting a Dataverse environment

6. When we select an environment, the tables that are in it will be displayed so that we can select them:

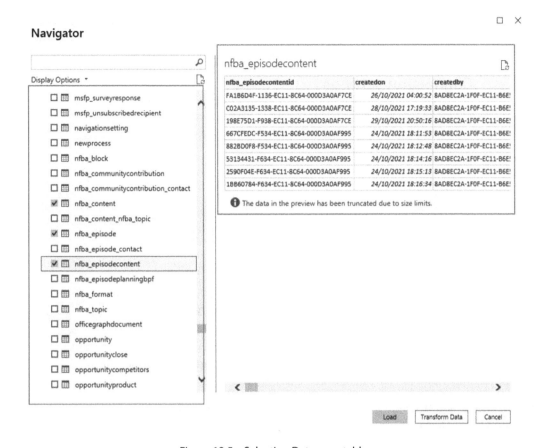

Figure 12.5 – Selecting Dataverse tables

7. Once selected, we will be able to load them or transform the data with Power Query:

Figure 12.6 – Selecting Load or Transform Data

> **Note**
>
> Selecting **Transform Data** will open the Power Query editor, which will allow us to create measurements, transform formats, and even hide columns of the data source we are connecting to. This last action is really useful when working with Dynamics 365 Customer Engagement as a data source.

8. Finally, we must select whether we want to import the data or set up a live connection with **DirectQuery**:

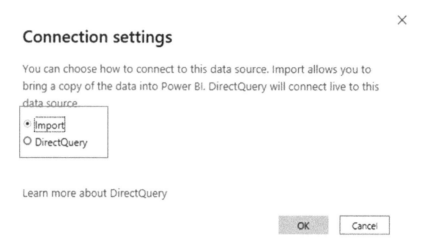

Figure 12.7 – Selecting Import or DirectQuery

When importing the data, the selected tables and columns will be imported into Power BI Desktop. As the creator, we will be able to build the reports using the imported data. To see the updated data since the last import, we will have to refresh the data source.

DirectQuery creates an online connection between Power BI and the data source. No data is copied, so it works all the time with the current data.

> **Note**
> Currently, there are several limitations of DirectQuery. Considering that it is a Microsoft investment area, it is recommended to consult the official documentation when considering using it to have the most updated information.

Once the connection is complete, we are ready to build our reports.

Configuring Azure Synapse Link for Dataverse

On the other hand, it is very common in enterprise scenarios to find a more complex architecture where we do not connect directly to Dataverse to consume their data for analytical purposes. For this, we can configure data export to Azure Data Lake, using Azure Synapse Link for Dataverse.

Azure Synapse Analytics is an analytics service that allows us to integrate data at the data level, store it, and perform analytics on large volumes of data. With Azure Synapse, we have Azure Data Lake as a storage solution, which will allow us to automatically scale and keep Dataverse data connected, even if it is a large volume.

This option requires a certain level of knowledge of Azure, so I do not consider that it can be categorized exactly as no-code/low-code, although much of its configuration is by the user interface and without development.

Power BI Apps

As I mentioned in the introduction, Microsoft offers multiple Power BI applications that we can obtain and use by simply connecting to our Dynamics 365 Customer Engagement environment. Among the available applications, we can find Process Analytics for Dynamics 365, Sales Analytics for Dynamics 365 Sales, Omnichannel Insights for Dynamics 365, and Customer Service Analytics for Dynamics 365:

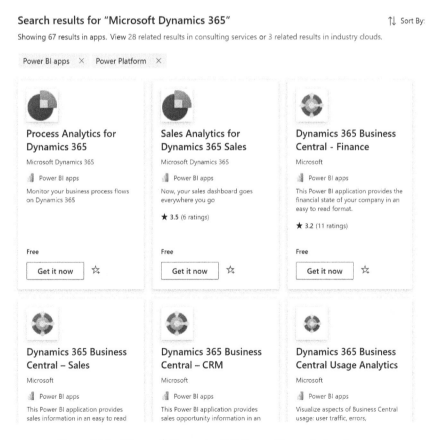

Figure 12.8 – Microsoft Dynamics 365 Power BI apps in AppSource

As we can see, one of the ways we can find and make use of these applications is from AppSource.

AppSource is the Microsoft marketplace where we can find different applications from Microsoft 365, Dynamics 365, Power Platform, and Azure, as well as consulting services, partners, and industry clouds.

However, we can also get these applications from the Power BI service. For this, we have to do the following:

1. Log in to `https://app.powerbi.com` and select **Apps** from the side navigation bar:

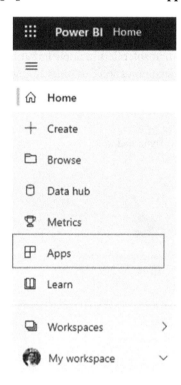

Figure 12.9 – The Apps section in the Power BI service navigation bar

2. Click on **Get apps**:

Figure 12.10 – The Get apps button

3. We can filter by Dynamics 365 in the search bar to get the Dynamics 365 applications developed by Microsoft or third parties, and select the application we want:

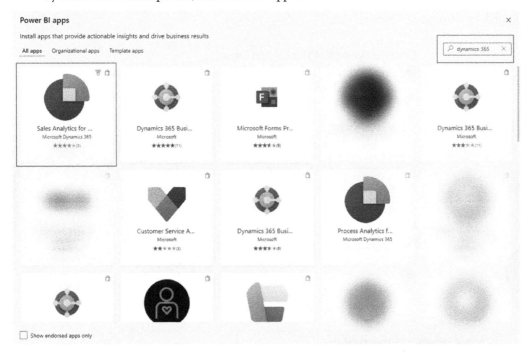

Figure 12.11 – Dynamics 365 apps in Power BI

4. Select **Get It Now**:

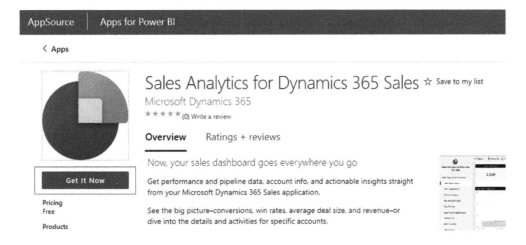

Figure 12.12 – Sales Analytics for Dynamics 365 Sales

On the side, we can see which products are supported/required by this application. In this example, the application requires Power BI and Dynamics 365 Sales.

5. Fill in the required information:

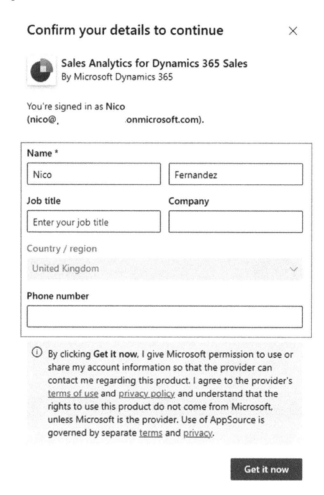

Figure 12.13 – Required data form

6. Accept that you wish to install the application:

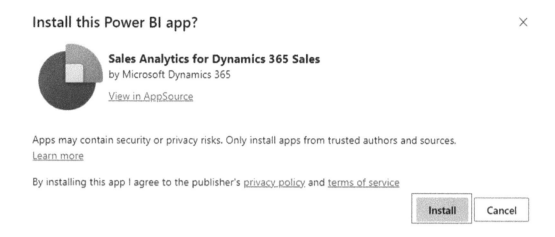

Figure 12.14 – Install app dialog

7.   Finally, we have to connect to our Dynamics 365 environment and start using the report:

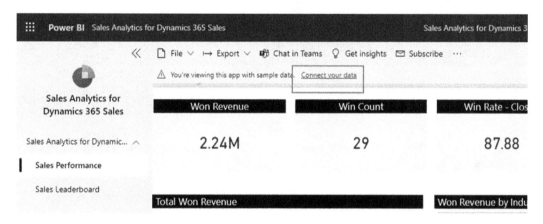

Figure 12.15 – Connect your data option in the installed app

These applications are a good way to start exploiting the data we have in Dynamics 365 Customer Engagement without prior knowledge of Power BI and taking advantage of the KPIs and graphs proposed by Microsoft as part of the applications.

Creating custom reports and dashboards

The first thing we need to do to work with Power BI Desktop to build custom reports is to understand the main components. Once we have the data connected to Power BI Desktop, there are three main areas of work:

- Report
- Data
- Model:

Figure 12.16 – Power BI Desktop areas

As we can see, these three work areas are located on the left-hand side of the screen, below the main ribbon.

Report

This is the area where we will build our reports and add the different visualizations we need. In the center of the screen, we will have the report area, where we can add different pages to the bottom page of the report. On the right-hand side, we have the data filters, the visualization configuration area, and the area where we can select the fields or create new measures:

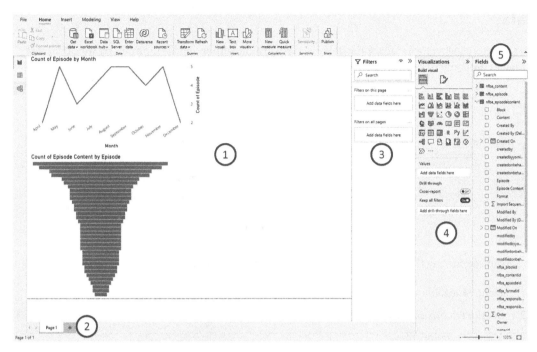

Figure 12.17 – Report area

In the preceding screenshot, we can see the following:

1. The area where we will design the report, adding the different visualizations that will be part of it.

2. The area where we can add new pages to the report and navigate between them.

3. The area where we can apply filters to the page where we are or to the whole report.

4. The area where we can select visualizations and configure them, defining the data they will represent.

5. The area where we can access the tables and columns.

In addition to working with the report, we can access the tables to work with their definition in detail from the data area.

Data

This is the area where we can see the data we are working with in detail. From there, we can access the tables, not only to see the data but also to work with it:

Figure 12.18 – Table tools actions

As we can see, among the available table tools, we can do the following:

1. Define the table name.

2. Set the table as a date table.

3. Manage relationships.

4. Create calculated fields, such as measures, quick measures, a new column, or a new table.

Finally, we can work with the data model, specifically in the model area.

Model

Finally, in the model area, we can work with data modeling. Here, we have a graphical representation of the data model we are working with, and can build new relationships between tables:

Figure 12.19 – Model area ribbon

Also, as shown in the preceding screenshot, from this area, you can create new measures, columns, and tables, as well as manage security roles.

> **Note**
>
> It is important to review the model and relationships that Power BI Desktop automatically creates when we connect Dataverse/Dynamics 365 Customer Engagement data because sometimes, they are not accurate.

Finally, once we have finished our report, to access it from Power BI, we will have to publish it. By doing so, we will be able to access it from Power BI, share it, and create dashboards based on the report visualizations.

Summary

In this chapter, we provided a high-level introduction to Power BI in the context of Dynamics 365 Customer Engagement. We started by understanding the possibilities we have to connect Dynamics 365 Customer Engagement data with Power BI. Then, we went through the most relevant components of Power BI Desktop so that we can start working with custom reports.

In the next and last chapter, we will learn how to create an embedded Power BI experience in Dynamics 365 Customer Engagement applications.

Questions and answers

1. Why would I use Power BI in the context of Dynamics 365 Customer Engagement?

    Answer: Even though Dynamics 365 Customer Engagement applications can create different components for data analysis, such as charts, dashboards, or reports, Dynamics 365 Customer Engagement's analytical capabilities are limited. Power BI will offer us advanced analytical capabilities, while not giving us the ability to create reports by consolidating data external to Dynamics 365 Customer Engagement.

2. What are the most common options for connecting Dynamics 365 Customer Engagement with Power BI for data analysis?

    Answer: The most common ways to connect Dynamics 365 Customer Engagement data with Power BI are as follows:

    *   Power BI templates by which we will have pre-built reports to start working with these

    *   The native Dataverse connector to connect directly to it

    *   Connecting through Azure Data Lake after configuring the data export through Azure Synapse Link

13
Embedded Dashboards and Reports in Dynamics 365 Customer Engagement

Throughout the book, we have reviewed the main capabilities that Power Platform offers to extend Dynamics 365 Customer Engagement applications. In this last chapter, we will conclude by learning how to integrate Power BI within applications such as Sales, Marketing, Customer Service, and Field Service.

Dynamics 365 Customer Engagement offers us the possibility of integrating with Power BI for advanced data analysis. Some of their applications, such as Marketing or Omnichannel Engagement Hub, come with report and dashboard templates, some of them embedded in Dynamics 365 Customer Engagement. By embedding Power BI in Dynamics 365 Customer Engagement, we introduce users to new integrated work scenarios.

As we saw in *Chapter 12*, we can make use of Power BI to build reports and dashboards based on Dynamics 365 Customer Engagement data. Among the native capabilities of Power BI, we will be able to access these components from the following:

- The Power BI web application
- The native Power BI mobile application
- From Teams, as an embedded experience

However, Power Platform has a deep integration between the different solutions, which allows us to think of other ways to consume Power BI reports, dashboards, or widgets. Among these, we can find the following:

- Embedding Power BI widgets in a canvas app
- Creating a model-driven app dashboard page with a Power BI component
- Embedding a Power BI report in a model-driven app form

As we have discussed previously in this book, when we talk about the capabilities we have in a model-driven app, we have to include Dynamics 365 Customer Engagement applications in that analysis, since they are model-driven apps.

In this chapter, we will focus on Power BI integration scenarios within a model-driven app, which will allow us to empower users.

At the end of the chapter, we will learn how to integrate Power BI within Dynamics 365 Customer Engagement and identify some practical use cases for which this integration is a recommended solution.

In this chapter, we will cover the following points:

- Embedding Power BI as a Dynamics 365 Customer Engagement apps dashboard
- Designing forms with embedded Power BI reports

Technical requirements

To work with Dynamics 365 Customer Engagement, it is necessary to have an environment with one of the supported licenses. However, the topics covered in this chapter do not require any Dynamics 365 application.

The following are required for this chapter:

- Any Dynamics 365 Customer Engagement license (any of the available ones) with administrator permissions in an environment
- Any Power BI license
- Power BI Desktop
- A supported browser

> **Note**
> It is important to remember that for a user to access a Power BI report or dashboard, even if it is embedded in Dynamics 365, the user must have the correct Power BI license and be authorized to consume the content.

Embedding Power BI as a Dynamics 365 Customer Engagement apps dashboard

Dynamics 365 Customer Engagement applications natively offer us multiple panels that we can use without requiring any configuration. Most of these panels will be Dynamics 365 Customer Engagement dashboards, which we can use to quickly adopt the Dynamics 365 Customer Engagement applications, and we can even take them as a reference to create our custom panels or modify the native ones based on our needs.

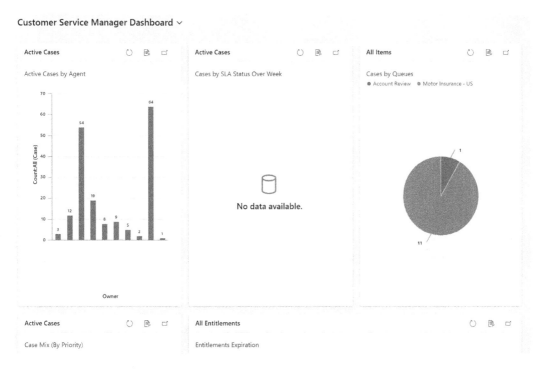

Figure 13.1 – Classic dashboard in Dynamics 365 Customer Service

In the preceding figure, we can see an example of a classic native Dynamics 365 Customer Service application dashboard. In *Chapter 3*, we saw how we can create our own native dashboards to extend Dynamics 365 applications.

Additionally, some of the Dynamics 365 Customer Engagement applications also offer us out-of-the-box Power BI dashboards, as in the example of the **Customer Service historical analytics** or **Knowledge analytics** dashboards, from Dynamics 365 Customer Service.

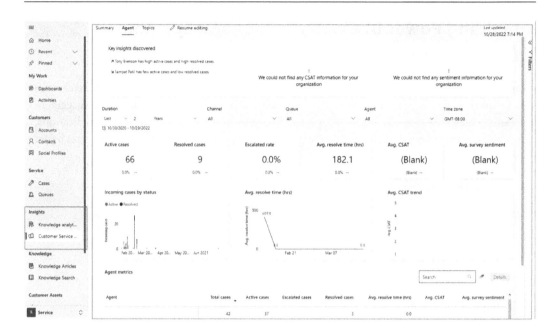

Figure 13.2 – Customer Service historical analytics dashboard in Dynamics 365 Customer Service

In the preceding figure, we can see the example of the **Customer Service historical analytics** report in the Customer Service Hub application.

However, we can also add our own Power BI components in our applications to use as dashboards. For this, we will need to do the following:

1. First of all, you need to have created the report or dashboard in Power BI.

2. Then, you need to open a solution where we have the Dynamics 365 application to edit it.

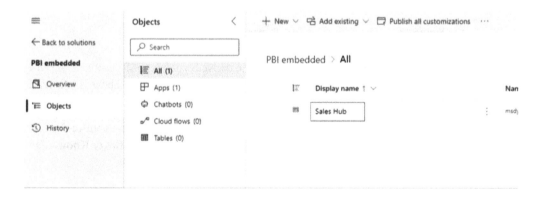

Figure 13.3 – Sales Hub app in a solution

3. Add a new Power BI report by clicking on + **New**, then on **Dashboard**, and finally, on **Power BI embedded**:

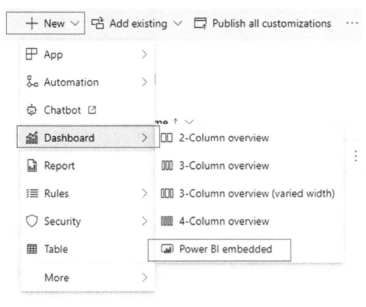

Figure 13.4 – Adding a new Power BI embedded component in a solution

4. In the quick creation form, fill in the data and select the report:

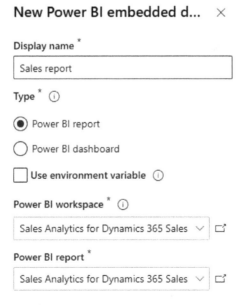

Figure 13.5 – New Power BI embedded form completed for a report

Add a dashboard by clicking on + **New**, then on **Dashboard**, and finally, on **Power BI embedded**:

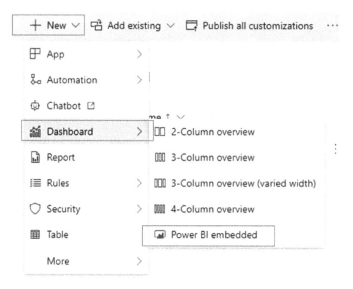

Figure 13.6 – Adding a new Power BI embedded component in a solution

5.   In the quick creation form, complete the data and select the dashboard:

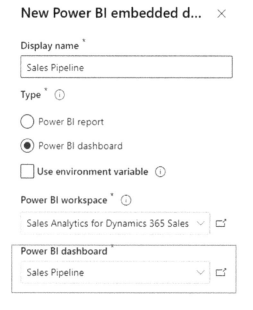

Figure 13.7 – New Power BI embedded form completed for a dashboard

6. Once you do that, you will have the report, the dashboard, and the application in the same solution:

PBI embedded > **All**

	Display name ↑ ∨	Name ∨	Type ∨	Managed ∨
	Sales Hub	msdynce_saleshub	Model-Driven App	Yes
	Sales Pipeline	Sales Pipeline	Power BI Embedded	No
	Sales Report	Sales Report	Power BI Embedded	No

Figure 13.8 – Solution with the app and Power BI embedded components

7. Select the **Edit** option in the application menu:

Figure 13.9 – Edit option in the app menu

8. From the command bar, or in the **Pages** section, you can add another page by clicking on + **Add Page**:

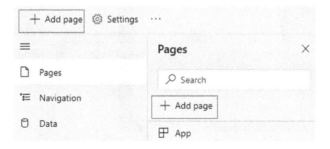

Figure 13.10 – Add page option in the app modern designer

9. Select **Dashboard** as the page type:

Display charts and tables from multiple entities to visualize data on a single page.

Figure 13.11 – Select a page type

10. Select the dashboard and the report, and click **Add**:

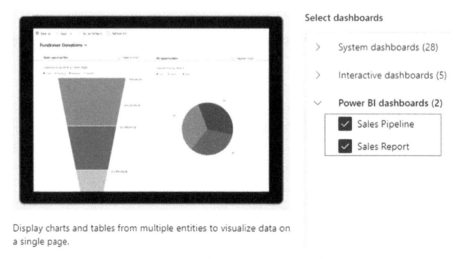

Display charts and tables from multiple entities to visualize data on a single page.

Figure 13.12 – Select Power BI dashboards

11. After publishing, go to the application, and within **Dashboards**, you will now see both the dashboard and the Power BI report:

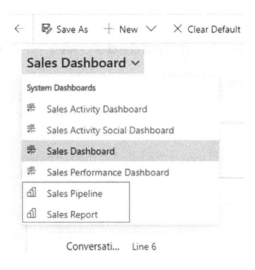

Figure 13.13 – Power BI dashboards in Sales Hub

12. When selecting the new embedded Power BI component, the application will load it and show it as part of the Dynamics 365 Customer Engagement application, regardless of whether it is a dashboard or a report.

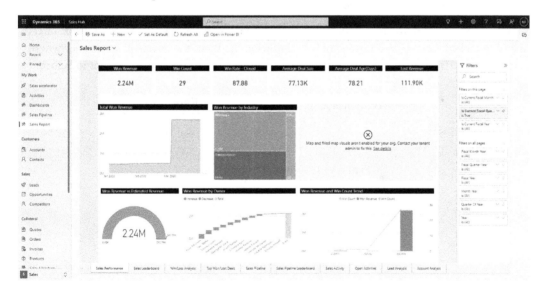

Figure 13.14 – Example of a Power BI report embedded

As we can see, what was unthinkable a few years ago, and meant a complex requirement to solve, Microsoft has managed to make quick and easy. Without the need for any code, we can add advanced Power BI reports and dashboards to our Dynamics 365 Customer Engagement applications.

Designing forms with embedded Power BI reports

Another way we can embed Power BI reports in Dynamics 365 Customer Engagement applications is by embedding a Power BI report in a record. This can be very useful to extend the 360-degree view of the customer, incorporate telemetry data to customer assets, or add an advanced report to a project, for example.

It is worth remembering that Power BI reports may have data from Dynamics 365 Customer Engagement, but also data from other systems where we may have relevant data for the business. By embedding a report, we will be able to pass the context of the record in which we are located, and thus facilitate the consumption and interpretation of the data.

Currently, it is not possible to embed a report in a form through configuration. In other words, there is no no-code option that allows us to embed a report in a form. However, as we have already seen several times, one of the key features of Power Platform is that it allows us to take a pro-code approach when needed.

In this particular case, we could consider that the proposal that Microsoft makes to embed a Power BI report in a form is a low-code approach, limiting with pro-code, because even though the steps are documented and you just have to follow them, it requires editing the XML of the solution. This can be somewhat complex for a citizen developer.

However, the **Power BI Embedder** solution built by **Ivan Ficko**, available in the **XRMToolBox**, offers us a tool to embed a report in a form simply by knowing the ID of the Power BI workspace where the report is, the ID of the report we want to embed, and the URL of the report we want to embed.

Figure 13.15 – Power BI report URL

As we can see in the previous figure, both the workspace ID and the report ID can be obtained from the report URL. Once we have this data, we will have to do the following:

1. Open **XRMToolBox**.

2. The first thing we will have to do is to connect our environment. For this, click on **Connect**:

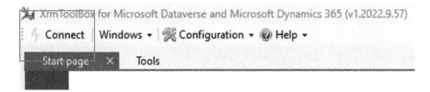

Figure 13.16 – Connecting the environment in XRMToolBox

3. To add a new connection, click on **New connection**:

Figure 13.17 – Creating a connection in XRMToolBox

4. There are different options to connect to the environment, and it will depend on the environment/ tenant you want to connect to. In this case, we will connect through **Connection Wizard**:

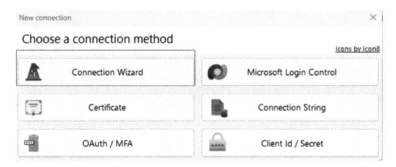

Figure 13.18 – Connection dialog – Choose a connection method

5. We add the URL of our environment:

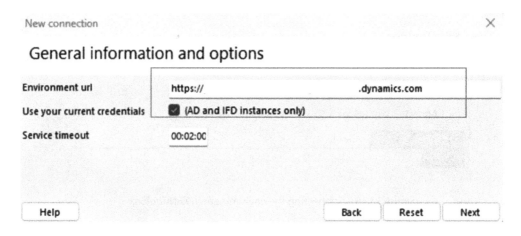

Figure 13.19 – Connection dialog – General information and options

6. Then, we indicate the credentials we will use to connect:

Figure 13.20 – Connection dialog – User credentials

7.   Finally, we have to give a name to the connection:

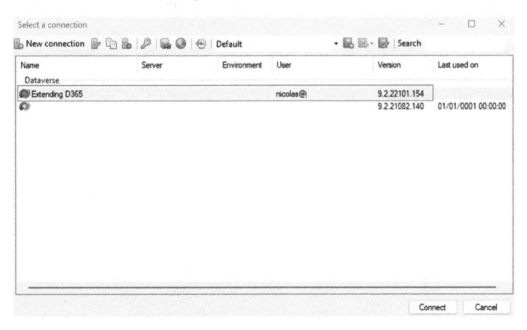

Figure 13.21 – Connection dialog – Connection validated

8.   Once the connection is created, we will see the available environment when we click on **Connect**:

Figure 13.22 – Select a connection in XRMToolBox

9.   Once selected, we need to look for the **Power BI Embedder** tool:

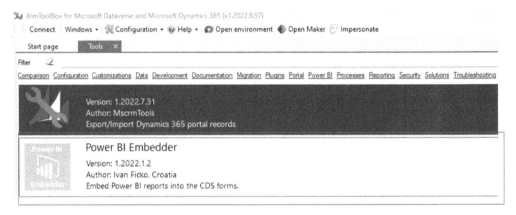

Figure 13.23 – Selecting Power BI Embedder

10.   There, we will have to indicate the following:

I.   The table we want to work with, the form, and the section where we want to embed the report

II.   The workspace ID (Group ID) and the report ID

III.   The number of rows we want the report to occupy:

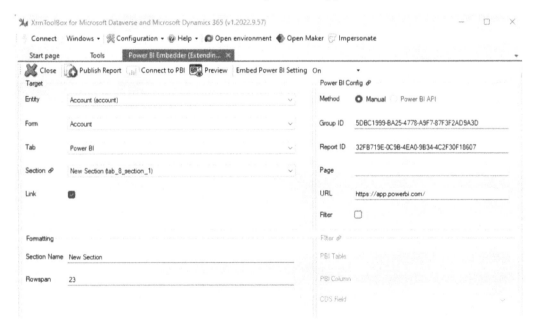

Figure 13.24 – Configuring Power BI Embedder

11. Finally, we have to publish it:

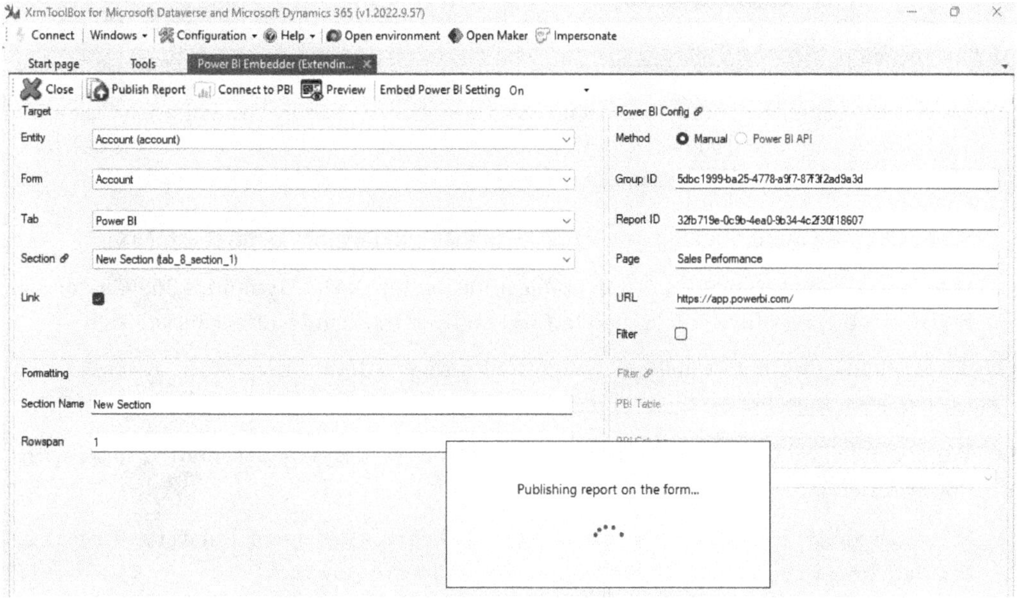

Figure 13.25 – Publish Report

As we can see in the previous figure, once we finish publishing, the report will be available in the table form. Since we have not indicated which record we are in, the report does not have any kind of context, so it will present the same information in all the records. However, at the time of publishing, we could pass parameters to filter, indicating the table and field of Power BI, and the field of the **Dataverse/ Dynamics 365 Customer Engagement** table.

Summary

In this last chapter, we have seen different ways we can use to embed a Power BI report in the context of a Dynamics 365 Customer Engagement application. Whether as a dashboard or as part of a table form, we can empower users by offering them advanced reports and dashboards for their daily work.

We started by discussing the data consumption options that Power BI offers us, and then went into the possibilities we have for embedding a Power BI component into a Dynamics 365 Customer Engagement application. We went step by step through how to use Power BI reports and dashboards as a system dashboard. We ended with another step-by-step guide on how to use a community tool such as **XRMToolBox** to embed a report in a form, with a no-code/low-code approach.

With this chapter, we can end the book, although I hope that you do not end your formative route. This book was intended to serve as a trigger, to help you visualize advanced Dynamics 365 Customer Engagement solutions, powered by Power Platform. We went through each of the core capabilities of extending Dynamics 365 Customer Engagement with Power Platform.

We first established common concepts of what no-code/low-code is, and why Dynamics 365 Customer Engagement can be considered a no-code/low-code platform. Then, we started to cover the different Power Platform components that we can use to extend our applications:

- We saw how we can extend the data model with the flexibility that **Dataverse** offers us

- We discussed how to create custom applications on top of the **Dynamics 365 Customer Engagement** applications model, and those key aspects to extend native applications

- We introduced artificial intelligence with **AI Builder** and mixed reality in Dynamics 365 Customer Engagement processes and applications

- We discussed real examples of how we can empower users by automating tasks with **Power Automate**

- We reviewed key concepts when processing data with **Power Automate**, **Dataverse**, **Power Fx**, and **dataflows** in the context of Dynamics 365 Customer Engagement

- We analyzed and saw how we can create bots without the need for code with Power Virtual Agents, both for customer-facing and internal processes

- Finally, we saw what options we have to exploit Dynamics 365 Customer Engagement data with **Power BI**, and how to embed Power BI reports in Dynamics 365 Customer Engagement applications

I hope this book has served to help you come up with new solutions in your Dynamics 365 Customer Engagement projects, extending the applications with Power Platform.

Index

`Packt.com`

Subscribe to our online digital library for full access to over 7,000 books and videos, as well as industry leading tools to help you plan your personal development and advance your career. For more information, please visit our website.

Why subscribe?

- Spend less time learning and more time coding with practical eBooks and Videos from over 4,000 industry professionals

- Improve your learning with Skill Plans built especially for you

- Get a free eBook or video every month

- Fully searchable for easy access to vital information

- Copy and paste, print, and bookmark content

Did you know that Packt offers eBook versions of every book published, with PDF and ePub files available? You can upgrade to the eBook version at `packt.com` and as a print book customer, you are entitled to a discount on the eBook copy. Get in touch with us at `customercare@packtpub.com` for more details.

At www.`packt.com`, you can also read a collection of free technical articles, sign up for a range of free newsletters, and receive exclusive discounts and offers on Packt books and eBooks.

Other Books You May Enjoy

If you enjoyed this book, you may be interested in these other books by Packt:

Implementing Microsoft Dynamics 365 Customer Engagement

Mahender Pal

ISBN: 9781838556877

- Explore the new features of Microsoft Dynamics 365 CE

- Understand various project management methodologies, such as Agile, Waterfall, and DevOps

- Customize Dynamics 365 CE to meet your business requirements

- Integrate Dynamics 365 with other applications, such as PowerApps, Power Automate, and Power BI

- Convert client requirements into functional designs

- Extend Dynamics 365 functionality using web resources, custom logic, and client-side and server-side code

- Discover different techniques for writing and executing test cases

- Understand various data migration options to import data from legacy systems

Mastering Microsoft Dynamics 365 Customer Engagement - Second Edition

Deepesh Somani

ISBN: 9781788990226

- Manage various divisions of your organization using Dynamics 365 customizations
- Explore the XRM Framework and leverage its features
- Provide an enhanced mobile and tablet experience
- Develop client-side applications using JavaScript and the Web API
- Understand how to develop plugins and workflows using Dynamics 365
- Explore solution framework improvements and new field types

Packt is searching for authors like you

If you're interested in becoming an author for Packt, please visit `authors.packtpub.com` and apply today. We have worked with thousands of developers and tech professionals, just like you, to help them share their insight with the global tech community. You can make a general application, apply for a specific hot topic that we are recruiting an author for, or submit your own idea.

Share Your Thoughts

Now you've finished *Extending Dynamics 365 Customer Engagement Apps with Low Code*, we'd love to hear your thoughts! Scan the QR code below to go straight to the Amazon review page for this book and share your feedback or leave a review on the site that you purchased it from.

`https://packt.link/r/1803232315`

Your review is important to us and the tech community and will help us make sure we're delivering excellent quality content.

Download a free PDF copy of this book

Thanks for purchasing this book!

Do you like to read on the go but are unable to carry your print books everywhere? Is your eBook purchase not compatible with the device of your choice?

Don't worry, now with every Packt book you get a DRM-free PDF version of that book at no cost.

Read anywhere, any place, on any device. Search, copy, and paste code from your favorite technical books directly into your application.

The perks don't stop there, you can get exclusive access to discounts, newsletters, and great free content in your inbox daily

Follow these simple steps to get the benefits:

1. Scan the QR code or visit the link below

https://packt.link/free-ebook/9781803232317

2. Submit your proof of purchase
3. That's it! We'll send your free PDF and other benefits to your email directly